CORSA ROSA

A History of the Giro d'Italia

Brendan Gallagher

B L O O M S B U R Y
LONDON · OXFORD · NEW YORK · NEW DELHI · SYDNEY

Bloomsbury Sport
An imprint of Bloomsbury Publishing Plc

50 Bedford Square   1385 Broadway
London   New York
WC1B 3DP   NY 10018
UK   USA

www.bloomsbury.com

BLOOMSBURY and the Diana logo are trademarks of Bloomsbury Publishing Plc

First published 2017

British Library Cataloguing-in-Publication Data
A catalogue record for this book is available from the British Library.

Library of Congress Cataloguing-in-Publication data has been applied for.

ISBN: TPB: 978-1-4729-1880-2
epub: 978-1-4729-1881-9

2 4 6 8 10 9 7 5 3 1

Typeset in Adobe Garamond Pro by Deanta Global Publishing Services, Chennai, India
Printed and bound in Great Britain by CPI Group (UK) Ltd, Croydon CR0 4YY

To find out more about our authors and books visit www.bloomsbury.com.
Here you will find extracts, author interviews, details of forthcoming events
and the option to sign up for our newsletters.

To cycling's other prisoners of the road — those colleagues whose enduring if occasionally gallows humour, linguistic excellence, radical driving, insatiable thirst for cycling talk and ability to function without sleep make the 'impossible' job of covering a Grand Tour one of life's great pleasures.

CONTENTS

CONTENTS

INTRODUCTION

The Giro d'Italia may have been created in the image of the Tour de France but it very quickly created its own identity and unique style and its own heroes. The fact that it stands full comparison with the Tour, the world's biggest annual sporting event, serves only to underline what an extraordinary bike race and sporting spectacle it has become in its own right.

Colder, steeper, often higher, snowier, wetter, foggier, muddier, dustier and yet often more colourful than the Tour, the Giro can also be noisier, harder, friendlier and arguably more beautiful. With the Italian love of drama and intrigue, it has also witnessed more than its fair share of low-life cheating, skulduggery and rank unsportsmanlike behaviour in the ruthless pursuit of glory, fame and financial gain.

Historically the Giro has usually started in late April or the first week of May. Barely a month separates the end of the Giro and the start of the Tour these days and increasingly the dramatis personae are very different, with few GC riders now attempting the double. Its early season slot sets the tone, with the weather as uncertain as the riders' form, and the elements can play a massive part in the narrative of the race particularly in the Dolomites and the Alps. The possible wintry condition of those big climbs, and therefore their scheduling as late as possible in the race, also ensures that the Giro builds to a natural crescendo in the last four or five days. Yet the rest of the Italian peninsula is so rugged and hilly that the decisive move or break can occur at any time.

The media interest and hype in the Giro is considerable, and following it can be a chaotic but more informal and intimate experience

1

than the Tour. The crowds are often huge – particularly in the city finishes and mountaintops – and the *tifosi* are perhaps the most knowledgeable and passionate fans in the sport. Like them, we should appreciate the enormous challenge the riders face each year in this most brutal and beautiful of all cycling's contests.

Brendan Gallagher
April 2017

1

'NECESSITY', THE MOTHER OF INVENTION. ORIGINS OF THE GIRO D'ITALIA

The origins of the Giro d'Italia are not difficult to discern. A young nation, increasingly obsessed with the bike both as a means of transport and recreation, looked over the border and enviously viewed the growing success story that was the Tour de France. Italy badly wanted the same for itself and shamelessly copied the idea and basic format. The Giro may have very quickly established its own identity and narrative – gloriously so in fact – and buried deep within its origins there are undoubtedly other much nobler elements but the first edition in 1909 was a commercially driven carbon copy of the Tour de France. The two great races share the same DNA, tapping into the growing mania for cycling. Both were also instigated by harassed newspaper executives looking for an irresistible long-running story to boost circulation and advertising in order to stave off bankruptcy, preferably killing off the opposition in the process. The financial imperative underpinned everything even if the main selling point was the romanticism of the challenge and the heroism and individual stories of those involved.

In France the megalomaniac who was Henry Desgrange seized the opportunity offered by the suggestion of a Tour de France and fashioned a race in his own extraordinary image. A considerable cyclist himself – he was an early holder of the Hour record in 1893 – Desgrange was fascinated by the ultimate challenge of circumnavigating France and pushing man to the limit, but as sports editor of *L'Auto* what he wanted most of all was to start making money and see off his main rival *Le Vélo*. The successful running of the 1903 Tour de France killed two birds with one stone in this respect and, although there were tough years ahead, the Tour was up and running. Meanwhile in Italy a similar scenario was unfolding. *La Gazzetta dello Sport* was the Italian equivalent of *L'Auto*, a sports-orientated cycling-friendly newspaper that was frankly struggling a bit. It had tried various wheezes such as printing on yellow and then green paper and had eventually settled, in 1898, on a rather distinctive pink. Founded on April's Fool Day 1896 just ahead of the first of the modern-day Olympics in Athens, it published twice a week, first on Friday to carry features and preview the weekend's events and then on Monday to bring news of everything that had unfolded.

In its first year *Gazzetta* had merged with the specialist cycling paper *Il Ciclista e La Tripletta* and had been quick to embrace the relatively new sport of cycling. The newspaper's cycling correspondent Armando Cougnet, who had joined the newspaper as a wet-behind-the-ears 18-year-old in 1898, had been despatched to France to cover both the 1906 and 1907 Tours and had distinguished himself with his thrilling accounts although there was no particular Italian angle to report. He was, however, in the ideal position to observe how such a monumental stage race had developed and was organised logistically. The newspaper's hands-on involvement in cycling had started in 1905 when it organised the Giro di Lombardia and continued apace in 1907 with the soon to be famous Milan–San Remo one-day classic which, curiously, morphed out of a race for motor cars the previous year. That 1906 car race produced just two finishers but the vanity of the town's mayor had been tickled and he was soon persuaded to help sponsor a bike race from Milan to the Mediterranean resort town.

Testing the human body and spirit to the limit, along with developing technology, was a big theme in the first decade of the twentieth century and it perhaps helps to see cycling in that context. In 1907 the Peking–Paris motor-car race was established while 1908 saw the Arctic expeditions of Robert Peary and Frederick Cook and the Antarctic *Nimrod* expedition of Ernest Shackleton, who trekked to within 97.5 miles of the South Pole. Also in 1908 aviator Wilbur Wright – who ran a bicycle repair company with his brother Orville called the Wright Bicycle Exchange – entertained invited French guests with a series of short flights around a field near Le Mans, while the following year French aviator Louis Blériot became the first man to cross the English Channel in a heavier than air aircraft. Everywhere pioneers were pushing the limits and the boundaries. The 1908 Olympics in London underlined this, being organised on a grand scale, and there was a significant leap in human performance in virtually all disciplines. One of the most noteworthy, headline-grabbing, performances of those Games came from the diminutive Dorando Pietri from Carpi in Italy who won the hearts of the sporting world for his brave efforts in the marathon when, having seemingly run the opposition to a standstill, he himself started to crack with the finish in sight at the White City Stadium. The distressed Pietri collapsed a number of times and at one stage started running in the wrong direction before being helped through the tape by officials, an act which led to his disqualification. Pietri was denied his gold medal but became a big celebrity in Italy and earned over 200,000 lire as a professional in the next three years before retiring to run a hotel in San Remo.

There was a widespread appreciation of, and fascination with, extremism and cycling fed into those sentiments. Nobody quite knew what the limits were either for the riders or their bikes and that sense of tackling the unknown was already at the heart of the Tour de France where Desgrange had set out with the idea of organising a challenge so difficult only one rider would be left standing by the end. To survive would constitute victory in Desgrange's world. Over the border, Italy, with its huge mountain landscapes, thousands of miles of glorious coast, the rainy north and arid sun-baked south, was a land of extremes just like France. And just like France the Italian working classes had taken to the bike as an essential form of transport and those of a more competitive or compulsive nature had also adopted this mode of transport as their sport of choice. A Tour of Italy – a Giro d'Italia – was frankly a race waiting to happen. It was when not if.

Gazzetta clearly had a strong relationship with cycling in place but hitherto had lacked the financial clout to seriously consider a Giro d'Italia. That wasn't critical until 5 August 1908 when Tullo Morgagni, *Gazzetta*'s sports editor, got word that a rival newspaper, *Corriere della Sera*, was seriously considering launching a Giro d'Italia in conjunction with giant bike manufacturing company Bianchi the following year. A disgruntled former employee of Bianchi, Angelo 'Mici' Gatti, had contacted Morgagni with the news that very morning and the editor immediately realised that it was crunch time. What was vitally important now was who would emerge as the organisers and owners of the race? Who would reap the rewards and harvest the prestige? Time was of the essence. *Gazzetta* had to be seen to be first with the idea. *Gazzetta* had to scoop *Corriere della Sera* whose original initiative the race was.

Suddenly there was the kind of explosion of activity that journalism, with its own insatiable adrenalin-fuelled need for drama, occasionally produces although the choreography of this particular episode was frenzied even by newspaper standards. On 5 August Morgagni sent a telegram to Cougnet who was in Venice on business: 'Without delay necessity obliges *Gazzetta* to launch an Italian Tour. Return to Milan, Tullo.' The harassed Morgagni also sent a similar telegram to the newspaper's main investor, Emilo Costamagna – Cougnet was also a smaller investor at this stage – who was on holiday in Mondovi, summoning his boss to a meeting in Milan the next day. As a rule editors – certainly the wise ones who value their jobs – don't interrupt their proprietor's summer vacation unless they absolutely have to. But needs must. This was serious.

The following day the 'big three' met in *Gazzetta*'s offices on Piazzale Loreto in central Milan and within the space of one manic working day the Giro d'Italia was born. Cougnet, as the man who had seen how the Tour de France was run at a practical level, would have been the key individual in these discussions and as the only man who understood the mechanics of staging such an event immediately carved out a key role for himself as race director for the best part of 40 years. Next day's *Gazzetta*, which appeared less than 48 hours after the panic-stricken Morgagni had hurriedly kick-started the process, proclaimed that the newspaper would be staging the first Giro d'Italia the following May. The race would be 3,000km long – a figure rather plucked out of the air – and there would be prize money of 25,000 lire, capital which, at the time of going to press, *Gazzetta* certainly didn't possess. In its front-page editorial the newspaper stated: 'The *Gazzetta dello Sport*, pursuant with the glory of Italian Cycling, announces that next spring will see the first "Giro d'Italia" one of the biggest, most ambitious races in international cycling.'

As Cougnet later commented, in his autobiography, about the Giro's birth: 'Like all babies that you hear, it squealed its way into life in the columns of *Gazzetta*.' The die had been cast even if there was a large element of self-fulfilling prophecy in their bold statements. Now the newspaper somehow had to make this happen, and in a way that would suggest permanency and an ongoing annual event. In many ways the actual cycle race was the least of their worries although heaven knows that presented problems enough. But at least Cougnet had the basic template of the Tour itself to follow and to improve upon where possible. The paper had already dipped its toes into event organisation at the Milan–San Remo and the Giro di Lombardia and the public interest seemed to be growing in parallel with the general usage of bikes. Big one-day races had already been established while a number of velodromes has been built around the country to accommodate those who enjoyed track cycling. It was still a gamble, though. The bottom line was that this new event had to sell newspapers and advertising space in the newspaper or else it would be scrapped. *Gazzetta dello Sport* was not a charity. Much encouraged by the daily stories in the newspaper no fewer than 166 riders signed up for the race and, even though some dropped out towards May as the enormity of the challenge began to hit home, 127 competitors eventually made it to the start line in Milan.

The biggest problem was financial. *Gazzetta* had established this beast of an event literally overnight but didn't really have the wherewithal yet to stage it, as Cougnet again admitted when he looked back: 'Financially I was absolutely terrified. I was 28 years old and had a young family to support so if the thing collapsed it would threaten the newspaper and all our livelihoods. But our great project was announced and we resolved to make it happen by whatever means. We wrote about it in every issue, effectively begging for sponsorship.'

At which point happy chance intervened and a certain Primo Bongrani entered the stage, an influential friend of Cougnet and minor shareholder in the paper. Bongrani was also a clever if possibly bored accountant with the bank Cassa di Risparmio and, most importantly, the secretary of the Italian Olympic Committee. A considerable cycling fan, who had just returned from the grandiose 1908 Summer Olympics in London, Bongrani was enthused by the sound of this embryonic Giro d'Italia and immediately volunteered to take a further month's leave from the bank to start organising the necessary funds. Bongrani knew how to crunch numbers and wasn't afraid to talk money with those who might be willing to offload.

Bongrani negotiated successfully with a number of minor sponsors such as the fledgling motor-car manufacturers Lancia and also secured the full support – financial and otherwise – of the Italian Cycling Association. Without their official backing nothing could happen. With an eye to the future the travel agents Thomas Cook, well established in Italy, were engaged to sell spectator packages to the well heeled who might wish to follow the race from stage to stage and Bongrani then persuaded the Italian royal family to offer a gold medal for the winner. His finest achievement behind the scenes, however, was to boldly approach *Corriere della Sera*, still licking their wounds at missing out on the race, for financial assistance and the scheme he proposed was the donation of a then huge 3,000-lire first prize for the winner.

It was an audacious approach and yet why not? *Gazzetta*, having effectively gazumped their rivals, were now in full charge of the Giro d'Italia but *Corriere* had clearly demonstrated an appetite for such an event. They were also hurting badly having had their great project ruthlessly hijacked, but perhaps by sponsoring the winner of the first Giro they could recover some of the lost ground and again become synonymous with this wonderful race which was so laden with potential. Meanwhile, the final component of the financial package was put together by Francesco Sghirla, a *Gazzetta* stalwart who had helped organise the ill-starred Milan–San Remo car race. The eloquent Sghirla persuaded the Casino in San Remo to stump up all the other prize money. It had all been rather hurried and on the hoof but necessity is often the mother of invention. As Morgagni's original telegram had said: 'Necessity obliges Gazzetta to launch an Italian Tour.' The Giro d'Italia was up and running.

2

AN EVOLVING RACE MAKES ITS MARK (1909–13)

The first Giro d'Italia got underway at the unlikely hour of 2.53 a.m. on the morning of Thursday 13 May 1909 just outside the *Gazzetta dello Sport* offices on Piazzale Loreto in Milan. The brutally early *partenza* (depart) was to maximise the hours of daylight en route with an expected finish in Bologna 397km down the road sometime that evening, hopefully before night fell. It was an extremely tough introduction and would immediately sort the wheat from the chaff but actually Cougnet and his organisational team had generally reined themselves in. It was important that this inaugural Giro be seen to hit the ground running. Immediate comparisons would be made with the now established Tour de France and it was vital that the Giro should not fall at the first hurdle. It was also important that *Gazzetta* covered everything that moved – every storyline, every development in the *Classifica Generale* (General Classification, or GC) and with that in mind the newspaper now started publishing every other day.

So Cougnet kept the race comparatively short with eight stages totalling 2,445km – the shortest ever Giro – as the race largely described a clockwise route around northern and central Italy and taking in Bologna, Chieti, Naples (the southernmost point), Rome, Florence, Genoa and Turin before returning to Milan on 30 May. At least two, sometimes three, rest days had been allocated between stages which immediately established the commercial value of being a start or finish town with racers, camp followers and media requiring accommodation throughout. The roads were poor, especially in the countryside away from the big cities and towns, and it was undeniably arduous, but in this first edition at least it didn't appear the Giro's aim to 'break' all the riders as was always the case at the Tour when Desgrange was in charge. Come the big day 127 riders went to the start line, the vast majority hugely inexperienced adventurers more than anything.

In keeping with the Tour de France at this time the GC was to be decided on a points system with riders being awarded one point for a stage win and two for second place and so on down to last place. The rider with lowest total of points at the end of the eight stages would be the overall winner and although it seems antiquated now it was in reaction to the infamous 1904 Tour de France when wholescale cheating – by riders and fans – made the calculating of accumulated time for each rider problematical. On the subject of cheating, the Giro was immediately able to profit from the hard-earned experience of the Tour by insisting that every rider be photographed at the start line of each stage, to ensure that the rider arriving at the finish was one and the same. The Giro also introduced regular mid-race checkpoints – normally at some remote spot – where riders had to sign in and produce their photo identification, again to ensure that they were completing the full course.

As the riders gathered at the *Gazzetta* offices the day before the race to register and receive their race numbers, their bikes were stamped with their own names and this *la punzonatura* ceremony became part of the Giro tradition with a big crowd gathering to support their favourites. The *Gazzetta* offices physically became race headquarters, mission control and for the duration of the race updates would be posted in the windows of the offices with crowds gathering around for the latest information ahead of publication of the latest standings in the paper the following day.

Professional teams entered and their riders enjoyed the assistance a team-mate can provide during the race itself and the back-up of knowing that there would be a mechanic to tend their bikes and that a hotel room, no matter how modest, awaited at the end of a stage. However, the majority of riders at this stage were plucky 'independents' – *isolati* – who were totally on their own, on and off the bike. Many were either unemployed or poor rural workers and accommodation was random to say the least with many a rider taking refuge in a friendly farmer's haybarn. Every rider who completed the Giro was guaranteed 300 lire, more than enough to feed a family for three to four months, so, apart from the big-name cyclists, the peloton also consisted of those who simply looked on the race as a job of work, a source of much-needed income.

The 1909 race was a very Italian affair but five overseas riders made it to the start line, including two former winners of the Tour de France. Other French riders had wanted to enter such as Maurice Brocco, Emile Georget and Jean-Baptiste Dortignacq from the Alcyon team but pressure was put on that trio to race instead at the Tour of Belgium, a much more fruitful market for the team sponsors. Of the French riders who did compete the star turns were the dashing and ever-popular Lucien Petit-Breton – French-born but raised in Argentina – who won the Tour de France in both 1907 and 1908, and Louis Trousselier, who had won the Tour in 1905. For Petit-Breton his first Giro was a painful experience, having to abandon at the end of stage one after a nasty crash earlier in the day in which he dislocated his shoulder as he descended near Lake Garda – reportedly while eating a piece of chicken to refuel ahead of the first serious climb of the Giro. It was disappointing for rider and organisers alike but the presence of such a big hitter at the launch of the inaugural Giro had helped immensely. Trousselier was very competitive in the early stages but was badly hampered on stage four when nails thrown on the road by the Italian fans caused him to puncture, and he was beset by further punctures and crashes on the following stage after which he abandoned.

There was enough competitive racing in Italy prior to the 1909 Giro for there to be a clear form guide and one or two riders stood out. Luigi

Ganna, the so-called 'King of Mud' who was known for his strength in difficult conditions, rode for the Atala-Dunlop team, and had won Milan–San Remo earlier in the year. He started as the clear favourite and lived up to that billing by eventually winning the GC. Carlo Galetti, twice a winner of the Giro di Sicilia, was also tipped to go well and didn't disappoint either with a hard-earned second place.

Before that there was a deliciously predictable incident with three riders, who had obviously been reading accounts of various ruses on the Tour de France, being withdrawn from the GC contest after being found catching a train during stage two. Vincenzo Granata, Andrea Provinciali and Guglielmo Lodesani had all been spotted boarding the train at Ancona with their bikes, but although Provinciali chose to head for home in disgrace the others continued to race for stage honours and prize money, the organisers seeing no need to disqualify them from the race altogether.

Giovanni Rossignoli, a powerful rider from Pavia in Lombardy, produced a strong performance to win stage three into Naples but generally lacked a sprint finish which counted heavily against him in a race decided by such a Points system, and he eventually finished third. It is interesting to note, however, that he would have won the 1909 Giro by 37 minutes if accumulated time had been the criteria used. Of course Ganna and Galetti might have ridden very differently had time been the deciding factor but nothing should disguise what a strong effort Rossignoli put in day after day. He was the iron man of the peloton.

There was some fun and games on those final stages. On stage seven an unruly crowd at the finish in Turin persuaded Cougnet to finish the stage six kilometres down the road in Beinasco which caused a deal of confusion and ill feeling. Then, on the final day, with an estimated crowd of 30,000 at the finish, there was more chaos when a police horseman fell in the press of the crowd with the knock-on effect of causing a crash in the bunch. There had already been a good deal of drama with the leader Ganna flatting twice in the final 70km. On the second occasion he seemed unlikely to catch the leading group but the organisers salvaged a potentially awkward situation by closing a set of railway barriers to halt the lead group until the race leader had regained contact. Ganna was a worthy winner, though, and grateful recipient of the 5,325 lire first prize which went a long way towards financing the bike manufacturing company he had always dreamed of owning. His bikes and sponsored teams were to feature prominently in future Giri although his own riding days were far from finished at this stage. In the early days of his cycling career he had still worked as a stonemason, attributing his exceptional fitness to daily 100km round trips to work on various jobs. As he stepped up onto the podium to receive his winner's garland, Cougnet, ever the journalist, asked the new champion how it felt. *Mi brucia tanto il cu'* he answered in language borrowed from the building sites he had once worked on. My arse is on fire!

Cougnet smiled broadly. Not just the first Giro winner but a first great quote. The Giro was up and running and so was *Gazzetta dello Sport*.

Galetti emerges as the Giro's first big star

By any criteria the inaugural Giro in 1909 was a huge success with big crowds at all the starts and finishes and it had an immediate impact on the fortunes of *Gazzetta*. In fact, to a very real extent the race and the paper became one entity, each massively dependent on the other, and it is rather amusing at this safe distance to observe the musical chairs and internal politics that kicked off as those most intimately concerned fought for control of what clearly had the potential to become a cash cow, although in these early editions it was far from that. The admirable Tullo Morgagni, that human ball of energy whose alert thinking, flurry of telegrams and hurriedly arranged meetings had played such an important role in the Giro's birth, didn't even see the year out as he was replaced by a new sports editor, Emilio Colombo. Morgagni was history. The fight to take credit for, and control of, a success story was underway.

Yet again there is a parallel here with the Tour de France where Desgrange, admittedly a man of huge talent and drive in his own right, was quick to take all the plaudits for himself and bask in the power and glory after the inaugural 1903 Tour when in fact his chief cycling correspondent, Géo Lefèvre, was the true architect of the race.

At *Gazzetta* the new sports editor Colombo had no intention of being tied to the office chair and insisted on following the Tour personally and producing his own rather lame byline reports. Meanwhile, in 1911 Cougnet bought out Costamagna as the owner of *Gazzetta* although he in turn quickly sold to a publishing house Sonzogno who augmented the *Gazzetta* board with two hard-nosed businessmen in Arturo Mercanti and Edgardo Longoni. Costamagna, meanwhile, did not disappear from the scene and, rather like Colombo, insisted on accompanying the Tour and filing voluminous high-profile reports under his own cod byline 'Magno'. Costamagna had a very decent if occasionally florid turn of phrase and you suspect he enjoyed his annual three-week tour of Italy enormously, writing about a sport he clearly loved and individuals he admired immensely.

At this distance it's difficult to keep track of *Gazzetta*'s internal politics, but the two main players were Colombo, the hands-on 'front of house' sports editor who wants to take full credit for the glory of the Giro, and the cycling fanatic and workaholic fixer and chief cycling correspondent Cougnet who not only ensures the race happens but rules it with a rod of iron. In their own ways they were a formidable team and the race, indeed the national institution, that developed on their watch is their legacy.

These early days were a stressful, dynamic and experimental time as the Giro's founding fathers sought to nurture this embryonic event – and of course to maximise its commercial value and transform it into a guaranteed source of income. Partly, though, it was also their highly tuned journalistic instincts which motivated the movers and shakers at *Gazzetta* to always try and top the last 'story' – whether it be the previous year's Giro or indeed the Tour de France which they continued to monitor closely. There was an explosion of ideas coming out of *Gazzetta's* cycling think-tank, some of which hit the bullseye while others died quietly, never to be mentioned again.

Some were obvious. When the dust had settled the 1909 Giro was considered perhaps a little 'soft' in comparison to the Tour so steps were quickly taken to rectify that. The 1910 Giro was increased from eight to ten stages with a total distance of 2,987km and this appeared to have an immediate effect with only 20 of the 101 starters making it back to Milan. Meanwhile, in 1911 another two stages were added to make the Giro a 12-stage race of some 3,358km which resulted in a similar rate of attrition. In two years the race distance increased by 910km. The 1911 Giro was also the first time a really high Alpine climb was included, with the peloton breaking through the 2000m barrier on the climb to Sestriere on the French border on stage five.

So far so good: all very logical and progressive; nor were there any arguments with the decision to award 51 points to every rider who finished lower than 50th which saved the organisers the trouble of laboriously counting everybody in hours after the race had finished, with the circus looking to pack up and move on. But then came 1912, an appalling wrong turn from which the race had to hastily extract itself the following year. It was a humble minion – the paper's horse-racing correspondent – who seemed to be identified as the villain rather than those much bigger names who ran the race and accepted the accolades when it was universally praised. What the Giro actually did in 1912 was to try and respond to the massive contradiction that has always hung over Grand Tour racing. These races are 'won' by individuals who take all the glory, honour and prize money and stand atop the podium alone, yet everybody within the sport accepts the eternal truth that Grand Tours are won by teams.

So, in the pioneering spirit that existed at the time, the 1912 Giro attempted to address this by making it a team race. The race would be won by a collective not a single individual. Together they would stand on top of the winner's podium. A noble thought with much merit but emotionally counter-intuitive. When the public witnesses a single rider crossing the line triumphantly in splendid isolation, they instinctively attribute victory to that individual. In that defining moment appreciation of their mates who have busted a gut along the way to make such a victory possible is suspended, a process much accelerated by *Gazzetta*'s own lionisation of the individual and his story.

In 1912 you could only enter the Giro as a member of a team with the organisers stipulating they were looking for four-man teams, although ultimately they relaxed that a little and allowed teams of three. Initially there had also been the hope that the many cyclists who had been recruited into the bike divisions of the Italian Army – the *Bersaglieri* – would be released to form regimental teams but this idea did not find favour with the military authorities who in the end consented to just one composite team of soldier-cyclists to compete. Nor was the new team scoring system always easy to follow with a team being awarded four points if they produced the stage winner and two if they placed two riders in the top ten. Additionally, all teams that finished each stage with a full complement – the same number of riders they started the day with – earned another point. No matter how much *Gazzetta* hyped the idea they failed miserably to sell it to the teams or the public. At the start just 54 riders from 14 teams took the line, this in a race that just three years earlier had seen 127 riders gather in the middle of the night at Piazzale Loreto. It was a disappointing response and even before the race got underway plans were being hatched to return the Giro to normality in 1913.

While all these changes were taking place the one constant was the enduring excellence of Carlo Galetti who, having finished runner-up in 1909, won the next two Giri and to all intents and purposes won in 1912 as well when he was manifestly the strongest rider in the Atala-Dunlop squad which won the team event. The Giro had its first superstar rider and hero. Nicknamed '*il Scoiattolo dei Navigli*' – 'the squirrel of the canals' – by *Gazzetta*, the Milanese rider was a terrific all-rounder and won the 1910 Giro in commanding style although there was the prospect of a strong French challenge early in the race before that receded in controversial style. The redoubtable Petit-Breton was back for another assault on the title while Jean-Baptiste Dortignacq and Constant Ménager were also highly rated.

Dortignacq was a streetwise veteran who had finished second in the infamous 1904 Tour and third the following year and in 1910 he was going strongly at the Giro. When he won stage two Ménager moved to second in GC and Petit-Breton third. The French invaders were putting some stick about and the Italian peloton – normally a fractured and jealous collection of riders who were conscious of proudly representing their regions and provinces as well as their employers – for once responded as one on stage three to crush the French trio. The top three Italian riders – Galetti, Ganna and Eberardo Pavesi – were allowed to escape up the road to roll over the finishing line 22 minutes ahead of the peloton. Order of sorts had been restored at the top of GC with Galetti taking a convincing win, a situation that was reinforced when his nearest rival, Petit-Breton, had to abandon through injury at the end of stage three when in second position.

The dangerous Dortignacq still looked strong and showed up well in the brutal mountainous stage four from Teramo to Naples but failed to appear at the start of stage five after becoming ill overnight and abandoning. The Frenchman was so violently sick that Italian police launched an investigation, suspecting foul play in the form of poisoning. Nothing was proved, however, and, as is the way with Grand Tours, the circus had moved on before there was proper time for reflection and possible action. The French threat, one way or another, had receded, and it was pretty plain sailing for Galetti thereafter although he had to recover from an unfortunate crash with a hay cart on the final stage into Milan to claim his first title.

In 1911 the race started and finished in Rome, a departure from the norm designed to celebrate the 50th anniversary of the Unification of Italy. In a triumphant editorial emphasising the quasi-missionary and stage-building qualities of their race, *Gazzetta* gushed: 'It is not only a sporting exercise that engages Italian cyclists from such a variety of regions, in a battle of dialects and personalities on the roads of the south, barely known by the rest of Italy. It is also true patriotic work of acquaintance, swiftly turning to brotherhood, greeting and smiles.'

The ever popular Petit-Breton – a big crowd favourite in Italy since winning the first Milan–San Remo in 1907 – was back for yet another tilt at the Giro and this time mounted a very strong challenge. Third time lucky perhaps? He won the mountainous stage five from Mondovi to Turin in spectacular style and continued to place so well that by the end of stage nine Petit-Breton became the first overseas rider to lead the GC. On stage ten, in a six-man break, Petit-Breton found himself outnumbered by five Bianchi riders and stood little chance but he was still second in GC behind Galetti going into the penultimate stage, a rugged 345km run from Bari to Pompeii, when he crashed and was again forced to abandon.

Petit-Breton always brought a whiff of class and panache to proceedings and was much admired by Costamagna, aka Magno, who wrote a eulogy in *Gazzetta* to the departing Franco-Argentinian: 'The best of the class. A superior man of great class, a courageous and fair athlete; a perfect gentleman … this magnificent champion, truly an expression of the Latin race … his elegant silhouette, an attractive figure of a lord competing with dignity on the field of professional glory and money was saluted everywhere with true sporting enthusiasm.'

With Petit-Breton's challenge alas coming to nothing the field was clear for Galetti although there was a flurry of excitement later on stage 11 when a herd of water buffalo charged the peloton and caused much disruption and dismay to the tired riders. Dispirited towards the end of a very long race, the riders staged a strike and decided to finish the race in Pompeii, some way short of the official finish line in Naples where a large crowd had gathered. They later promenaded into Naples and received a very boisterous reception from the unhappy crowd. The race finished without further controversy back in Rome after a routine stage 12 although it is worth noting that the rock-solid Rossignoli would have again taken GC – by some 33 minutes – had accumulated time been the criterion.

Following the aberration of the 1912 'Team Giro' it was back to a more normal format in 1913 and *Gazzetta* had clearly not been too discouraged by its moment of madness because they continued to publish on a daily basis. Cycling was still its staple diet although football was beginning to make modest inroads. The 1913 Giro was the last to be decided by the Points system and was contested entirely by Italians with 99 mustering at the start in Milan ahead of the 341km ride to Genoa. Italy's war with Turkey, which resulted in them annexing Libya, had garnered much international disapproval and there was an unofficial boycotting of the event during these two years. The eventual winner of the race, Carlo Oriani, was a cyclist whose career had been interrupted by army service, having finished fifth in the 1909 Giro before he joined one of the Bike Divisions of the *Bersaglieri* who were rapidly becoming an important component of the Italian Army.

On his return to cycling action, having served in Libya, Oriani answered a late call to ride for the army team in 1912 and won the Giro di Lombardia on 27 October 1912, nine days after he had been demobbed following the cessation of hostilities. Although he didn't win a stage in the 1913 Giro his consistency was difficult to match and Oriani eventually finished six points ahead of Eberardo Pavesi with Giuseppe Azzini in third. Galetti, seeking a fourth Giro title in as many years, had not looked in prime form at the start and in any case was forced to abandon during stage four with a damaged ankle.

Ganna dug deep to finish fifth overall while the 1913 Giro was also notable for the first appearance of a 20-year-old Costante Girardengo who finished sixth in GC having also won the Italian championship earlier in the season. The Giro was to hear much more about the man from Novi Ligure in the coming years.

The 1913 Giro was the crowning achievement for Oriani who was, alas, one of the many professional cyclists to lose their lives in the First World War, killed at the Battle of Caporetto in fierce fighting at the Piave River on or around 10 November near Kobarid in what is now Slovenia. Oriani didn't succumb to wounds received; rather, he died of pneumonia after spending a long time in the icy waters of the Piave. Some reports say he was forced to try and swim the river to escape German and Austro-Hungarian forces while others suggest he dived in in an attempt to save a drowning colleague. He was taken to hospital and fought bravely for his life but eventually died on 3 December 1917, soon after his wife had arrived.

Even amidst the catastrophe of the rout at Caporetto his death touched the nation, or at least the cycling fans. Rather than allow him to be buried in a mass grave in the region, *Gazzetta* raised the funds via donations to the newspaper for the body of its former Giro champion to be transported back home; Oriani was eventually buried in Sesto San Giovanni just south of Cinisello Balsamo where he had spent much of his childhood.

3

1914: THE TOUGHEST BIKE RACE IN HISTORY?

The 1914 Giro is still considered by many to be the most gruelling and demanding bike race in history. After the 1912 debacle which nearly killed the race stone dead, and a 1913 race won by a rider who failed even to win a stage, the stakes were high. The Giro was a worthy race but it was lacking the drama and pathos of the Tour and, frankly, required a bit of a relaunch. At the 1913 Tour de France the cycling world – and the *L'Equipe* readership – had lapped up the story of second-placed Eugène Christophe on the Tourmalet climb and his epic ten-kilometre walk to find a blacksmith, where he was required to mend his own broken forks before continuing: the stuff of legend and still spoken of a century later. The Giro didn't seem to be producing similarly spell-binding stories of men *in extremis* so the *Gazzetta* think-tank looked for ways to up the ante.

The 1914 Giro was to be the toughest bike race the world had ever seen. It would take the riders to the very edge of what could be achieved physically by mankind and in so doing look to fulfil Desgrange's stated aim concerning the Tour de France: namely that it should be so tough that ideally only one rider would be able to complete it. The other big change worth noting was the overdue switch from the Points system to decide the GC winner to accumulated time. The Points system often encouraged fairly boring, tactical racing and also tended to penalise the true endurance athlete who was not fully rewarded for his virtuosity in getting away from the pack – or his main contenders – and winning by a considerable time margin. There were also, initially, plans to introduce a cut-off system after each stage to eliminate the laggards and the calculation was that the back markers should not be more than one hour per 100km behind the stage winner's time but, as we shall see, that hurriedly had to be abandoned.

Cougnet and his team rolled out an absolute beast of a course. Nobody could accuse them of half-measures. It had been condensed to just eight stages again, five of which were to be in excess of 420km, which would necessitate midnight starts, which in turn would make sleep deprivation a major factor. The 1914 Giro came at you from all directions. The average stage length was 80km longer than in 1913 and a full 114km longer than the inaugural Giro just five years earlier. Only the 340km stage two, from Cuneo to Lucca, could objectively be described as a regular stage. The other seven all included serious mountainous territory to a greater or lesser extent. There was to be only one rest day between stages so it was also the intensity of the race which helped make the 1914 Giro go down in infamy. In terms of actual length – 3,162km – it lagged a long way behind the Tour de France of that year, which was the longest in history at 5,405km, but in degrees of difficulty it was unsurpassed. The average length of time in the saddle per stage for the winner was just under 17 hours with the eighth and last man home averaging more than 19 hours per day.

On top of this, the riders had to contend with appalling weather. A slightly later than usual start date of 24 May should have increased the chances of good weather but a cruel later winter hit northern Europe that year and the 1914 Giro was contested in conditions more akin to January and February. Stage one largely took place in a howling winter storm that blew for 36 hours and the majority of the other stages were affected by torrential, often icy, rain. Factor in primitive roads which immediately turned to mud, the woollen clothing riders wore which quickly became sodden, the spare tyres, tools and food they all had to carry and the heavy, mainly fixed-gear bikes they rode and you begin to get the picture. Just eight of the 81 riders who set out from the start crawled back to Milan a fortnight later. It was carnage. And even then there wasn't an undisputed winner, with the need for a long-running court case before Alfonso Calzolari was officially declared the victor. Cougnet and *Gazzetta* couldn't have been happier. So many stories to write about, so many tales to tell and a daily edition to fill. Where to start?

An estimated crowd of 10,000 gathered outside the *Gazzetta* offices just before midnight on 24 May to cheer the riders on their way. The newspaper had left nobody in any doubt as to how tough the course would be in their many preview articles and anticipation was keen, although nobody could have predicted what unfolded. A quality field had assembled, including the winners of all the previous Giri and the top ten from the year before although it was still very much an Italian race with just a handful of overseas riders contesting the issue. The ever-gallant Petit-Breton was back again in the Atala team with fellow Frenchman Paul Duboc, another tough character who had seemed set to win the 1911 Tour de France before abandoning with what some claimed was poisoning. Supporters of the leader, Gustave Garrigou, were suspected but nothing was ever proved.

Another intriguing competitor was Freddie Grubb, the first British rider to start a Grand Tour. The 26-year-old Londoner was a bit of an oddball, a single-minded, cantankerous, teetotal, non-smoking vegetarian health addict – but he had performed great deeds as an amateur. Grubb had briefly held a world record of 351 miles covered in 24 hours and his record of 5 hours 9 minutes and 41 seconds for the London–Brighton–London stood for 14 years. At the 1912 Olympics in Stockholm he won a silver medal behind South Africa's Rudolph Lewis in the 315km individual time trial – a far cry from the ITT distances of today. Grubb completed the distance in 10 hours 51 minutes and that fine ride anchored the GB team comprising himself, Leon Meredith, Charles Moss and William Hammond to a silver medal behind Sweden in the team competition. Off the back of those performances he was encouraged to quit his amateur status and race professionally on the Continent. The 1914 Giro was to be his first major professional race. And last. Sadly, he couldn't then regain his amateur status after the 1914 Giro and so his promising racing career was over. Grubb wasn't the only one to suffer. Also in the Atala colours were the ever-reliable Giovanni Rossignoli, Giuseppe Contesini and Gino Brizzi and the expectation was that one way or another they would make the race. Instead, to a man, they had all abandoned by the end of stage one.

By all accounts it seems the apocalyptic weather set in about two hours into the stage as the race swept out on a long loop towards the north-west in the direction of Arona on Lake Maggiore before the *percorso* turned south and headed for Cuneo via the mighty Sestriere climb near the French border. The tempest started with a solid 60–70mph wind howling through the Po Valley, scattering debris on the course and destroying much of the Giro signage so that a number of riders took wrong turns when they became detached from the leaders. Riding in the pitch-dark is no fun at the best of times let alone into an approaching storm, a torrential downpour that didn't cease for 36 hours, which turned gradually into hail and sleet as the riders climbed in height. Icy rain, howling winds, the dark of night, caked in mud and already frozen to the bone, the peloton limped into Arona where many riders then punctured on nails local partisan fans had thrown on the road. The motivation behind such senseless behaviour is always difficult to comprehend but such sabotage tactics had quickly become commonplace on the Tour de France and 'fans' on the Giro were determined to follow suit. Their actions were well-orchestrated, indeed *Gazzetta* had got wind of them and offered a 1,000 lire award for tip-offs as to where and when but to no avail.

A succession of punctures was ruinous for many riders who had to stop and lost body heat as they tried to mend them in the dark with frozen hands in the rain and sleet. Habitually most riders carried two or three inner tubes but, once they had been used, unless they were a member of one of the 'big' teams who had a support vehicle there was virtually no way of finishing the stage. At least ten riders had abandoned before the peloton had even reached the foothills of the Sestriere climb where it was already snowing heavily ten kilometres below the summit and beyond that, should anybody successfully fight their way to the top, lay another 130km to the finish in Cuneo.

Petit-Breton was among the many riders who abandoned at the foot of the climb near Susa although few did it in such spectacular fashion. His team had been beset by mechanicals and he himself had already suffered a couple of morale-sapping punctures when he was abruptly stopped by a third. As he contemplated another repair he saw his team car approaching and ripped off his sodden, mud-caked jersey in anticipation of at least getting a clean, dry replacement. Alas for Petit-Breton the Atala team had already run out of spare kit; this was the final straw for Petit-Breton who reportedly 'flipped' and rode off up the road and into the storm bare-chested, howling with frustration before collapsing in a hysterical heap. Petit-Breton then repeatedly threw his bike at the team car. Magno's 'attractive figure of a lord competing with dignity' had cracked good and proper. Cycling in general, and the Giro in particular, can reduce the very best to gibbering wrecks of humanity.

Atala's team of *galácticos* decided to quit along with their revered leader Petit-Breton. Not one of them made it to Cuneo that evening, including Grubb. Shocked by the severity of the course and the racing, Grubb decided that road racing on the Continent was not for him although he had chosen possibly the toughest day on a bike in history to make his judgement. Disillusioned, he returned to Britain and concentrated his efforts on starting a bike shop in Brixton, south London, which eventually morphed into FHG Bikes, a significant name on the British cycling scene between the two world wars.

For those who 'conquered' Sestriere there was still a long ride to Cuneo and it was Angelo Gremo who eventually won the stage in a time of 17 hours 13 minutes and 55 seconds, just over 14 minutes ahead of Carlo Durando and Alfonso Calzolari who were the next arrivals, riding in together. The youthful Costante Girardengo was in fourth at 44 minutes and 20 seconds while in fifth was the 1909 winner Ganna – the King of Mud – who endured a dreadful time but battled on bravely. A kidney infection, however, forced him to abandon before the start of stage two. The reigning champion Oriani was seventh man home at 1 hour 7 minutes. Last man to arrive in Cuneo was Mario Marangoni, just 19, who was 7 hours and 14 minutes behind the stage winner. In total he was in the saddle for 24 hours and 7 minutes and Marangoni, being an *isolato*, had to then go and find himself some hot food and accommodation. He must have been a remarkably resilient young man, though, as he finished last in all the first five stages before abandoning on stage six.

Only 40 of the 81 starters finished in Cuneo although three of those were later disqualified for taking a tow. Harsh given the circumstances but rules are rules – except for the Giro leader who was not disqualified but, rather, incurred a 3-hour penalty when he was penalised for exactly the same offence later in the race. Of those who finished that first stage just 24 were within 4 hours of the winner's time. Under the new regulations that Cougnet had announced the remainder of the peloton should have been eliminated there and then but the race director relented and quietly shelved that rule for the rest of the race. Only three of the *aspiranti* – the least experienced and totally amateur members of the peloton – survived the day and only 14 of the *isolati*. Cougnet was far from unhappy, though, in fact he was quietly ecstatic: 'The retirements add prestige to the performance of the survivors and so to the race itself,' he later wrote.

Stage two on 26 May – down to Savona and then along the Ligurian coast – was the only comparatively flat stage of the 1914 Giro although there were still steep hills and mountain passes to negotiate. Relatively speaking it was the calm after the storm although of the 37 riders who started the day a further ten were forced to abandon as the after-effects of stage one continued to be felt. It was, however, an important day in terms of the GC race because it was the day when Alfonso Calzolari, third man home on stage one, took a grip of the race, breaking decisively on Passo del Bracco and riding alone for the final 125km to record a memorable stage win, finishing 24 minutes ahead of second-placed Giuseppe Azzini with the consistent Girardengo in third. With the overnight leader Gremo being forced to abandon – his Peugeot team were already down to just one rider and the team manager issued orders to withdraw from the race – Calzolari now found himself just over 1 hour ahead of Girardengo in the overall rankings which seemed a comfortable enough position but in fact, on this race anyway, was still some way short of being a decisive margin. On the 1914 Giro when things went wrong they went catastrophically wrong.

Cycling history has not been kind to Calzolari, who has been rather dismissed as a freak winner of a freakish race, but although he never won another bike race in his life after 1914 that is not altogether fair. In 1913 he had finished fifth behind winner Odile Defraye in a high-class Milan–San Remo, riding home alongside the winner of stage one of the 1914 Giro Angelo Gremo. He also won the prestigious Giro dell'Emilia that year, finishing ahead of Giovanni Gerbi and Gremo to name just two other quality riders. Calzolari was a very decent and unusually durable rider who produced his best form when it mattered, under the most testing of conditions, while others were either found wanting or were unlucky. He placed fourth or better in six of the eight stages on the Giro. It should be added that, having been deprived of five years of his career by the First World War, he still returned to record two second places in the first two stages of the 1919 Giro and was third overall after seven stages when he was forced to abandon. But for the war, the name of Calzolari might have featured more prominently in the history of cycling.

Stage three from Lucca to Rome, the longest stage in Giro history at 430km, had loomed large ever since the route had been announced but a desperate, lone 330km break from Lauro Bordin had the effect of settling the race down, with all the main contenders happy to ride as a group for most of another 17-hour day to first contain and then catch the Bianchi rider. Bordin, from Crespino in the Veneto, had taken advantage of the race stopping at a railway barrier just 15km into the day and slipped away on what still ranks as the longest solo break that competitive cycling has ever witnessed. When Bordin was eventually caught, just under 14 hours later, the ambitious Girardengo decided to press the issue and escaped for the second of his 30 Giro stage victories. The other big names contested a bunch sprint 2 minutes back while the battling Bordin hung on well in the final couple of hours to finish tenth some 16 minutes behind the stage winner. Another brutally long day – in fact the longest stage in Grand Tour history – but the surviving riders coped much better, with just one more rider abandoning as 26 riders made it safely to Rome.

Drama on stage four

Girardengo may have been a sure-fire star of the future but he was still a young man and cracked spectacularly on the rugged Monte Bove climb near Macerata on stage four from Rome to Avellino, losing 3 hours in the process. His time would come after the First World War but in both the 1913 and 1914 Giri he had already left his calling card and started to win a fanbase.

The narrative of another long, testing day was dictated by the Bianchi rider Giuseppe Azzini who had started the day in sixth place fully 1 hour and 47 minutes behind the leader Calzolari. The man from Gazzuolo in Lombardy had nothing to lose and pressed hard while behind him it is just possible that a spot of skulduggery was afoot as the peloton, most notably the Bianchi team, looked to clip the wings of the race leader. Calzolari had to cope with a tyre mysteriously flatting while he went into the commissaries' control tent to sign in at the Avezzano checkpoint midway through the stage, while on another occasion he picked up a second puncture when he and a number of other riders had to carry their bikes around an obstruction in the road, almost certainly down to saboteurs, and had to mingle with the *tifosi*. Whatever the truth of the matter, by the end of stage four Calzolari's lead was down to just over 1 hour with Azzini beginning to mount a credible challenge.

Azzini, who had finished third overall in 1913 after leading the race at the end of stage seven, was on a roll now and went on the attack again on stage five, on what was the shortest stage of the Giro, being a piffling 329km although littered with testing ascents at Lo Scorzo, Pietrastretta, Serra dei Palmenti and Matera. It was prime territory for a break and with Calzolari only having one team-mate to lean on – Clemente Canepari, who had gone into the race as the team leader – the race was blown apart with Azzini arriving in Bari 1 hour and 3 minutes ahead of Calzolari. Suddenly, well in the space of two stages, Azzini had recouped over 1 hour and 48 minutes and by the end of stage five was the new leader in GC, 89 seconds ahead of Calzolari. On paper the race was now Azzini's to lose. With four Bianchi colleagues still going strongly, the odds were heavily stacked in his favour but at that juncture the unseasonal weather, which had been rolling around northern Italy since the start of the race, intensified and shifted down to central Italy and contributed to another mind-boggling stage that will go down in the annals. The 428km run from Bari to L'Aquila was always going to be epic with climbs all over the place – Montecorvino, Vinchiaturo, Cinquemiglia and Poggio Picenze – but what you don't expect to get in central Italy in June is sleet, snowstorms and freezing conditions. For the second time the 1914 Giro morphed from a race into a battle for survival and by the end of the day there were just 12 riders left standing.

Azzini, so strong and dominant in the previous two stages, had again been going well when he suffered a massive crack. With about 30km of the stage left and with the weather at its worse, Azzini simply disappeared from sight and wasn't discovered until the next day when he was found feverish and disorientated in a farmer's hay barn where he had sought refuge. It might just have been sheer physical exhaustion, a driven individual pushing too hard in his pursuit of victory, but the crude use of drugs, such as strychnine and cocaine to mask the pain and suffering, or drugs to induce an artificial feeling of wellbeing, was by now commonplace in the peloton. With no reliable water en route, riders were also apt to fill their two metal bidons with red wine most days and as is well known now alcohol does not always mix well with such drugs, especially when the individual is in an already weakened state.

The brave backmarker Marangoni also ground to a halt on this hellish stage which was won by Luigi Lucotti in 19 hours 20 minutes and 47 seconds, the longest-ever winning stage time in Giro history. All this drama, however, took a back seat to the row concerning the leader Calzolari who, it was claimed, had taken a tow along with Clemente Canepari and Carlo Durando on the Svolte di Popoli climb about 45km from the finish in L'Aquila. The Bianchi team lodged the complaint with the race commissaries – no surprise there – but Canepari added fuel to the fire by admitting his own guilt and claiming that the car had been driven by a friend of Calzolari. Of course Canepari might have had his own axe to grind having gone into the race as Stucchi's number one rated rider. He would not have enjoyed the indignity of having to ride as a domestique to Calzolari.

It was all very messy and contentious. One race official claimed to have witnessed the incident but his evidence wasn't compelling and it was the race leader under scrutiny here. If there had been no question about his guilt, logic suggested that he be thrown off the race, as was the fate of the three cheats on stage one, but Cougnet was having none of it. A compromise was put in place whereby the three riders were relegated to last place on the stage and given the same time as the last rider who finished plus 1 minute. It sounded like a devastating blow but as all those concerned were riding high in GC there was effectively no change in GC other than Calzolari now being back in the lead. And commandingly so. With the abandonment of Azzini he was now 1 hour and 56 minutes ahead of second-place Pierino Albini.

The remaining 12 riders were out on their feet by now and there appears to have been a truce of sorts for the last two stages which were both 17-hour-plus monsters that nonetheless finished in bunch sprints. Albini took line honours in both, the 429km stage into Lugo and the final 420km ride into Milan but it made absolutely no difference to the provisional GC. Calzolari was the winner in 135 hours 17 minutes and 56 seconds, which was 1 hour 57 minutes and 26 seconds ahead of Albini, with Luigi Lucotti of the Maino team third at 2 hours 4 minutes and 23 seconds. Enrico Sala was the only *isolato* to finish so his fifth place won that division, and one of the most remarkable rides of all was that of *aspiranto* Umberto Ripamonti, just 19, who was the only rider in that class to finish. He came home in eighth and last place, 17 hours 21 minutes and 8 seconds behind the winner. The previous year the precocious Ripamonti had finished 30th on his Giro debut but there is no trace of him again in the cycling world until 1925 when he suddenly appears on the Giro start list and yet again he gets to the finish safely in 32nd position. A proven stayer if nothing else.

And then the fun really began. The 1914 Giro d'Italia still wasn't over. The Italian Cycling Federation had been monitoring events and ruled that Calzolari really should have been thrown off the race for taking a tow on the stage into L'Aquila and declared Pierino Albini the winner. There was an uncanny parallel with an early Tour de France dating back to 1904 when the French Federation disqualified 12 riders, including the first four in the provisional GC, for taking rides with taxis or trains in the most chaotic of Tours which had seen riders repeatedly attacked and injured and generally go in fear of their lives. After that race Maurice Garin, Lucien Pothier, César Garin and Hippolyte Aucouturier were all retrospectively disqualified and banned and Henri Cornet, who had finished nearly 3 hours behind Maurice Garin in the provisional standings, was declared the victor.

Untypically Desgrange accepted this without a fight. Cougnet, however, was violently opposed to the Federation interfering in what he considered to be his race and, having witnessed the entire 1914 Giro at first hand, he knew that there had definitely been a campaign of sorts within the peloton to discredit Calzolari and to prevent him from winning. The rider himself let it be known that in Bari, at the end of stage five, he had been offered double the winner's prize money by a complete stranger to throw the race. This doesn't altogether ring true either because Calzolari had lost the overall lead that day and was something of a long shot to regain that time – this, remember, was ahead of the dramatic snowy stage into L'Aquila. It was all very contentious with passions running high and, good newspaper man that he was, Cougnet also knew that this was a great soap opera of a story which would continue to sell newspapers during cycling's winter months and at a time when much of his readership might otherwise be understandably preoccupied with the opening salvos of the First World War.

Cougnet instituted proceedings against the Italian Federation and in February 1915 the courts ruled that Calzolari was indeed the winner of the 1914 Giro d'Italia. The Federation, though, were in trenchant mood and appealed the decision, and still the race wasn't won for sure until July 1915, 13 months after it had finished, when the appeal court also ruled in favour of Calzolari. By then the world was at war and the race with all its arguments and bitter polemics, and just eight finishers, a fading memory.

1914 Giro d'Italia Final Classification

1 Alfonso Calzolari (Stucchi) 135hr 17mins 56sec
2 Pierino Albini (Globo) + 01hr 57mins 26sec
3 Luigi Lucotti (Maino) + 02hr 04mins 23sec
4 Clemente Canepari (Stucchi) + 03hr 01mins 12sec
5 Enrico Sala (*isolato*) + 03hr 59mins 45sec
6 Carlo Durando (Maino) + 05hr 12mins 12sec
7 Ottavio Pratesi (Alcyon) + 17hr 21mins 08sec
8 Umberto Ripamonti (*aspiranto*) + 17hr 21mins 08sec

4

COSTANTE GIRARDENGO AND THE GIRO'S FIRST GOLDEN AGE (1919-25)

After the monstrosities and deprivations of the First World War sport had a major and sometimes unrecognised part to play as people's lives got back to something resembling normality. Part balm but mostly pure escapism, sport offered an alternative universe in which you could battle and 'fight' an opponent and achieve honour and glory without killing a fellow member of the human race.

That was certainly the case with cycling and the Giro. For the fans and the *Gazzetta* readers there was the chance to immerse themselves in the drama in which the worse scenario for the combatants was a crash and a broken limb. Meanwhile, for the most talented riders the sport now offered a genuine route out of the poverty to which most were accustomed. Out of this came an explosion in sport generally and the Roaring Twenties was certainly a golden decade for the Giro, when the race really came of age. This decade spawned two of the all-time greats of Italian cycling in Costante Girardengo and Alfredo Binda and a wonderfully varied supporting cast that included a third rider, Giovanni Brunero, whom some would also bracket with that immortal duo, and Alfonsina Strada, the only woman ever to 'complete' a Grand Tour racing against men.

Cycling in Italy had kept its head above the water even in the war with many of the big races like Lombardy and Milan–San Remo running in some form or other, although staging a nationwide Giro in such circumstances was obviously impractical. *Gazzetta* was still there, both reporting and organising, and 30,000 copies of the newspaper were transported up to the battlefront every week to be distributed among front-line troops as they tried to maintain a connection with home and normality. When peace eventually came, the seventh edition of the Giro got underway on Wednesday 21 May 1919 in Milan. Cougnet, recognising that the 1914 race, for all its sensational newspaper-selling qualities, was probably a tad over the top, reined in a little by reducing the average stage length to 298km from 395km and increasing the number of stages from eight to ten.

In the immediate aftermath of the 1914 race *Gazzetta* had originally outlined radical plans to switch from eight to 15 stages with an average length of just over 200km for the 1915 race to further reduce the strain on riders and increase revenue from those towns and cities hosting the starts and finishes. Then war intervened and come 1919 Cougnet opted for a midway house. It was still, by most standards, a brute of a course with many of the neglected roads, or those damaged by the fighting in the north, in even worse condition than normal. Certainly the *corsa rosa* was tough enough for only 15 riders to complete.

The 1919 Giro was undoubtedly also significant in that it appeared to portray a united Italy so soon after the First World War; indeed, it started just 13 days after a national referendum had voted to declare an Italian Republic and elections for the first properly national assembly. In an editorial on the day the race started *Gazzetta* stated: 'It is not true, it is not possible that Italians can not be united. Italians know that divided they will perish, united they will rise again. The Giro d'Italia is serving a purpose greater than the race itself. Neopoletans, Torinesi, Lombards and Laziani, Venetians and Emilians, all Italians, all regions with a single society and a single heart await the Giro as a mirror in which they can recognise each other and smile.'

At that start line on 21 May a good proportion of those competing were recently demobbed soldiers from the *Bersaglieri* cycling regiments that had proved so effective and resourceful. The army had let the ex-soldiers keep their bikes and many were now racing them, having stripped off the attachments used to carry machine guns and stretchers. The 1913 Giro champion Carlo Oriani, a proud member of the *Bersaglieri*, had been killed in action during the war and would have been known to many of the peloton while there would also have been a doffed cap to Petit-Breton, last seen hurling his bike against his team car in stage one in 1914. Petit-Breton had joined the French Army Driving Corp and was heavily involved in the famous Taxis de la Marne episode in the first days of war – in September 1914 – when every available driver and vehicle, including the Paris taxi fleet, was pressed into action to transport French troops to the First Battle of the Marne as the Germans closed on the French capital. Elsewhere he served extensively close to the front but Petit-Breton was actually 20 miles behind the lines when he was killed on 20 December 1917, reportedly swerving on the road in the middle of the night to avoid a horse and cart being driven erratically by its drunken owner.

Costante Girardengo started the 1919 Giro like a man who, at the age of 26, understandably seemed intent on making up for lost time. As a 20-year-old he had made his Giro debut back in 1913 and made his mark by winning stage six and finishing a promising sixth overall, while the following year he won the longest-ever stage, the 430km marathon from Lucca to Rome although that came at a cost and he later had to abandon. Now, though, he was in his physical pomp and about to embark on a winning streak that saw him win seven of the ten stages in 1919 when he led the Giro from start to finish, the first man to achieve that. It was after yet another stunning win, on stage eight, that the admiring Emilio Colombo christened him *campionissimo*, champion of champions. As Girardengo had yet to win the Giro – and actually only ever won two of the 11 Giri he contested in a lengthy career – this could perhaps be viewed as a slightly premature anointment of godlike status. Colombo, however, was never one to hold back and there is no doubting the genuine excitement Girardengo's winning streak caused. Post-war Italy was in the mood to celebrate heroes.

Girardengo was a compulsive serial winner – he was to finish his career with 30 stage wins at the Giro – who had little interest in minor placings. It was first or nowhere as far as he was concerned, as he proved in the Italian National championship which he won on nine occasions – the first in 1913 and the last in 1925 – and Milan–San Remo which he won six times, a record to this day beaten only by Eddie Merckx. He was a genuine all-rounder. There were a couple of great wins in the mountains among that impressive haul of Giro stage wins and even flat stages in Italy can be distinctly lumpy, but for a while he was unstoppable in the bunch sprints which Cougnet was cleverly trying to encourage. A modern-day equivalent is perhaps Peter Sagan, formidable on every terrain except perhaps in the very high mountain stages.

The flamboyant nature of Girardengo's wins in the bunch finishes partly explains his what we would now term celebrity status. Although growing massively in popularity with readers following the race from afar in *Gazzetta*, the stages were so long and often so remote that the only practical opportunity to 'experience' the race live, to be there in person and support your rider, was at the finishes. These were staged as often as possible in velodromes or stadia which also had the advantage of allowing the organisers to charge an entrance fee. Often Girardengo was the star of that show. Before and after the various stages, although by no means a matinee idol he was a snappy dresser and good with the fans. He possessed a certain charisma and x factor.

The media loved him and, of course, the photograph invariably featured most prominently after each stage was the clichéd shot of the stage winner heading the charging bunch and coming through the line, hands aloft. Not much change there. Meanwhile, from 1921 a film crew accompanied the race and although they did make heroic efforts to race ahead and take the occasional mid-race action shot up in the hills, once again the money shot was always the closing 100m or so of each stage. When the film was eventually edited and distributed around the country for fans to watch at cinemas, the winners of the bunch sprints featured time and time again. Girardengo was gold dust. The film crew knew exactly who to concentrate on as the pack charged towards the camera.

Girardengo's virtuosity was easy to understand; no wonder he became Italy's first superstar cyclist and one of only three Italian riders and Giro gladiators to be anointed *campionissimo*. Mussolini even ordered that all trains travelling through his hometown of Novi Ligure should stop at the local railway station as a mark of respect, whether they actually needed to or not. But who was this warrior on wheels, so diminutive that he sometimes looks like a jockey on a horse in photos and earned the less than flattering nickname of 'the Novi Runt' or *faina* (weasel).

As the fifth of nine children born into a poor farming family just outside Novi Ligure Girardengo had to fight his corner for both food and attention from the start. Later his father moved the family into town where he ran a bar-tabacchi. As a youth he discovered bikes by becoming a delivery boy, a common tale among early Italian cyclists, and after school he worked in a local factory before gaining employment at the Alfa-Romeo factory. As his two pre-war Giri rides demonstrated he was a precocious talent and had logged up two National championships and a Milano–Torino title before hostilities intervened. During the restricted wartime racing programme he took Milano–Torino for a second time and won his first Milan–San Remo in commanding style in 1918 with a daring 180km break, a sweet moment after the disappointment of 1915 when he was first across the line but was disqualified for taking the wrong route. It wasn't all plain sailing, though. After that Milan–San Remo triumph Girardengo nearly died, falling ill during the Spanish flu epidemic that devastated Europe during the latter stages of the war. It was touch and go but perhaps the strength and resilience he had built up as a road cyclist saw him through. Certainly he returned as formidable as ever.

Stucchi-Dunlop gathered a mighty *squadra* (team) around Girardengo which included Clemente Canepari, Angelo Gremo and Ezio Corlaita. Encouraged by his formidable trainer and masseur Biagio Cavanna, Girardengo was also quite modern and monastic in his approach to training, preparation and nutrition and is even said to have abstained from sex before a big race. That said, he was a habitual chain-smoker. Girardengo's stock couldn't have been higher after his triumph at the 1919 Giro which he won virtually at leisure with Gaetano Belloni 51 minutes and 56 seconds adrift in second place while Belgium's Marcel Buysse, riding for the Bianchi team, made a small piece of history in third by being the first non-Italian rider to claim a place on the podium. In the 1919 season Girardengo also won a third Italian championship, another Milano–Torino and the Giro di Lombardia as well as the Giro del Piemonte and Giro dell'Emilia. He was untouchable, different class, but cycling can humble even the great champions as Girardengo was about to discover in his next Giro appearance.

In terms of severity the 1920 Giro was right up there in second place behind the 1914 edition with only ten of the 49 riders successfully negotiating the eight stages and 3,300km of distinctly variable road conditions to make it back to Milan. And among those was the *campionissimo* himself. It had all gone horribly wrong on stage one from Milan to Turin when he crashed badly in the icy rain on the descent of Monte Ceneri. Not only was he badly battered and bruised, he had to repair his bike and while he was doing that Belloni and his Bianchi team had no hesitation in going on the attack, as was the norm in those days. There were no gentlemen's agreements about not attacking the leaders or reigning champion when they crashed or suffered a mechanical; it was every man for himself. So Bianchi ploughed on and, although Giuseppe Olivieri took the stage in just over 12 hours and 13 minutes, Belloni finished with the same time and put nearly 12 minutes into Girardengo who had bravely remounted and emptied the tanks to limit the damage and finish in fifth place. It had been a huge effort, fuelled mainly by the adrenalin that a bad crash often temporarily pumps into the system, but there was a big price to pay. Bruised and sore, Girardengo was not in good shape when he lined up for the second stage in Turin city centre after a day's rest for the 378km ride to Lucca, and from the start it was obvious that the *campionissimo* was suffering like a dog. The end came when he abandoned at Molassana in hilly terrain north of Genoa with fans fearing for his health and requisitioning an empty cottage nearby to lay their sick and injured champion out on a bed to recover.

It was a blow – for Girardengo obviously but for *Gazzetta* and their race as well – and first there had to be an inquest to extract maximum mileage out of the story. There had been suggestions that Girardengo had been angered at accusations of an illegal wheel change or that his morale had dipped after the unfortunate crash on stage one. That he lacked the stomach for the fight and that if he couldn't finish first he wasn't interested in finishing at all. There might just be an element of truth to the latter but it was way too early in the race surely to throw the towel in and the champion had shown plenty of spirit in trying to chase back on at the end of stage one. It was all good debating fodder for *Gazzetta* but there is no reason on this occasion to doubt Girardengo's insistence that his problems were entirely physical and clear for all to see.

Without their great champion to write about and to command the narrative, the 1920 Giro became a bit scratchy and contentious. For a day or two the crowd's ageing favourite Gerbi – 'the Red Devil' – was the main topic after being disqualified for taking a tow from a motorbike only to be reinstated *sub judice*. At the start of stage four in Rome there was a demonstration demanding that Gerbi's original disqualification should stand but by the end of the stage to Chieti it was all academic anyway with Gerbi, perhaps shocked by the strength of feeling against him that morning, deciding to retire.

With Girardengo out of the way this was undoubtedly Belloni's opportunity to strike and claim a big win for himself in a career in which he became labelled, rather unfairly, as the eternal second, the *eterno secondo*. It is true that on no fewer than 25 occasions Girardengo beat him into second place and undoubtedly theirs was a master–pupil relationship but, equally, it is true that Belloni won 43 races in his distinguished career including five Monuments – three Giri di Lombardia and two Milan–San Remo races – and finished his career with 12 stage wins in the Giro. That is hardly the palmares of an out-and-out loser. He was also a phenomenally successful Six Days racer both in Europe and the USA where he became a big star at the Madison Square Garden. So successful and lucrative was the latter that he didn't retire until the age of 43 – who in their right mind resists such low-hanging fruit? – and was on first-name terms with all the waiters and barmen on the transatlantic liners as he moved between Italy and New York.

Angelo Gremo was of much the same mind and as the 1920 Giro progressed around Italy was the only other serious contender for GC honours. Gremo, an impressive winner of Milan–San Remo in 1919, was also a Bianchi rider but with the rest of the massively diminished peloton trailing a long way behind it became a two-man battle. At the end of stage six it was Gremo who seemed to hold the upper hand with a lead of 9 minutes and 58 seconds over Belloni but stage seven was to prove decisive, a savage 349km from Bologna to Trieste over the still war-damaged roads of the Veneto and Trieste region.

Belloni had been biding his time and was unstoppable as he launched his bid for glory mid-race. Only Ugo Agostoni – more than 4 hours behind on GC – had the heart to follow and was rewarded with a fine second place behind Belloni but Gremo suffered grievously, finishing 42 minutes behind, his GC hopes smashed. The *eterno secondo*, for once, was *numero uno* while Girardengo licked his wounds back in Novi Ligure. At some stage somebody was going to pay for this.

With his wit and willingness to accept the superiority of the people's choice Girardengo with good grace, Belloni was a big favourite with the *tifosi* and his win was extremely well received. Looking at pictures of him with his wild hair, his wrestler's physique – he had been a promising Greco-Roman wrestler before injuring a thumb in a factory accident – and jovial sunburned face you just know he would be good fun to talk to. When questioned, in 1919, about Girardengo's perennial dominance over him he replied: 'I will never be a *campionissimo* but the names of a few pretty girls will be etched on my heart.'

So the two post-war Giri to date had produced two popular winners and a wealth of stories. Cougnet and *Gazzetta* were happy enough but in an ideal world normal service would be resumed in 1921, which for them meant a clutch of spectacular wins by Girardengo leading to an inevitable and rapturous welcome back in Milan for the champion of champions. And for a while that appeared the most likely scenario with Girardengo embarking on one of his irresistible surges in which he claimed the first four stages of the race with sprint finishes at Merano, Bologna, Perugia and Chieti. The strong Stucchi team were able to contain the half-hearted attacks with relative ease and the peloton seemed resigned to its preordained fate. With those four wins in the bag he was obviously leading the GC at the end of stage four although Belloni, in second place overall, had kept him close company and was officially on the same time as Girardengo in the overall standings.

And then came stage five, a tough Apennine passage from Chieti to Naples, and yet another reminder that you take nothing for granted in bike races. A momentary loss of concentration, a touch of wheels, a crash and Girardengo was on the deck with a damaged bike and badly wrenched back muscles. Two seconds before he had been in the form of his life and looking unbeatable, yet now, suddenly, he was grovelling in the dust and watching those at the front of the peloton look back with some relish before they attacked with a vengeance. Eventually he effected a repair of sorts and climbed back on and tried to give chase, but this time it was utterly pointless and just outside Isernia on the Cinquemiglia Plateau, he climbed off for the second year in a row, a broken man. At which point he reportedly drew a cross in the road and said: 'With this cross I signify that I Costante Girardengo from Novi Ligure will never again pass this point on my bicycle.' Given his utterly exhausted and emotional state such theatrical eloquence seems doubtful and it is possible Colombo added a degree of drama to his report. An alternative version has Girardengo saying, '*Girardengo si ferma qui*' – Girardengo stops here – which sounds much more plausible. Whatever the story, for the second year running the race would have to survive without its star attraction. *Gazzetta* naturally mourned Girardengo's departure although it should be pointed out that at the start of stage five, and despite more than 50 hours of racing, there were four riders within 9 seconds of Girardengo on GC. Not even at halfway, and with some big climbs to come, the race was by no means over.

It was time for the prospective winner to make a move and again the cards appeared to be falling for Belloni who assumed the lead at the end of stage five and then increased his advantage to over 1 minute at the end of stage six, the run from Naples to Rome. But there were other exceptional riders in this race who, like Belloni the year before, were biding their time to strike. Foremost among these was the handsome, enigmatic, consistently underrated and indeed slightly tragic figure of Giovanni Brunero – the pride of the Canavese region but seemingly not held in the highest regard elsewhere.

Brunero was a natural climber despite his strong muscular build and was also powerful on flat and rolling terrain – what the Italians call a *passista-scalatore*, a rider good on the flat and in the mountains. His only real weakness on the road was that he possessed no sprint finish which meant that his victories were largely a result of dogged persistence. It wasn't always exhilarating to watch and his real genius was often employed on remote mountains and passes where few were on hand to witness its devastating effect. Generally, his *modus operandi* made it difficult for *Gazzetta*'s wordsmiths to launch into purple prose and almost impossible for the film crews to capture but he was nonetheless a stunning talent. It would be safe to say he would be much more appreciated today than he was in his pomp.

By the time he arrived at the 1921 Giro Brunero was no callow youth; he was nearly 26 and had experienced much on and off the bike. He had won the Italian amateur championship two years earlier and later in 1919 turned professional for the Legnano team before winning the Giro dell'Emilia in 1920, when he beat Girardengo and Belloni. That same year he came second in the Giro di Lombardia and recorded a fifth place in Milan–San Remo. In short a major new talent was moving among the domestic Italian peloton. All this would probably have happened much earlier but Brunero spent part of the war fighting in the 5th Regiment of the *Bersaglieri* although his circumstances changed when both his parents died within a short space of time. Brunero reportedly stumbled on his father's death when, getting off the train on the way home for a week's leave, he spotted a funeral cortège. On enquiring who had died he was informed it was his father. In the wake of the death of both their parents – his mother had died not long before her husband – Brunero and his younger brother were moved away from the front and ran a small bike shop in Cirie from which he based his training and assault on the cycling world. This was a very determined man with the bit between his teeth and, like so many of the most successful riders down the years, he was being driven on by difficult circumstances in his personal and emotional life.

Brunero went to work on stage seven on the road to Livorno. He didn't rout the field but somehow he managed to escape a select group including not only Belloni but Alfredo Sivocci, Bartolomeo Aymo, Marcel Buysse, Angelo Gremo and Federico Gay. And having made the break he rode with the strength of two men to hang on and win the stage by 2 minutes and 1 second, all the others arriving together. His audacity had earned him a 52-second lead over Belloni in GC. There were still three stages to go and the gutsy Belloni went on the attack and managed to win two of them but Brunero, with good support from his Legnano-Pirelli colleagues, tracked him masterfully and eventually took this first Giro from Belloni by 41 seconds. In third place, nearly 20 minutes behind in this two-horse race, was Brunero's loyal helper Aymo. Italy had a new Giro champion but there appeared to be little love for the unspectacular Brunero. After the race, Colombo wrote to Brunero in rather awkward self-serving terms, realising that his newspaper probably hadn't done full justice to Brunero and his win and was, before his withdrawal, perhaps rather too partisan in its support for Girardengo: 'I write because my heart and my conscience compel me to, because I want you to understand my affection and my most sincere compliments … I confess that during the opening stages I wasn't very enthusiastic. I believed that given your references to lack of form you intended to retire.'

Draw your own conclusions from that. Meanwhile, the intriguing prospect of a rematch hung in the air all winter and throughout the spring calendar and, in fairness to the Girardengo disciples, Brunero certainly needed to repeat his fine debut win in the Giro, against the man considered to be the *campionissimo,* before he could be accorded the same status.

The race of a thousand arguments

And so to the 1922 Giro, so cantankerous and bad-tempered that it was soon dubbed the race of *mille polemiche* – thousand arguments or disputes. The ill feeling had possibly started earlier in the season when Brunero walked off with Milan–San Remo after he and Girardengo were comfortably in the lead and heading for a sprint, which the *campionissimo* would have won as sure as night follows day, when both had been brought down by a stray spectator on the course about two kilometres from the finish. Some reports suggest it was an official.

Brunero recovered quickest and although the incident itself was not captured surviving footage shows him rolling over the line in first place with a rather sheepish look on his face, while a few moments later a clearly angry and agitated Girardengo arrived home in second place. There was plenty of unfinished business between the two protagonists going into the Giro.

It all kicked off on stage one and the 326km run from Milan to Padua, quite a lumpy stage which included Colle San Eusebio and Pian delle Fugazze. Enough climbing for Brunero to immediately attack and make his mark on the race and perhaps silence some of the doubters who were still questioning the quality of his win 12 months earlier. By the time he reached the Fugazze he was alone out in front having already put 10 minutes into the main contenders, but on the descent into Riva del Garda he crashed and broke a wheel which threatened to undermine all his good work. What happened next was commonplace but under the regulations of the day illegal. Brunero waited for the chasing peloton which included his Legnano team-mate Sivocci who gave his team leader a wheel from his bike (although 'gave' is probably being too generous: a price will almost certainly have been agreed, even among team-mates).

There then followed a convoluted process: Alfredo Sivocci in turn 'borrowed' a wheel off another Legnano rider, Pietro Linari, who in turn negotiated a wheel from Franco Giorgetti. The final transaction involved Giorgetti obtaining a wheel from humble independent Ruggero Ferrario who, by a process of elimination, was the rider left with just one wheel on his bike. Ferrario carried his bike and Brunero's broken wheel to the checkpoint at Riva del Garda, at which point race officials, who had missed the entire pantomime, became aware that something was afoot. Meanwhile, up at the front of the race Brunero had recovered from his mishap and was going like a train, eventually winning the stage from Belloni by nearly 16 minutes with an off-colour Girardengo a further 22 minutes behind. Given that the previous year's race had been won by just 41 seconds, this already seemed an unbeatable lead and, predictably, there was uproar and much concern among the vanquished.

Girardengo's Maino team had seen and heard what had gone on with regard to Brunero's dodgy wheel change even if the Giro's officials had missed it and immediately filed an official complaint, as did Belloni's Bianchi team. The daggers were out for Brunero, who, disregarding the legality of the wheel change for a moment, had clearly crushed the other contenders on the road and was in the form of his life. Initially Cougnet threw Brunero out of the Giro but Legnano, arguing with some justification that such wheel changes were commonplace in the peloton and rarely punished, even if this was an extreme and convoluted example, lodged an appeal. If the judges zealously pursued every alleged case of borrowed or purchased wheels over the coming days and weeks it would be a very small peloton indeed that returned to Milan.

Eventually the judges reconsidered their decision and the reigning champion was allowed to stay in the race *sub judice*. This, however, didn't appease Bianchi or Maino who were on the warpath and felt, probably rightly, that this was the crucial battleground of the 1922 Giro. The race was going to be decided by this decision. Big players in the world of Italian cycling with Girardengo being the ace in their pack, they put renewed pressure on the judges to seek clarification from the Italian Cycling Federation – the Unione Velocipedistica Italiana (UVI). But with the limited communications of the day, the ruling only came when the race had reached the end of stage three in Bologna, a bunch sprint won by Belloni. The UVI's call was that Brunero should be retrospectively docked 25 minutes for his wheel change on stage one and that the stage victory and prize money be given to Belloni. The GC was recalculated accordingly that evening in Bologna, and Belloni found himself leading Girardengo by 1 minute 15 seconds, with Brunero trailing 3 minutes 5 seconds in fourth.

Belloni and Girardengo were back in the lead but Brunero was still in the race and with a number of big mountain stages to come was still very much in contention. The Bianchi and Maino teams were in no way appeased and the very real and embarrassing possibility of losing to Brunero despite his 25-minute penalty loomed large.

Taking all that into consideration they took the unprecedented decision of withdrawing from the Giro. The race leader and the man in second place were quitting and going home, along with their team riders. They opted for the moral high ground – not a summit often visited by cycling during this period – and again a friendly press and the *tifosi* seemed largely to support them.

But the Giro waits for no man and, despite all the arguments and chuntering in the background, the now diminished peloton was back on the start line at Pescara two days later. Although the GC race was now clearly going to be between Brunero and that relentless trier Bartolomeo Aymo, there was also the chance now for some lesser names to chase stage wins and to enjoy their day in the sun. Stage four provided immediate evidence of this with Alfredo Sivocci, Pietro Linari and Luigi Annoni providing the podium in an eight-man sprint in which Aymo and Brunero had safely attached themselves. The GC at the end of stage four looked very different from two days earlier, with just two names – Aymo and Brunero – surviving from before Maino and Bianchi had withdrawn.

It was a two-horse race and again Brunero made his decisive move on stage seven between Rome and Florence when he won convincingly to move ahead of Aymo in GC, a lead he consolidated on stage eight between Florence and Santa Margherita, when he and Luigi Annoni worked well in a long break before the former rolled over the line first. The plucky Aymo hit back with a stage win of his own in Turin but was never seriously going to challenge his team leader and Brunero wrapped the race up impressively by soloing into Milan nearly 6 minutes ahead of the pack to win his second Giro on the bounce. Still the applause was a little muted, respectful rather than rapturous for the diminished peloton. Brunero just shrugged: it was the others' decision to withdraw from the race. You have to be in it to win it.

It was time for Girardengo to take stock. That was three Giri in a row now which, for one reason or another, he had failed to complete let alone win. He could point to bad luck and the slings and arrows of outrageous fortune that confront every Grand Tour cyclist. The decision to withdraw when leading in the most recent Giri, however, was entirely down to him and his team. Did he really feel so strongly about Brunero's dodgy wheel change – something he himself would have done on a number of occasions in his career without penalty – or had he found a convenient way of sidestepping the ignominy of defeat? Something had to change and only person who could make that happen was Girardengo himself and in 1923 he demonstrated exactly why he was indeed a great champion and so revered. This was the season in which he set the record straight by winning everything, not just the Giro. Rejuvenated, he won the Italian championship (yet again), Milan–San Remo, Milano–Torino, the Giro del Veneto and the Giro della Toscana but, of course, it is his stage-winning exploits at the Giro that are remembered above all else. He was a man on a mission.

The insatiable Girardengo won eight of the ten 1923 stages on offer but although the race turned into a sprintfest and his winning margin in GC was only a remarkably slim 37 seconds, the key to his victory was winning a very hilly stage six across the Apennines from Naples to Chieti when even Brunero could not get away and had to be content finishing second with the same time. Had Brunero been able to make the break that day and win, even by just a minute or two, the whole complexion of the race might have changed but Girardengo was absolutely determined to re-establish his authority and fought off a joint effort by Brunero and his colleague Aymo to animate the race in the high hills which incorporated the climbs at Vinchiaturo, Rionero Sannitico and Fontanella. It was a deeply impressive performance especially in an area of the country that had caused him so much grief; indeed, at one point they rode past the exact spot on the Cinquemiglia Plateau where Girardengo had abandoned two years earlier, making a cross in the dusty road.

Girardengo had ridden the entire race flawlessly this year with everything working out as planned. He took the first sprint in Turin but was happy enough to cede the race lead to Aymo the following day which featured a hilly run to Genoa. Quite why Aymo, Brunero's top domestique went for the win and not Brunero himself is not clear because this was always going to be one of the few opportunities to put time into Girardengo on a *corsa rosa* that favoured the quick men. Regardless, the net result was excellent for Girardengo. Aymo and the Legnano team had assumed the lead but was only 1 minute and 15 seconds to the good and the *campionissimo* had a clutch of flatter stages and mixed terrain stages to get tucked into. In quick succession he clocked up wins in Florence, Rome (after another strong performance in the hills) and Naples before reclaiming the leadership in Chieti. Thereafter it was a procession on much easier terrain with only Alfredo Sivocci in Mantua interrupting his remarkable sequence of stage wins. Girardengo was back where he belonged, on top, although in quieter moments he might have reflected that 37 seconds was quite a slim win the GC. The margins were still fine.

The 1923 Giro was notable for one other performance that occasionally gets overlooked and even slightly derided, namely a fifth place in GC in his only Giro appearance by a wild and haunted looking *isolato* named Ottavio Bottecchia. As an unknown debutant going up against the big names and their organised teams that was an exceptional result; it's just that when you place his solitary Giro ride against what he subsequently achieved at the Tour de France it rather pales into insignificance. This was, however, the first real glimpse of an astounding and unusual talent that was to burn brightly for a couple of years across the border.

The 1924 Giro was ill-starred from the start with the painful culmination of a power struggle between the teams and the race organisation. Bianchi and Maino had flexed their muscles two years earlier by withdrawing Belloni and Girardengo when they were leading the GC after the Brunero time penalty. Cougnet stood firm on that occasion but then the following year Girardengo's phenomenal tally of eight stage wins seemed to redress the power in favour of the teams. How could you have a Giro d'Italia without Girardengo or indeed Brunero, the man most likely to topple the *campionissimo* if he faltered? Or that great crowd-pleaser Belloni or, indeed, the slightly mysterious Bottecchia from the Veneto, the man who had lit up the 1923 Tour de France and become the first Italian on the podium there?

These were the star names, the talent, and they thought it was right they start demanding bigger money from their teams. The teams pleaded poverty and decided to ask for appearance money from the organisers, but Cougnet would never agree to that dangerous precedent and dismissed any such notion. At which point all the top teams promptly withdrew. The Giro was in real trouble but Cougnet sensed that if they could get through this test of their resolve they would break the teams' opposition for good. In the long term Italian cycling teams could never exist without the opportunities, afforded by *Gazzetta*, of racing in the Giro d'Italia, Milan–San Remo and the Giro di Lombardia. Great riders come and go but they are nothing without the great races in which they can display their talents.

It was time for a charm offensive for those who were happy to compete without making a fuss. For 1924 therefore everybody racing the Giro would be given free board and lodging for the duration, an offer which attracted 90 starters. Each competitor was given a daily food allowance of a quarter of a roast chicken, 250 grams of meat, two prosciutto and butter sandwiches, two jam sandwiches, three raw eggs, two bananas, 100 grams of biscuits and 50 grams of chocolate along with as many oranges and apples as the rider wanted or could carry. Yet the field badly lacked stardust and dynamite. Witness a distinctly underwhelming top five in the final GC: the American-born Giuseppe Enrici, Federico Gay, Angiolo Gabrielli, Secondo Martinetto and Enea Dal Fiume. No names to set your pulse racing there. It should probably have been the year that the worthy Bartolomeo Aymo – deciding to compete as an *isolato* – should have triumphed but he crashed out on stage three.

As a newsworthy story capable of selling newspapers the race was only saved by the presence of an extraordinary trailblazer – Alfonsina Strada – who to this day is the only woman ever to 'compete' in a male Grand Tour.

Born Alfonsina Morini in a poor family of ten in Castlefranco Emilia, her story according to the *Gazzetta* version was that her father swapped ten chickens for her first rusty bike which was intended to help her run errands and chores. She then started riding for pleasure on Sunday mornings, telling her mother instead that she had been to church. Eventually everybody was in on the secret and she started racing against the local men, the local press soon christening her 'the devil in a dress'. Her career received a further boost when she married the cycling-loving Luigi Strada in 1915, Luigi giving her a new man's racing bike as a wedding present, the same bike she was to ride in the 1924 Giro.

Cycling lore has it that she entered the Giro under the name Alfonso Strada which fooled the organisers who only realised they had a woman in their race the day before it began in Milan when everybody gathered for registration. Frankly, you have to take that with a pinch of salt. This is a lady who started and finished both the *Gazzetta*-organised 1917 and 1918 Giri di Lombardia, placing 31st and last in the former and 21st in the latter when she beat a number of men. Those rides were big stories, Alfonsina was the media's darling and already quite a celebrity in her own right, a friend of many of the top male riders and an instantly recognisable figure. It is inconceivable that her participation in 1924 was in any way random or unexpected. It was a clever ploy to breathe a little life into a Giro that would otherwise have died on its feet.

Come the start Strada lined up with number 72 pinned to her jersey and, although finishing stage one, a 300km run to Genoa won by Aymo, with the stragglers, she made the cut and was good to go for stage two.

In Florence she was 56th out of 65 finishers and finished 2 hours and 6 minutes behind the stage winner, Federico Gay, a respectable time given that the winner's time was the best part of 12 hours. And so she battled on day after day with the crowd on the road and the travelling press corps concentrating as much on her plucky rides as the battle for GC which had developed into a race between Enrici and Gay. It was on stage eight, a nasty hilly day from L'Aquila to Perugia with the rain sluicing down and winds blowing hard that Strada really began to suffer with a series of punctures and crashes – one badly bruising a knee – which resulted in her missing the cut. At one stage her handlebar snapped but an ad hoc repair was effected by using a broom handle donated by a housewife on the roadside. She wasn't the only rider in trouble, however. Gay had endured a poor day and was now over 40 minutes behind Enrici. The GC race was all but over but there were four stages still to go, the Giro having reverted to a 12-stage format.

All of which probably helped Strada as she pleaded to be allowed to continue. Colombo, Cougnet and the judges conferred and came up with a compromise agreement. She had to be withdrawn from the official classifications but she would be allowed to 'race' on with the peloton and the organisation would continue to provide free board and lodging. This was too good a story to end prematurely. And so she raced on, covering every last centimetre of the 3,613km course, eventually finishing some 30 hours behind Enrici. To put that into perspective, only 38 of the 97 starters completed the race. Strada succeeded where 59 men failed.

It is salutary to note, however, that 12 months later, when peace had broken out again between the teams and the organisation, and the luminous presence of Alfredo Binda had arrived like a meteor to light up the scene, Strada was surplus to requirements. Her enlightened participation in 1924 is a strange episode and ultimately, alas, a pyrrhic victory. She had served her purpose and was no longer wanted. Now there were genuine male stars to lionise again *Gazzetta* reasoned that readers wouldn't be interest in a woman rider trailing home in the gloaming after the finish had been dismantled.

Indeed, the rest of Strada's life has a slightly melancholic tinge. She continued racing in exhibitions, novelty races, walls of death at the circus, and as late as 1938 she set the female world record for the hour, covering 32.58km at Longchamp in Paris. After her husband Luigi fell ill, she was his carer until he was hospitalised and died in 1946. She remarried in 1950, a former cyclist Carlo Messori, and they ran a cycling shop in Milan. Messori had started to write her biography when he also died young. She closed the shop, discovered motorbikes rather late in life and treated herself to a 500cc MotoGuzzi on which she cut quite a dash. Alas, the bike was to play a part in her death after she had been riding it one day to the Tre Valli Varesine event. Returning home, she was trying to restart her motorbike when she collapsed, suffering a fatal heart attack.

5

THE DESPOTIC REIGN OF ALFREDO BINDA (1925-33)

By 1925 peace of sorts had broken out, or at least an uneasy truce. The big teams and major players had made their point and vented their spleen and although they could in no way claim a victory it had been a shot across the bows for *Gazzetta*. A race like the Giro cannot flourish without its star riders and personalities. Take away the x factor and soon it would become just another bike race. As it happened the Maino and Bianchi teams didn't compete in 1925 but their star names still mustered in new colours with Girardengo and Belloni riding for Wolsit. Brunero and the Legnano team were back and from the outside looking in it seemed like a straightforward tussle between Girardengo and Brunero with both riders looking to become the first rider to win three Giri individually.

Pre-race, though, *Gazzetta* was trumpeting the cause of a young Italian émigré, Alfredo Binda, who was returning from Nice just over the border to make his debut in the Legnano team alongside Brunero. It was a good call. The next superstar of Italian cycling – the next *campionissimo* – was about to announce his presence to the wider world in the most spectacular fashion. Originally from Cittiglio near Varese, Binda had arrived back in Italy as a 22-year-old and in less than a decade rewrote the record books and in a very real way redefined what could be achieved on a bike. A genuine all-rounder in that he could excel in all departments, Binda was also a calculating and ruthless racer. Although not academic – that opportunity was denied him – Binda was intelligent and measured in everything he did. Combine those exceptional physical and mental attributes with a robust constitution and the result, eventually, was five Giri titles and 41 stage wins. Binda's dominance of the race became such that, by the time he had won 33 stages in the previous five editions, the organisers paid him to stay away from the 1930 Giro, in many ways the ultimate compliment.

One of Binda's nicknames was 'the dictator', fairly self-explanatory given his dominance and the inevitability of victory, but perhaps his kinder moniker – '*la Gioconda*', the Mona Lisa – captures him better. He undoubtedly possessed the inscrutable smile of the *Mona Lisa*; we see it in almost every picture of him. He tends to look pleased with himself – with good reason – but there is also another slightly more unnerving quality he shares with Leonardo's masterpiece. He is observing you just as the *Mona Lisa* seems to do. Even in repose you sense a hyperactive enquiring mind which misses nothing.

Binda's cycling style fascinated the critics who constantly struggled to do it justice. The words effortless, floating, stylish and perfect all appear frequently in contemporary reports and the absence of any obvious excessive physical exertion was puzzling and rather defied analysis. He appeared to spin along like a modern-day rider doing a gentle recovery ride, requiring no more effort to climb steep gradients than to ride on the flat. That, of course, was his genius, making the difficult look easy and the unlikely inevitable. French cyclist René Vietto memorably noted of Binda that: 'If you put a cup of milk between his shoulders at the foot of a mountain, he would cross the summit without spilling a drop. He was at one with his bike. Elegance, purity, he was an artist. He was the epitome of beauty in action.' But he had worked hard to become this good. Study images of Binda from 1925 onwards and you see a fantastically honed and strong-looking athlete, and if you start examining his palmares before he arrived back in Italy its shows a driven man packing in thousands of kilometres of high-quality racing and training over very tough terrain. Slightly under the radar over the border in France, Binda was unstoppable in 1923–4 riding for the La Française team. He was putting in the hard yards. There were 29 wins in all including Nice–Nice, the Mont Cauvaire, Nice Trophée du '*Petit Journal*', Circuit du Provençal, Toulon–Nice, the Mont Faron climb and two victories in the annual Nice–Puget–Théniers–Nice event.

As early as 1923 Girardengo and Belloni were alerted to his talent when a young Binda went steaming past them high on the slopes of Mont Chauve (better known as Mont Ventoux) at the conclusion of the Nice–Mont Chauve race. This was the apprenticeship which went largely unseen by the parochial Italian fans even though the young man tearing it up in France was one of their own. Strangely, the lack of any obvious suffering, struggle and inner torment meant that for many years he was admired rather than loved. Binda was so extraordinarily good that he wasn't a rider the *tifosi* could identify with though his results were incredible and his style peerless. With his good looks, slicked-back hair, perfectly pressed trousers and apparent playboy lifestyle in the resort of Alassio, Binda was from another world altogether. In some pictures you even see him lounging around post-race in the sort of dressing gown more usually associated with Noël Coward.

If there was indeed the hint of a playboy about him, appearances can be deceptive. Although he famously stayed single until the end of his competitive career and was perceived as playing the field for much of that time, he shared Girardengo's aversion to mixing sex and cycling. In 1949, when he was coaching the Italy squad at the Tour de France, he clashed with Fausto Coppi who wanted his wife Bruna to accompany him. Binda refused him this and was quoted in the press as saying: 'A real professional should concentrate exclusively on his job. When I was winning I permitted myself one sexual encounter a year.'

Binda was difficult to pigeonhole. The tenth child of 14 – parents Maffeo and Martina were another prolific Italian couple – Binda grew up initially in Cittiglio, close to Lake Maggiore, and a strong musical strain ran in the family. Brothers Albini and Benito played the trombone and the saxophone respectively while Alfredo took up the trumpet and together they played in the town's marching band. Later, when his cycling career took off he inevitably became known as 'the Trumpeter of Cittiglio' and you wonder if a sense of timing and rhythm might in some small way account for the languid riding style, tapping out the smoothest of beats. A number of riders over the years have spoken of almost riding to an internal soundtrack and tempo as they try to ease their way through rugged, staccato terrain, smoothing out the harsh edges, in their minds at least.

Bringing up 14 children was not easy and there was little prospect of employment in Cittiglio, so eventually Binda's parents sent Alfredo, aged 16, and a younger brother, Prima, to stay with an uncle in Nice. Initially, Alfredo earned his keep as a plasterer although much of his spare time – he had one day off in midweek as well as weekends – was spent riding with the local Nice Sport Cycling club or on his own up in the mountains close by. He was a regular at the Vélodrome du Pont Magnan where he developed a love for the track as well and worked on his devastating sprint finish. His talent was obvious to all and by the age of 21 he had signed for small local professional team La Française with whom he claimed those first important victories.

The 'breakthrough' moment came when, at the end of 1924, he decided it was time to test his mettle against the top Italian riders at the Giro di Lombardia. His main objective was to win the 500-lire prize awarded for the first man over the Ghisallo climb but, having accomplished that, he hung on to finish fourth behind Brunero, Girardengo and Pietro Linari. The subplot, though, was that ahead of the race he had written to Eberardo Pavesi – the 'lawyer' – who was *directeur sportif* for Lagnano saying that he hoped to ride at Lombardy and hinting that he might be available should he feel so inclined to sign him for next season. There was even a suggestion doing the rounds that Binda was on the point of applying for French citizenship – by now he was mainly talking in the *Nasasrte* patois of the Nice area rather than his native tongue.

Pavesi recognised Binda's outstanding talent, his only reservation being whether Binda's form could transfer across from the smooth paved roads of the South of France to the much rougher surfaces he would encounter on the Giro and the Italy's one-day classics. Binda's showing in the 1924 Lombardy offered reassuring evidence that 'the Trumpeter of Cittiglio' could make music anywhere. Pavese offered Binda 20,000 lire a year and 5,000 for every Classic he won. Much emboldened by Pavesi's interest, Binda held out for a week or two for a slightly larger basic wage and eventually the deal was done. In no time at all an avalanche of prize money rendered his basic wages fairly insignificant anyway.

That was the Alfredo Binda who made himself known to the Giro officials in Milan the day before the 1925 Giro d'Italia. An incredible ride was about to begin. The 1925 Giro boasted a quality field and a tough-looking 3,520km course spread over 12 mainly hilly or mountainous stages. Girardengo and Brunero, first and second at Milan–San Remo a couple of months before the Giro, were the big favourites as they renewed their battle from 1923, but Belloni was always competitive, Linari was a quality sprinter although this wasn't a sprinter-friendly course and Binda was an exciting if unproven talent in a Grand Tour.

It was tight and cagey to start with and at the end of stage four, from Pisa to Rome, Girardengo led Binda in GC although they both shared the same time, Girardengo being considered the leader by virtue of his win on stage two in Arenzano. Unwittinglyly, however, Girardengo had already made a tactical error which was to come back and haunt him. On stage three the *campionissimo*, seemingly in generous mood, had ridden hard to help his *gregario* Pierino Bestetti take a much-valued stage win, a reward in advance for the hard work that Girardengo would undoubtedly require from his man in the long days ahead. All of which was admirable except that one of Girardengo's other team-mates – and very good friend, Belloni – was having a bad day at the office and would himself have appreciated a helping hand and a little TLC from Bestetti and indeed Girardengo. As a former Giro winner Belloni felt he was entitled to rather better from his colleagues and was not a happy man when he trailed into Pisa 16 minutes behind the stage winner. He and Girardengo might be firm friends and frequent travelling companions but that was out of order. Just because he was the eternal second didn't mean there was any reason to treat him as a second-class citizen.

Fast-forward to stage five from Rome to Naples and the sporting gods offered Belloni a chance to get his own back when Girardengo suffered a puncture. Belloni instantly went full gas and drove home a decisive break to win the stage with Binda in close attendance. Binda took over as the race leader with a fuming Girardengo at 5 minutes and 32 seconds and the Herculean efforts of Girardengo to close that gap – and Binda's implacable resistance – provided the narrative for the rest of the race.

By way of celebration, and possibly to demonstrate how fit and fresh he felt, Binda wandered over to the marching band that had been entertaining the crowd at the Arenacia Track and borrowed a trumpet to give a solo rendition of a couple of rousing tunes before making his way to the podium. The subliminal message was very strong.

Still, the Giro wasn't even at halfway and nobody was throwing the towel in just yet. Indeed, in many ways what transpired was one of Girardengo's finest moments, the old gunslinger bravely taking on the new hotshot. Could he somehow ramp up the pressure and expose Binda's relative inexperience on Italian roads? Binda looked as if he was in control but would he, like others had done before, crack at some unlikely point when all the stresses and strains of a race suddenly manifest themselves in a crisis? Girardengo kept plugging away – his pride and reputation at stake in his own mind at least – yet, despite reeling off four stage wins in the second half of the race, he simply could not shake off Binda who rode effortlessly on his shoulder with that inscrutable smile, shadowing his every move. When Belloni led the peloton home in Milan by winning the stage win, Girardengo was still 4 minutes and 58 seconds behind. He had pulled back just 34 seconds in the final seven stages, 2,051km of full-on, eyeballs-out racing. The new *campionissimo* – for Binda was surely now that – was unbreakable, a man of granite as well as genius.

It was the changing of the guard but the cycling world seemed stunned more than anything else and some attempted to explain away Girardengo's defeat by the two or three punctures he had suffered, including that costly one on stage five when Belloni led an attack. Remarkably, Binda didn't have a single puncture. Or was it so remarkable? Well aware that the big question mark against him was his inexperience on rough Italian roads, the new man had taken the key decision to ride with stronger, tougher, heavier – and slightly slower – 500-gramme tyres as opposed to the sleeker 390-gramme tyres the rest of the top riders utilised. He sacrificed a little speed for extra reliability. Yes, he probably was still a little lucky to suffer no punctures at all but he had done everything possible to encourage such good fortune.

Girardengo was nonplussed and there is a wonderfully evocative picture of the two of them on the podium which speaks volumes. A garlanded Binda seems slightly bemused, bored almost – another race, another win – while Girardengo completely ignores Binda's presence and looks defiantly at the camera assuming the pose of the winner almost as if he was still in denial. He was a factor again in the early stages the following year but, poignantly, 1925 was the last time he completed the Giro d'Italia, even if he kept plugging away until 1936.

These two giants of the early years of the Giro's history had no real rapport with each other; their relationship was very different from that of Girardengo and Belloni where there was a well-established hierarchy. When two athletes are equals and seeking the same goal simple cordiality is probably the best we have any right to expect. Anything more is a bonus. It is said that later that year, in the winter, when Binda and Girardengo were made an offer they couldn't refuse to ride together in the Milan Six, they didn't even shake hands or say goodbye at the end of a long week living and racing together. The *campionissimo* was dead. Long live the *campionissimo*.

The 1926 Giro, a famously wet and muddy edition featuring more than 200 starters, was billed as the Binda–Girardengo rematch but steadfastly refused to follow any preordained script and ended with Giovanni Brunero becoming the first rider in history to win a third, individual, GC title at the Giro. That chain of events started as early as stage one with Binda crashing while descending the Serra climb between Milan and Turin when he also managed to damage his brakes. His first inclination was to retire – in fact technically he probably did retire – but frantic Legnano officials persuaded him to remount and continue. He wasn't too badly injured and if he could limp home there were still stage wins to aim for while, with his help as a *gregario di lusso*, or super-domestique, there would be every chance of making Brunero very competitive against Girardengo.

So Binda made his way to Turin as safely as possible, finishing 37 minutes behind the stage winner Domenico Piemontesi, which was some 18 minutes behind Girardengo. The decision seems to have been made there and then for Binda and Brunero to switch roles which seems slightly premature given the Giro's justified reputation as being a race in which there can be huge swings of fortune from one day to another. Still, emotions were high and two days later, during stage two, it was Brunero who shadowed Girardengo all day long as they gave gentle pursuit to Piemontesi who bagged himself a second stage win to consolidate his lead in GC. Girardengo and Brunero crossed in second and third just under 3 minutes behind with Binda making his unhurried way home in tenth place, a further 6 minutes back.

Some 45 minutes behind the race leader and 25 minutes behind Girardengo with Brunero safely tucked in alongside Girardengo, Binda was well and truly off the leash. The trumpeter was free to make some noise and in his own inimitable way he won six of the last ten stages. The great man started picking off his wins on stage three with a stunning victory over the lumpy route from Genoa to Florence when he soloed in 4 minutes and 30 seconds ahead of Brunero with Girardengo another 30 seconds back. That had been fun and with the gauntlet thrown down Girardengo responded a little although he was canny enough to realise that Brunero and the course itself were now the opponents, not Binda, and he needed to avoid getting dragged into a one-on-one tussle with his conqueror from 12 months earlier.

The three rode together at the head of the peloton on stage four hammering everybody into submission, including Piemontesi, who cracked in the Cimini Hill, abandoning and, according to *Gazzetta*, throwing himself into a ditch in despair. The events of the day catapulted Girardengo into the GC lead with Brunero second and the big three continued to dish out the punishment in stage five which Girardengo again won although he gained no time on Brunero who he now led by 2 minutes and 36 seconds with Binda at 24 minutes and 55 seconds.

Binda took the sprint as the big names again dominated stage seven, after which came the pivotal stage and another Girardengo abandon, this time with an unspecified sprain in the Abruzzo en route from Foggia to Sulmona. Girardengo had certainly shown no signs of injury until this point – two stage wins and a second place in the previous three stages – and the exact nature of the injury never came out although the ever-supportive *Gazzetta* wrote that 'he had honoured the *maglia tricolore* with his valiant efforts'.

Perhaps we are too cynical these days but you look at that unfolding scenario and wonder if Girardengo might have done the maths and decided there was no hope of winning and little purpose in continuing. Brunero was in splendid form and his *gregario di lusso* Binda was off the leash and making mischief at every possible opportunity. Barring accidents and crashes there was no realistic way he could counter that duo. Better, perhaps, to abandon when in front, harvest the usual sympathy vote around yet another example of his infamous 'bad luck' in the Giro, and leave a few doubts hanging in the air as to the definitive quality of Brunero's third Giro win. It was an odd affair no matter how you look at it.

Following Girardengo's withdrawal it really was a promenade to the finish in Milan. Binda helped himself to that Foggia–Sulmona stage and three others, including the final day, while Brunero happily tucked into his slipstream to win the GC by over 15 minutes from Arturo Bresciani of the Olympia team with Binda in third just over 19 minutes behind. Despite this record third Giro for Brunero he still he struggled to get the plaudits he deserved. *Gazzetta* was all geared up to laud the new *campionissimo* Binda or to celebrate a miraculous return to winning ways from Girardengo. A Brunero win, albeit that he was a worthy and classy individual, remained a hard sell. The *Gazzetta* think-tank went into lockdown again in their smoke-filled offices in Milan and came up with the radical idea of awarding a 1-minute time bonus – *abbuoni* in Italian – for stage wins in the 1927 addition and to increase the number of stages to 15.

In racing terms it was a conscious decision to award the crowd-pleasers and to that end the stages were also made shorter and flatter. Financially, growing the race to 15 stages resulted in more starts and finishes – and more cities and towns bidding to host the travelling circus. You can see the logic but in racing terms anyway it backfired spectacularly as it provided the launching pad for a remarkable despotic winning run from the hungry Binda which nearly brought the Giro d'Italia to its knees.

In the next three Giri – 1927, 1928 and 1929 – Binda won 26 of the 41 stages contested and, of course, given that domination, won the three General Classifications virtually unchallenged. In 1927 he took 12 of the 15 stages available and although the organisation had another re-think on granting time bonuses for all stages the following year Binda was on a roll. In 1928 he limited himself to just the six stage victories although there were in fact seven for the Binda family with his brother and loyal *gregario* Albino taking stage eight from Rome to Pistoria, while in 1929 Alfredo blew the race to pieces with a run of eight consecutive stage wins (two to nine). He also crossed the line first on stage 13, a sprint finish in Alessandria, but he and the top four finishers were all disqualified for dangerous racing and the stage awarded to the grateful Mario Bianchi.

It should be added that Binda also won the Italian championship in all these three years, won a hat-trick of Giri di Lombardia between 1925 and 1927, won the inaugural World Championship in 1927 and was an outstanding winner of Milan–San Remo in 1929. His consistency was staggering, especially in the Giro. Grand Tour riding at this stage of the sports' development was the Wild West, on occasions just one step removed from bare-fist bar-room punch-ups. To impose such order and routine, such predictability on such random chaos, was and remains mind-boggling. There were huge unruly pelotons – 258 riders in 1927 and an all-time record of 298 in 1928 – full of riders of mixed ability making big crashes a daily occurrence; the rough Italian roads and tracks made mechanicals inevitable while, given the extremes of weather and climate, just staying healthy was a massive challenge. Despite all this, Binda reduced one of the great adventures in sport to a procession.

Binda is paid *not* to ride in the Giro

It is difficult to think of many comparable examples of such total individual domination in a given sport – the remarkable Donald Bradman certainly, perhaps Pete Sampras in his pomp at Wimbledon, and Usain Bolt. So absolute was Binda's mastery that the Giro organisers ultimately had to find a way of getting him not to compete in 1930, an artificial hiatus which took a little of the momentum and steam out of Binda's career. It was also a lifeline to battered opponents who picked themselves off the floor and continued when otherwise they might have quit.

Binda's 'removal' from the Giro for being too good really was an extraordinary episode. By the end of the 1929 Giro the truth is that most *Gazzetta* readers were bored to distraction from consuming the same old story and viewing pictures of the same victory pose virtually every day. There was no variety and very little human interest and, perversely, the public rather grew to resent their greatest champion. When Binda stood atop the winner's podium in Milan in 1929, for example, he was greeted with a volley of boos and jeers.

Colombo was apparently having none of that and wrote one of his more trenchant, less flowery pieces in which he made his displeasure quite clear: 'He has won the Giro again, in extraordinary fashion, though it's really not important how he won. This athlete, who has elevated Italian cycling to a different level, who has delivered us our first World Championship, deserves better. By all means offers him less of your applause but don't ever whistle at a great champion again.'

Fine words from Colombo but words are cheap and Binda, aged just 27, hadn't even reached his peak yet. This problem needed solving sooner rather than later. In no time Colombo and the ever-practical Cougnet, alarmed at the prospect of another Binda stage-winning fest in 1930, were conducting clandestine meetings with Legnano owner Emilio Bozzi and trying to explain to Bozzi how his rider was destroying the Giro and the profound knock-on effect this would have on the Italian cycling industry. It would, of course, also result in the near-certain collapse of *Gazzetta* although Colombo preferred not to dwell on that. Instead he made the radical suggestion that Binda miss the next Giro which would give the sport and readers new names to concentrate on. Perhaps instead Binda could, for once, look to the Tour de France.

Henri Desgrange was a massive admirer of the great Italian champion and had frequently pressed Binda to skip the Giro one year and tackle Le Tour. Bozzi contacted both Binda and the *directeur sportif* (DS) Pavesi. The rider himself, as well as being instinctively against such a deal, was also furious that Colombo had not had the guts to contact him first. After his four titles in five years and 26 stage wins in the last three editions Binda was the Giro and the Giro was *Gazzetta*.

Pavesi, though, could see a certain logic in the suggestion. He believed he had uncovered a fine young rider in Luigi Marchisio who could win the Giro in Binda's temporary absence, and the sportsman in him also fancied the idea of Binda attempting the Tour de France and Legnano pulling off a famous double even though the bike company had no interests in France and there would be little or no financial advantage in winning the Tour. Another meeting was arranged at the *Gazzetta* offices, this time between all the interested parties, and the savvy Binda had sniffed the wind and knew where this one was heading: Colombo was a newspaper man first and a cycling fan second, just as *Gazzetta* was a commercial organisation first and a race organiser second.

Binda's priority now was to extract maximum benefit from the situation. As expected Colombo and Cougnet lavished great praise on the *campionissimo* and his record-breaking achievements before suggesting that he show the true Olympian virtues of a champion and step aside for one year to allow other lesser mortals the opportunity to shine. That would allow Italian cycling to regenerate around an open and competitive 1930 Giro, after which he would be welcomed back with open arms.

Few opposition cyclists had ever outfoxed Binda and unsurprisingly he arrived in Milan armed with a few facts and figures. At the very least he would expect to win six stages in the 1930 Giro although it would probably be more. And of course he would also, barring an act of God, expect to win his fourth Giro on the trot. Add all that up and the winnings he would have to forego and the cost to *Gazzetta*, should he withdraw at the organisers' request, would be a minimum of 22,000 lire. The newspaper's top brass were dumbfounded, but, caught off guard, they couldn't argue with Binda's logic and reluctantly agreed to his demands.

'It was my best Giro,' Binda said many years later. 'I didn't just get the prizes without riding but I took up about ten contracts on the track in France, Germany and Belgium. The records say I won the Giro five times but I consider I won it five and a half times.'

Binda was on a financial roll and now entered into similarly clandestine negotiations with Desgrange and the Tour de France who were desperate for the world's greatest cyclist to appear in their race. Desgrange was adamant that the Tour, like the Giro, would never pay appearance money and he went to his grave insisting that was the case, but shortly before Binda himself died in 1986 he revealed that he had been paid appearance money to ride in the 1930 Tour de France. Binda, it seems, agreed to ride the Tour on a daily rate equivalent to the appearance money he had already been receiving at those top track meetings during the Giro. You can only doff your cap and admire one of sport's great coups. To be paid the winner's fee for not competing in the Giro is outstandingly good business by any criteria, but then to be also paid, in advance, for simply turning up on a daily basis at the Tour de France regardless of whether he won or not was off the scale. It certainly demonstrates the power his virtuosity had now bought him within the sport but it was also indicative of a pretty ruthless and calculating attitude from Binda. You can see why the *tifosi* often withheld their unreserved love for him.

In Binda's absence Marchisio, just 21, justified Pavesi's faith in him by climbing strongly to win a worthy if unspectacular Giro. Seemingly close – Marchisio beat Luigi Giacobbe by 52 seconds and Allegro Grandi by 1 minute 49 – the race in truth lacked star quality and excitement despite being hyped by *Gazzetta*. Marchisio himself was certainly a genuine talent but he was a cyclist who burned brightly at the start of his career before a rapid and sad decline.

Meanwhile, when he arrived at the 1930 Tour de France Binda understandably appeared a little demob happy and less focused than usual. The driving need to win wasn't there. He lost 1 hour after a crash and a mechanical on stage five – Bordeaux to Hendaye – but bounced back with brilliant back-to-back stage wins the following days in Pau and Luchon, the latter after a brutal mountain day.

In the next stage – another mountain classic from Luchon to Perpignan – he appeared at his dismissive best again as he raced ahead of the peloton on the first climb, the Portet d'Aspet, only to climb off and abandon in bemusing circumstances. Officially Binda claimed he felt he needed to rest up in preparation for the World Championship soon after the Tour in Liège – and in fairness he did win a famous victory in Belgium – but unofficially the rumour persisted that during the rest day preceding the stage he had received word that *Gazzetta* were trying to renege on their payment to him for not racing the 1930 Giro. There was a sudden urgent need to be back in Milan to sort that out and Binda's subsequent appearance at the 1931 Giro would suggest that any problems regarding the payment of his fee were indeed resolved.

The enduring mysteries of Bottecchia and Aymo

Away from the Binda narrative, which dominated the Giro in the late twenties, there are a couple of other storylines that clamoured for attention. A week after Binda's crushing victory and 12 stage wins in the 1927 Giro, just about the only Italian sportsman who could match his fame was found dead on a quiet Italian roadside, apparently the victim of a murderous attack. Just four years after winning the *Isolati* Classification in his one Giro appearance Ottavio Bottecchia was dead and in circumstances that sent a shiver down the spine of Italian cycling.

The war veteran, cycling star and high-profile anti-Fascist was found unconscious in a field by the roadside just outside the village of Peonis, close to the spot where his brother had been killed in a car accident just a month earlier. The great champion's skull was cracked, his collarbone broken and an arm as well. His bike, found nearby – he had been out on an early morning training ride – was in good repair and there were no tell-tale skid marks on the road suggestive of a hit and run motor accident. The coroner's verdict was sunstroke – almost certainly an act of clemency on the part of the local courts to ensure that his widow and two young children enjoyed the benefits of an uncontested insurance payout. Things start to get very complicated if a verdict of murder is returned and in this case murder it surely was. Police investigations indicated that the broken skull and abrasion to his face were seemingly the result of being hit by a rock, which clearly didn't tally with the sunstroke 'story', but they were told to drop the case.

Bottecchia, a stout socialist, never hid his anti-Fascist views and Fascist hit squads were known to be operating around this time. Some years later an Italian docker working in New York claimed on his deathbed that he was the hitman who had taken out Bottecchia, but are we really to believe that a professional hitman chose to beat a man's head with a rock in broad daylight? Another time a local farmer insisted he had seen this figure 'eating my grapes' in his vineyard so he picked up a rock and threw it at the intruder, felling him in an instant. Picking green grapes to eat in June? A shot so deadly from distance that it not only cracked the man's skull but also caused other fractures? It sounds unlikely.

The death of Bottecchia remains a mystery, and so in many ways does the lionisation of Giro stalwart Bartolomeo Aymo by Nobel Prize-winning author Ernest Hemingway. Aymo rounded off a stalwart career with third place in the 1928 Giro before finding his name immortalised in a small but key character, a heroic Italian ambulance driver in *A Farewell to Arms*, perhaps Hemingway's definitive book.

The choice of Aymo, who achieved a literary immortality greatly in excess of his sporting legacy, was a big call on the author's part. Hemingway, a big cycling fan, clearly needed to find a suitable generic Italian name but to opt for a well-known and current professional cyclist when the book was published in 1929 was unusual to say the least, but also deliberate. The individual in the book would automatically take on the characteristics of the athlete in real life, thus saving Hemingway the problem of having to spend valuable time and space characterising the soldier in the book. By brazenly name-checking Aymo, Hemingway was tapping into a considerable 'back story' that many will have been aware of.

All of which begs the question: what kind of rider and man was Aymo? What was his back story and the assumed knowledge many of the book's readers would share. He wasn't quite at the level of Girardengo, Brunero, Belloni, Bottecchia or Binda because essentially he wasn't a winner. But he was no mug either, claiming four podium finishes at the Giro – 1921, 1922, 1923 and 1928 – and two consecutive podiums at the Tour de France in 1925 and 1926. He was a stalwart, a man who just fell short physically compared with the very best of his era but a trier, a man who endured, who never gave up and who conferred dignity on the process of losing. He was at all times honourable and rose above much of the chicanery and backbiting that was commonplace in the peloton. He was a man who was happy to serve. Certainly when claiming his first two Giro podium places Aymo was very much the junior partner to his Legnano-Pirelli team leader, expected to rein in personal ambition to assist race winner Giovanni Brunero who was in any case an exceptionally talented rider and obvious team leader. Again in the 1926 Tour de France he also rode largely in support of the runner-up, Nicolas Frantz, his team leader at the high-profile Alycon team.

A number of additional factors may also have kicked in for Hemingway. Surviving portraits of Aymo show a handsome, modest-looking individual with more than a whiff of movie-star charisma, and

Hemingway was not above preferring aesthetically pleasing individuals in his books when it suited him. Hemingway might also have been tapping into a certain contemporary poignancy about Aymo. When he was writing *A Farewell to Arms* in 1928 Aymo was undertaking his final attempt to win a Grand Tour at the age of 39 and that would have been big news and fresh in his mind.

There was no recorded meeting between Hemingway and the real Aymo who seems to have virtually disappeared from public life after his retirement in 1930. Other than a brief obituary in *La Stampa* in 1970, which mentions that he subsequently ran a bike shop, nothing is known. Italian cycling journalists and historians have searched in vain but to no avail. Nothing, for example, is known of his reaction to Hemingway hijacking his name. His disappearance from cycling circles in real life seems as random and complete as his character's sudden death in *A Farewell to Arms*.

Learco Guerra becomes the first *maglia rosa*

It was a new, streamlined Giro to which returned Binda amid some fanfare in 1931 with just 109 riders contesting the 12 stages. The no-hopers among the *isolati* were beginning to fall out of favour with the organisers, who preferred dealing with well-organised teams and viewed the *isolati* as doing little more than making up the numbers, so although small the field was very competitive. *Gazzetta*, rather slower than usual in mimicking the Tour de France, had also finally decided to issue the leader of their race each day with a distinctive jersey and opted for pink in celebration of the paper itself which was famously printed on pink paper. It was considered an odd decision at the time and reportedly Mussolini wasn't terribly happy, calling it too effeminate, but the *maglia rosa* quickly obtained iconic status. Indeed, among sporting jerseys and shirts, it is probably second only to the Tour's yellow jersey. Initially the Fascist emblem of Mussolini's regime was embroidered onto the jersey but this was dispensed with after the Second World War.

Learco Guerra was the first rider to wear pink, winning the sprint into Mantua, and for a few brief years the dashing and extremely talented Guerra was the one Italian rider whose charisma put him on an almost equal footing with Binda. A would-be footballer from Bagnolo San Vito in Lombardy, Guerra only turned to cycling at the age of 26 when he finally quit football and within a year had won the Italian championship riding as an *isolato*. Strong, stocky and powerful he was known as 'the Human Locomotive' on account of his irresistible strength on flat stages. He was also handsome and photogenic and became one of the posterboy sportsmen for Mussolini's Fascist regime.

Guerra took stage two as well before Binda flexed his muscles, winning two of the next three mountain stages to take the overall lead heading towards Rome and a sprint finish at the end of stage six. The Giro was far from won – Binda's lead over Michele Mara was only 1 minute and there was a cluster of riders just seconds back with Guerra also in close attendance, having recovered from illness on the first mountain stage – but all the smart money was on Binda. And then the Giro blew apart, as bike races often do. Coming into the finish at Rome's Villa Glori horse-racing track Guerra and Binda were manoeuvring for a head-to-head battle when Binda crashed painfully although he quickly remounted and crossed the line 96 seconds behind stage winner Ettore Meini. Binda had badly injured his back, though, and had to withdraw in some distress midway through stage seven.

Two stages later, on stage nine, Guerra abandoned as well after crashing into an over-enthusiastic fan, which saw him hospitalised although there was no long-term damage. Indeed, he won the World Championship later that year in fantastic style in Copenhagen, routing the field in an extraordinarily long time trial with which the organisers decided to experiment. The GC was now a fight between Marchisio, Giacobbe and precocious climber Francesco Camusso, a second-year professional who had shown up well in a couple of stages the year before. It was all to play for and Camusso clinched it with a memorable coup on the penultimate stage from Cuneo to Turin.

Before the intimidating Sestriere climb Camusso slipped quietly off the back pretending to be concerned about a slow puncture and, when he was out of sight of the leaders, flipped his rear wheel around to change for a lower gear which he wanted to spin on the massive climb ahead. He quickly rejoined the front group and then, when the main climb started just outside Pragelato, he immediately went on the attack while the others stopped to make their own gear change. Camusso climbed beautifully – there have been few better Italian climbers – and enjoyed an inspired day on the descent to finish nearly 3 minutes ahead of Giacobbe and more than 6 minutes in front of Marchisio. The Giro was his.

The following year, 1932, was curious. Guerra was in fine stage-winning form with six of the best to please his adoring fans, but Binda seemed subdued and happy to work for the GC ambitions of his colleague Antonio Pesenti. The so-called 'Cat of Zogno' – his hometown – took the race by the scruff of the neck on stage seven when the peloton, expecting Binda to make his move, were caught dozing. Pesenti went nearly 4 minutes in front of the pack that day and, with Binda now watching his back, enjoyed an armchair ride to Milan where he finished over 11 minutes ahead of the second-placed man in GC, Joseph Demuysère. Pesenti was not a completely unknown quantity but he was another talent who blazed but briefly. He had finished third in the 1931 Tour de France and was to again go well in France just weeks after his Giro triumph with a creditable fourth, but after 1932 he never won another race of any description in a professional career that stretched all the way to 1939.

There appeared to be little wrong with Binda's form as such in 1932 – a couple of months later he won the World Championship in superb style in Belgium – so cycling fans and historians are entitled to wonder exactly what was going on during this Giro. Was there an injury he was protecting? Was he becoming a fat cat content to live off past glories? Or perhaps he was still working off his anger with the Giro organisers. They might have thrown their weight around and effectively determined when he could or couldn't line up at the start of their Giro but he, Alfredo Binda, would decide when he actually 'raced'. In 1932, for whatever reasons, it seems he didn't fancy racing. But in 1933 he most certainly did.

Learco Guerra, after a stunning win at the early season Milan–San Remo, was probably still the favourite going into the 1933 edition but it was a different, more focused Binda who turned up in Milan. It had now been four years since he had bossed the 1929 Giro and at the age of 31 there might not be too many more opportunities left to win the event. Guerra was quality, though, and the set-up of the race possibly favoured him. The *corsa rosa* now consisted of 17 stages, which brought down the average daily length, with fewer rest days. And for the first time the organisers added a King of the Mountains classification, contested over a number of designated climbs with points being awarded in descending order as the race crossed a summit. (Over the years, the climbers' competition gradually extended to all categorised climbs in the race, although it wasn't until 1974 that the *maglia verde* was introduced – changed to blue, the *maglia azzura*, in 2012 – for the leader of the mountains classification.) It also featured the first time trial in Giro history, a 60km run from Bologna to Ferrara in which he expected to defeat Binda by a considerable margin.

Initially a battle royal unfolded, a treat for all cycling fans, with Guerra taking three of the first five stages. Binda boxed clever, though, took time back with an outstanding breakaway victory on stage two and was handily set in fourth place at the end of stage five, less than 2 minutes behind leader Joseph Demuysère and just 15 seconds behind second-place Guerra who he had identified as his main rival. Then came another contentious finish at the Villa Glori in Rome with Guerra crashing in a sprint finish as he tried to go outside Binda. He claimed his great rival had thrown out an elbow – which in reality was just part of the normal rough and tumble – while the judges concluded that what had actually happened was that in taking the outside line Guerra had clipped a branch of the hedge that lined the racetrack. Whatever the truth Guerra was badly injured and much to his chagrin was forced to retire from what had been shaping up as one of the great Giri.

From there on it was plain sailing for Binda as, in one of his last great outpourings of virtuosity, he claimed five stage wins including that inaugural time trial which even he had expected to lose to Guerra. Only the weather threatened his fifth and last Giro win with the conditions on a seemingly innocuous stage 16, from Bessano to Bolzano, not far removed from the 1914 epic. Survival became the order of the day which Binda achieved before he crowned his triumph with a final-day victory in Milan. His win had something of a valedictory feel about it: it was his last great Giro triumph and this time he was greeted by loud cheering rather than jeers.

6

GINO BARTALI DOMINANCE IS CHALLENGED BY FAUSTO COPPI (1934–40)

With the benefit of hindsight we now know that Binda's years of pre-eminence and greatness ended in 1933 and that two of the 'greats' of Giro history and indeed cycling generally would very quickly fill that vacuum. The transition wasn't entirely seamless, however, and although Gino Bartali was the dominant figure in the run-up to the Second World War before his first, humbling clash with Fausto Coppi in 1940, other fine riders disputed the issue with great spirit and no little panache. The fans' favourite, Learco Guerra, steamed in for his much-anticipated first Giro success in 1934 and Vasco Bergamaschi enjoyed his brief day in the sun the following year. There was also a brace of victories for Giovanni Valetti, the second a stunning but curiously unheralded effort that still ranks among the very best in Giro history. In short, the run-up to the Second World War was a wonderfully vivid chapter in the Giro's history, full of strong personalities and, as we shall see, no little controversy.

Following Binda's return to winning ways in 1933, the last thing *Gazzetta* wanted was yet another victory by the *campionissimo* and the 1934 route was set up for Guerra in an unapologetically blatant fashion. It was the longest, 'flattest' Giro yet – 17 stages totalling 3,712km – and included two juicy individual time trials totalling 104km in which 'the Human Locomotive' could get up full steam. From being a race that two years earlier had no time trials, the Giro now had two. This was one gift horse that Guerra could not look in the mouth, a once-in-a-lifetime opportunity to nail the GC win that had eluded him. He was helped greatly in this mission, however, by Binda having to abandon after being hit by a police bike on stage six although until that point the reigning champion had looked disinterested and not in great nick. Certainly he wasn't in the top ten of the GC before his crash, and there was little evidence to suggest he was poised to ride himself back into form.

Despite ten stage wins, including one streak of five straight stage wins and another of four, Guerra's GC triumph was still hard-earned as the slender 51-second winning margin over Camusso indicates, the splendid climber eking out as much advantage as possible from the climbs that were on offer. And to this day there are those who insist Camusso was the rightful winner of the race after the controversial events of stage 13, a short but demanding 120km mountainous day from Florence to Bologna.

Going into the stage off the back of that second run of four stage wins Guerra was still vulnerable, leading Camusso by just 2 minutes and 27 seconds, and on this of all days Guerra was unwell, suffering from stomach cramps and nausea. Staying healthy for three weeks is often the unheralded secret to winning Grand Tours. Guerra suffered like a dog and as the peloton disappeared out of sight all looked lost as he 'abandoned' on the early slopes of the Passo della Futa, climbing off the bike and slumping into the back seat of his Maino team car. His race was clearly over. Or was it? Having stowed Guerra's bike, the Maino car drove off in pursuit of the peloton to rejoin the race and support their other riders and soon drew alongside the organisers' car which had dropped off the back of the group wondering what had happened to the *maglia rosa*. Cougnet and Colombo were ashen-faced when they saw Guerra slumped in the team car.

This wasn't in the script. Guerra was the race's poster boy; he had won nine of the 12 completed stages so far and was the star of the show and surely a deserving winning of this year's edition. It would be disastrous if he dropped out at this relatively late stage. The second time trial in two days' time had been staged specifically with Guerra in mind, the decisive moment of a historic Giro to crown his season of seasons at the age of 32. And so, remarkably, they persuaded Guerra to get out of the car, remount his bike and to continue on his way. It was an outrageous and frankly desperate intervention by officialdom and a stark reminder to all concerned that ultimately *Gazzetta* called the shots. Neither Cougnet nor Colombo had any compunction about interfering with or manipulating the race. Guerra had been driven an unspecified distance along the course before being persuaded to continue, but was not taken back to the place where he climbed off to continue his Giro. No: instead he started again from where the team car had drawn up alongside the *Gazzetta* car.

There is no conceivable way Guerra should have been allowed to continue under those circumstances but *Gazzetta*'s word was law, so much so that there is no record of Camusso's Gloria team – who presumably learned of the incident one way or another soon enough – raising an official objection. The cynics among you should feel free to speculate on whether certain inducements were offered to Gloria to show such a benevolent attitude.

It is also likely that a curious incident from stage nine came into play. On that occasion a tired and stressed Camusso got into a heated argument with an over-officious police officer at a feed station in Pescara, which at one stage seemed likely to result in his arrest. Cougnet prevented that by promising the policeman that 'his' rider would be severely reprimanded. Of course as the race and circus moved on that didn't happen but come stage 13, and the extraordinary decision to allow Guerra to rejoin the race, Cougnet will certainly have enjoyed a certain leverage over Camusso and his team. Having revived a little in the car Guerra grovelled his way into Bologna and had managed to limit his losses to such an extent that although dropping to third in GC he was still only 2 minutes 55 seconds behind Camusso, the new *maglia rosa*. If he could recover on the rest day all was not lost. Guerra was capable of inflicting huge damage on the 59km time trial from Bologna to Ferrara.

Which is pretty much how it worked out. Camusso, the classic pure climber who is found wanting in time trials, lost 3 minutes and 46 seconds to Guerra who eased into a 51-second lead overall, an advantage he protected comfortably in the three remaining stages to Milan. The ever-popular Guerra was praised to the hilt and his big trademark smile was much in evidence in *Gazzetta* the following day but it was all very unsatisfactory. Today the Court of Arbitration in Sport (CAS) would take less than five minutes to overturn the result and award the race to Camusso.

Guerra was back in stage-winning form the following year, adding another five to his palmares, but this time the race was blown apart on stage seven, a relatively short but furiously ridden mountainous day from Portocivitanova to L'Aquila which saw a young first-year professional, Gino Bartali, leave his calling card with a famous win. Relatively unknown and outside of the top ten in GC at the start of the day, Bartali was given his head and took full advantage with an impressive solo win. The young Tuscan eventually finished seventh overall but this was the stage that provided the narrative for the rest of the race because Guerra struggled to live with the young Bartali and trailed home 3 minutes and 22 seconds behind. It was Guerra's *gregario* Vasco Bergamaschi who withstood the onslaught better than most and it was Bergamaschi therefore who found himself in the *maglia rosa* that night, 1 minute 31 seconds ahead of Giuseppe Olmo. Guerra was a hugely experienced rider and could read the signs already. This was not going to be his year and from this point onwards he concentrated on stage wins and helping Bergamaschi in the GC race.

Bergamaschi, although not a stellar talent, was a rock-solid rider and with the leader's jersey on his back and Guerra in support eventually won in fairly routine fashion, the only real danger coming on stage 12, an arduous 317km run from Rome to Florence when he not only successfully fought off various attacks but actually won the stage itself. Come the finish in Milan he was over 3 minutes ahead of Giuseppe Martano of the Frejus team with Bianchi's Giuseppe Olmo in third place another 3 minutes back. Bergamaschi's 'helper', Guerra, finished fourth.

Nicknamed '*il Singapore*' by the distinctly non-PC *Gazzetta* on account of his undeniably Asian facial features, Bergamaschi certainly had a tale to tell his children and grandchildren because the 1935 Giro saw a rare coming together of the greats, albeit at varying stages of their careers and physical capabilities. Girardengo, aged 42, again went to the start line but had to abandon after the fourth stage. It was also the last Giro that the ageing Alfredo Binda completed. Binda finished 16th in GC and was runner-up in the final stage in Milan. And as we have seen it was also Gino Bartali's first Giro. As well as finishing seventh overall, the young tyro took the Mountains competition. That's not a bad trio of riders to have finishing in your wake, not to mention the other Giro champions who went to the start line – Guerra, Camusso, Marchisio and Pesenti. Bergamaschi was never to rise to the heights again but his day in the sun had been a sparkling affair.

The genius of Bartali becomes apparent

Gino Bartali had served notice in 1935 that his time was nearing and in 1936 he claimed the first of his three Giri in what was the start of a remarkable cycling career, and indeed life, which we now know, following revelations shortly after his death, including a clandestine but exemplary war helping to save and protect Jews within Italy who otherwise faced certain death. He was a towering sporting figure and massively important socially as well, being championed as the antithesis of the prevalent Fascism of the era in Italy.

Bartali was a famously devout Catholic, who would attend mass whenever possible even during the Giro or Tour de France, and would place a small statue of the Madonna on his dining table before saying pre-meal prayers. He was personally blessed by three popes during his career and his wedding mass was celebrated by the Cardinal of Florence, Archbishop Elia Dalla Costa, who became a close friend, and indeed during the war a fellow resistance worker fighting to save Jewish lives. Bartali was also an active member of the *Azione Cattolica* – a Catholic action group wanting and working towards social reform – and perhaps unsurprisingly Bartali found himself dubbed '*il pio Gino*', 'Gino the pious'.

But this man of iron was a fascinatingly nuanced character. Like many Italian Catholics he drank and smoked like a trooper and although apparently abhorring bad language he could be cantankerous and bad-tempered. He was a man of God yet later in his career showed little forgiveness and civility to his great rival Coppi. His religious beliefs were not soft or sentimental; rather, he was an unforgiving Catholic warrior, a prime example of Muscular Christianity. He even looked, as many commentators have observed, like a boxer with his strong features and squashed nose, the result reputedly of an early cycling accident.

He was canny and a survivor and learned to box clever under the increasingly cruel and despotic Fascist regime of Benito Mussolini. He hated both with a vengeance but they had the power to terminate his cycling career, livelihood and indeed life at a stroke and within Italian cycling there was still the vivid memory of Bottecchia's murder in 1926. Bartali wasn't fooled or suckered by the Fascists for one minute but knew he had to play their game. He made his protest by omission, always giving thanks to God in his moment of victory rather than to Il Duce. Somehow he managed to retain his integrity and independence of thought. When he raced in the Giro and the Tour de France – especially in his duels with Coppi – it seems his supporters were backing more than just a man on a bike; they were supporting by proxy Bartali's standards and approach to life.

Bartali was the third of four children, born in Ponte a Ema, a suburb of Florence. The family weren't grindingly poor like those of many Italian cyclists but they had to watch the pennies and by the age of 13 he had already left school and was working at the bike shop of his father's friend Oscar Casamonti. His interest in cycling was aroused at the age of ten when his father Torello bought him a bike to celebrate his first communion. With Casamonti fuelling his enthusiasm for the sport it soon became obvious that Gino was an outstanding natural talent on a bike, as indeed was his younger brother Giulio who was regarded by some as the even greater prospect. By the age of 17 Gino was the junior champion of Tuscany and when he turned professional with Frejus in 1935 he had won over 40 races as an amateur. Bartali was good on all terrain but imperious on long climbs. Time spent working in the bikeshop had encouraged an appreciation of developing bike technology, particularly in the area of gears and the refinement of the derailleur systems being perfected in the 1930s.

After his impressive Giro debut in 1935, and indeed a noteworthy victory at the Tour of the Basque country, the giant Legnano team swooped to sign Bartali. This was clearly a champion of the future and it was imperative that he ride in their colours the following year.

The 1936 Giro was another comparatively flat affair and in many ways turned into a sprintfest for the voracious Giuseppe Olmo, the Bianchi sprinter who was also a fine time-trial rider. Olmo was the early leader and eventually helped himself to no fewer than ten stage wins but with no time bonuses on offer – that seemed completely at the whim of the organisers from one year to the next – was unable to draw clear at the head of the GC. Bartali was in a seemingly innocuous ninth position at the start of stage nine but in reality was in the driving seat with the big mountain stage across the Apennines from Campobasso to L'Aquila offering up a virtual rerun of his jaw-dropping stage win the previous year. This time his performance was even more stunning. Having bided his time throughout the first week, he took off with a vengeance over the Macerone climb followed by the ascents of the Rionero Sannitico, Roccaraso and the Svolte di Popoli to finish over 6 minutes in front of the chasing bunch and go into a race lead of 6 minutes and 29 seconds. It was now his race to lose.

Not only was Bartali the best climber in the peloton but he had also mastered the Vittoria Margherita gear system pioneered by the Turin-based Nieddu brothers, Tommaso and Amedeo. The Margherita system, introduced barely 12 months earlier, was an improvement even on that initial system and incorporated a rod connected to the chain stay which enabled a skilful rider to push and move the chain while back-pedalling to change to a different sprocket and gear. It was a million miles away from today's electronically operated gears but equally it was a massive improvement on what had gone before, when the rider had to dismount the bike and flip the rear wheel over. It was a rugged, no-nonsense system and the tension wheel of the derailleur had enough ground clearance to generally make it immune from mud and puddles, a vital consideration given that road conditions were still often poor.

Bartali recalled the stage in his autobiography *La Mia Storia*, the day the cycling world had to sit up and take notice. 'They were the same roads with the same four climbs as the previous year. On the first, Macerone, I found myself at the front extremely easily so I knew I was the strongest. Then on the last climb I gave it everything and attacked. By the finish I had six minutes and the jersey which I was able to keep all the way to Milan without any great difficulty. I wasn't yet 22 but I had a fiancée, the national championship and the Giro. I had arrived.'

Indeed he had, although hanging on to the lead was perhaps not quite so incident free as Bartali remembered. Olmo stole 35 seconds back on stage 11, a short mountain time trial to Monte Terminillo, the first mountain *cronoscalata* in Giro history; Guerra crashed out on stage 13 when he collided with a horse-drawn carriage and broke an arm and then Bartali went missing mentally on a short half-stage – a pan-flat 106 kilometre run from Ferrara to Padua – which was held on the morning of the final time trial from Padua to Venice. Perhaps he thought he had the race won or perhaps he was conserving himself for the time trial but the leader somehow managed to miss the 31-man break and finished nearly 3 minutes behind Olmo who then put 1 minute 43 seconds into Bartali in the time trial. Suddenly the champion-elect only led by just over 2 minutes. More than a little shaken Bartali recovered to win two of the final three stages based around Lake Garda to claim his first Giro d'Italia. Impressive stuff but that mental lapse was perhaps a small pointer to the future. Bartali was a rider of immense tenacity and intensity and generally that blew the opposition away but when the latter was missing for whatever reason, or when an opponent matched that intensity, he could occasionally be found wanting.

Exactly seven days after his Giro triumph came the event that possibly fashioned the rest of Bartali's cycling career, the death of his brother and best friend Giulio in a racing accident. Torrential rain had swept through Italy and Gino's own event in Turin had been cancelled so he spent the afternoon travelling back home to Florence by train. During that time Giulio, 19, and considered the best amateur in Tuscany, was contesting a local race that had survived the weather and was descending in a lead group of three when they encountered a car parked where it shouldn't have been. The first two riders swerved to avoid it but Giulio, drafting in third place, didn't see it quickly enough and hit it full pelt at something in the region of 60kmh. He was taken by ambulance to hospital and for a while, conscious and talking coherently, it seemed he had made a miraculous escape. By the time Gino had been rushed to hospital from the railway station, however, his younger brother's condition had deteriorated with severe internal bleeding and a possible fracture to the skull. Like others who had gone to the hospital, Gino gave blood for the transfusions that were needed and prayed while his brother underwent extensive surgery. He came to briefly after the operation but then slipped into a coma and died holding his brother's hand.

The effect of such a personal tragedy on any sportsman can only be imagined and, given his strong faith, it was always likely to play out in one of two ways for Bartali: he would either reject religion altogether or he would become even more fervent as he turned to God in his hour of turmoil and need. Initially he gave up cycling and had a small chapel of remembrance built in his brother's honour at his parents' house, but after grieving long and hard he returned to the sport with an unforgiving and steely attitude. He was a man both in mourning and on a mission. The 1937 Giro was the race to relaunch his career and with that in mind he buried himself in training – he was notorious for his 400km endurance rides – and it was on just such an epic from Milan to Florence in March that he got caught in an unexpected snowstorm and arrived home with something akin to pneumonia. He certainly had a high fever and respiratory problems and was distinctly unwell for a while although he began to recover and by the time the Giro started outwardly he looked well enough. Outwardly.

Such was Bartali's class that, with the help of his strong Legnano team who took the first-ever team time trial staged at the Giro, he was able to ride within himself and still dictate the race. The combative Giovanni Valetti of the Frejus squad never gave up, however, and was still theoretically within striking distance of Bartali at the end of stage 18, some 2 minutes and 40 seconds adrift. Then came a Giro first, a high mountains day in the Dolomites which Bartali had long identified as the key stage with its climbs on the Costalunga and Rolle. Not quite at 100 per cent, Bartali had been trying to keep something in reserve and he piled on the pressure and beat Valetti and his strong *gregario* Enrico Mollo by over 5 and a half minutes. It was the decisive race-winning move and Bartali duly took his second Giro but it came at a physical cost. He was exhausted. He badly needed a complete rest. This was not a race he could just take in his stride.

At which point a long-simmering argument came to a head. The Italian Cycling Federation had received word from Mussolini's Ministry of Sport at the start of the season that Bartali, for the greater glory and honour of the Italian nation, must race in and win the Tour de France. Bartali was not totally averse to the idea of winning the Tour de France, but he was not a man who enjoyed being told where, when and how. He felt drained from his early season sickness and defending his Giro title and wanted to be in prime form before he tackled the Tour on his own terms. Next year perhaps? This was his line all season until, just 12 days before the Tour started, it was spelt out to him by the Federation that he would race in France or suffer the consequences. Bartali bit his tongue and travelled to France.

His Tour debut was not a happy experience with a nasty crash tipping him into the icy Colan River and sending him tumbling down the GC standings. After battling his way through four subsequent stages, however, Bartali, 17 minutes down on GC, was beginning to feel good again and was hoping for a strong finish in the Pyrenees when the Italian Cycling Federation, acting on a directive from up high, withdrew him from the race presumably, with defeat inevitable, to save face. Bartali, the warrior who never quit, was being forced to abandon. He despaired at the government's inept meddling in his career and that ire was further fuelled the following spring when he was informed he would not race in the Giro; he was to concentrate on the Tour instead. With a third straight Giro title there for the taking, Bartali was to be denied the chance. A word out of place, though, and his career would have been over so Bartali stoically got his head down and resolved to win the Tour de France in supreme style. And to dedicate it to God in heaven, not Il Duce – the only way he could make his protest.

The 1938 Giro, meanwhile, had to promote a race without its champion and obvious winner, not to mention his high-profile Legnano team, most of whom had been designated to ride with Bartali in France. Rather desperately *Gazzetta* dubbed the 1938 Giro the Race of Youth and a lacklustre edition was dominated by the increasingly impressive Giovanni Valetti. Of course in the absence of Bartali who, later in the year, recorded a sensational GC victory at the Tour de France, praise of Valetti was a little muted but nonetheless his riding in the Dolomites and in the mountain time trial was seriously impressive.

Valetti's forgotten masterpiece

Who was this new star of Italian cycling? Giovanni Valetti was from Avigliana just outside the city of Turin. The second of seven children, he left school at 11 to work at the city's famous Lancia factory and soon started cycling, joining the city's top club the Gruppo Sportivo Vigot. Tall and rangy, in no time he demonstrated himself to be enormously powerful on the flat and unexpectedly good going uphill. In fact the only thing he couldn't do was sprint but he was a talent nonetheless and he started to win local races. He enjoyed an early success in 1933 when he travelled south to win the Giro del Lazio.

Much encouraged, he started racing professionally, as an *isolato*, in 1935 and did enough to impress the renowned Turin-based team Frejus who had no hesitation in picking him for their 1936 Giro team as a *gregario* for their GC rider Olimpio Bizzi. In the event he proved the stronger man than his team leader and finished a very creditable fifth. The following season Valetti was one of the few riders who could challenge Bartali, this time finishing second in the Giro and recording his first stage win in Genoa. The upward trajectory was there for all to see again the following year when he won the Giro in Bartali's absence and then went on to record a highly accomplished win in the Tour of Switzerland.

And so to 1939. The return of Bartali was, of course, much anticipated and with a champion to promote in Valetti *Gazzetta* had little problem building the race up. Interest was high and with the race coverage on the radio much improved since its introduction in 1932, this was a contest fans could follow around the country, with regular rather breathless and sometimes erroneous updates followed by more measured résumés every evening. This battle would have a vast and far-flung listening audience. Valetti was undoubtedly a quality, improving, rider and Bartali recognised the challenge ahead, but the normal order of things would surely be restored. Bartali had won the Tour de France by more than 18 minutes the previous summer. Nobody could live with him, especially in the high mountains, and with an unusually early start planned for this Giro – 28 April – perhaps his biggest worry was that one or two of those high mountain passes in the Alps and Dolomites might not be open and that might possibly nullify his strongest weapon.

Both protagonists encountered problems early on. Valetti suffered a hunger knock on stage two and lost 5 minutes to Bartali who took the stage and the lead overall, the latter probably a little earlier than he would have preferred. It was Bartali who suffered the following day, a flat stage from Genoa to Pisa, when he contrived to miss a strong ten-man break containing Valetti and suffered badly in poor weather as his Legnano team struggled to limit the damage. Some reports mention that Bartali suffered a puncture, causing him to miss the decisive move, but on such a simple stage, and with such a strong team, the *maglia rosa* shouldn't really have leaked 7 minutes to the lead group. It was another example of Bartali's occasional vulnerability. When he wasn't quite in the zone, when his mind was wandering or perturbed, he could be vulnerable. The upshot of the incident-packed stage three was that Cino Cinelli – later to found the renowned Cinelli bike manufacturing company – took stewardship of the *maglia rosa* for the best part of a week. This suited the two main contenders as they tried to bring a little calm and order to their campaigns as the peloton navigated its way down the west coast of Italy to Rome and across the Apennines to Pescara. There was one day of particular note, however, a short (14km) but brutal mountain time trial from Rieti to Monte Terminillo which Valetti won, beating Bartali by 28 seconds. Physically Valetti was clearly right up there with the great man. Perhaps this wasn't going to be quite the procession that many had predicted.

Valetti was in the groove and regained the lead after a short but demanding mountainous half-stage – the peloton had ridden the 116km from Senigallia to Forlì that morning, won by Bartali but with Valetti and Cinelli in close attendance. The big tests up in the Dolomites still awaited but it was beginning to look promising for Valetti whose morale was further boosted in the second time trial, a fast, flat 40km stage from Trieste to Gorizia, which he won in fine style putting 2 minutes into Bartali. Approaching the big mountain passes Valetti was in a strong position, leading the race and 3 minutes 59 seconds ahead of Bartali.

The first mountain stage, with the Passo della Mauria the main event, ended in stalemate with Bartali and Valetti crossing the line together in Cortina d'Ampezzo behind stage winner Secondo Magni but the following day, a brutish 258km from Cortina d'Ampezzo to Trento, Bartali gave it both barrels, cresting the Passo Rolle first and putting Valetti into a world of pain. Valetti was dropped good and proper and had to dig very deep as Bartali took the jersey with a magnificent stage win finishing 7 minutes 48 seconds ahead of a shattered Valetti who dropped to fourth in GC, 3 minutes 49 seconds behind Bartali with two mountainous stages to go. As the peloton rested up in Trento, Bartali was odds-on to take his third Giro.

Rest days are welcomed by some but hated by others. They can slow a rider's momentum just as he is building up a head of steam or they can offer blessed relief and a chance to regroup for riders who have taken a kicking. The body can start seizing up as it attempts to go into recovery mode and modern-day riders religiously go for a short but sometimes strenuous ride to delay that process, to trick the body into thinking it's just another racing day. There can also be a tendency to brood and worry about the next stage and over-complicate things. We have no accurate record of what happened on the fourth and final rest day of the 1939

Giro, although throughout his career Bartali's preference was to rest totally, but we do know that the following day Giovanni Valetti rose Lazarus-like to produce the race of his life and beat Bartali – the greatest climber of his generation – by nearly 7 minutes to regain the *maglia rosa* in the most dramatic and impressive way imaginable. In poor weather that was to deteriorate further and result in more than 20cm of snow high on the passes ahead, Valetti went from the flag and immediately put Bartali under pressure. Initially only two riders went with him, Bartali and Valetti's team-mate Olimpio Bizzi, once his team leader but now his *gregario di lusso*. If nothing else it was a promising scenario: Valetti wasn't going to go down without a fight.

Without today's all-seeing TV coverage and communications there remains an element of doubt and mystery as to exactly how a long and dramatic day unfolded, but the nub of it is that Valetti was enjoying one of those magic carpet days when everything is effortless and Bartali was having to dig deep and not enjoying much luck. First he punctured, at which point Valetti and Bizzi attacked. Bartali tried to stay cool and decided to wait for a colleague to reach him rather than chase on his own. He was still the virtual leader. No need to panic.

Then Valetti punctured and decided to wait for Bizzi who he had begun to distance. At this stage, at Mezzan, some 90km from the finish, it is estimated that they had a 2 minute 30 second lead over Bartali, so Bartali was still leading the General Classification. At which point the gallant Bizzi, who could have been forgiven for harbouring a grudge against Valetti, who had basically usurped the team leadership from him in 1936, showed real class and nobility in emptying his tanks with a massive turn at the front into the elements that launched Valetti into his final solo attack and bid for glory. Onwards rode Valetti for well over 80km as his lead stretched to 3 minutes, 4 minutes, 5 minutes, until he eventually crossed the line 3 minutes 32 seconds ahead of Bizzi and 6 minutes 48 seconds ahead of a bedraggled Bartali who had endured another flat and delay while chasing. It was arguably the greatest individual ride in the Giro's history to this point, a sensational comeback story. And, given that, the rumour mill went into overdrive.

There were allegations that that Frejus team car had blocked the Legnano team car as it went to assist Bartali after his second flat by 'accidently on purpose' sliding on the icy surface and ending up sideways in the middle of the road. Others claimed to have seen the Frejus mechanic trash Valetti's punctured wheel when he flatted so they could execute a simple wheel change rather than a tyre repair. There are even those who believe there were Fascist agents out in the mountains that day conspiring to make life as difficult as possible for Bartali, the man who honoured God and not Il Duce. When most of the action takes place out of the view of officials, who knows where the precise truth lies? What we do know is that Valetti was immense all day long and had Bartali in trouble from the start way back in Trento. Great champion that he was Bartali made it a point of honour winning the final stage in Milan, but Valetti tracked him all the way and his winning margin remained at 2 minutes 59 seconds. Still only 25, Valetti was never going to top that and in fact scarcely tried. The following year Valetti finished 17th in the Giro and after surviving the war he never again contested a top-level race. He had beaten the great Bartali fair and square and life was never going to get better than that.

Fausto Coppi makes a stunning Giro debut

Having lost to Valetti, Bartali was determined to reassert his authority and pre-eminence in 1940 when racing continued unabated in Italy during the 'Phoney War' period of the Second World War. Nobody was under any illusions that it wasn't all about to kick off very soon but Italy hadn't yet officially entered the fray and a huge national event such as the Giro was handy for keeping people's minds otherwise occupied. In the event Mussolini declared war the day after the Giro ended. Bartali was on fire in the first half the 1940 season with wins at

Milan–San Remo and the Giro della Toscana as he set his steely eye on the Giro. He was fed up with being messed around by the Fascist authorities dictating when and where he should race and was tiring of a run of misfortune. It was time to put some stick about. Within the Legnano ranks, serving as a *gregario*, was a spindly but extravagantly gifted youth named Fausto Coppi who was just 20 but clearly destined for big things. But not quite yet surely. Legnano would be working for a Bartali win.

Bartali was well aware of Coppi's special talent, having at first hand witnessed him launch an audacious solo attack at the Giro del Piemonte in 1939 a couple of weeks after Bartali's defeat against Valetti in the Giro d'Italia. On this occasion Coppi was thwarted by a mechanical, a dropped chain, but recovered to finish a hugely impressive third behind Bartali, holding off a chasing pack single-handed.

Coppi was another rider from Piedmont, born in Castellania, the fourth of five children, to Domenico Coppi and his wife Angiolina. School was of no interest to him and indeed in the register at the school run by his auntie Albina it is recorded that he received a hundred lines – *I must go to school and not ride my bike* – at the age of eight after playing truant. The young Coppi had discovered an ancient rusty contraption in the cellar of his family home and had somehow got it up and running. By 13 he was working for butcher Domenico Melania in Novi Ligure with particular responsibility for delivering the prime, and often heavy, cuts to customers in the locality including, reputedly, Cosante Girardengo, the local boy made good. A timely gift of 600 lire from his uncle in the merchant navy enabled Coppi to buy a decent frame and race locally and at the age of 17 he was put in touch with Biagio Cavanna, the local masseur and trainer who had worked with Girardengo extensively as well as Binda and Guerra. By this stage the 20-stone, larger-than-life Cavanna, a former boxer, was virtually blind but continued to run what amounts to a cycling academy, arranging accommodation for young riders and organising their training in the minutest detail as well as monitoring their diet and social habits. It wasn't purely altruistic. Cavanna was also a wheeler-dealer who stood to earn a healthy commission from the big trade teams if they signed one of his riders, but he was nonetheless a remarkable trainer and huge influence on the young Coppi. He may have lived in a world of darkness but Cavanna could see the way ahead.

Although an amateur Cavanna's protégé Coppi was already training and living like a professional. Incredibly long-limbed and thin he had acquired the nickname 'the Heron' (*airone*) but was by no means an instant sensation; he lost more often than he won in those early years. But as those long legs started to gain strength and he entered tougher, longer, steeper races, his career started to progress apace. Awkward-looking on terra firma, his body made perfect sense when folded onto a bike. Man and machine were one. It has been suggested that Coppi's signing was somehow a surprise to Bartali but that seems unlikely. At the age of 19, Coppi already had the two strongest teams in Italy – Maino and Legnano – publicly chasing his signature and at one stage Maino had a signed agreement only for that to be torn up when Cavanna revealed that he had negotiated a better agreement with Legnano and their veteran but ever-alert manager Eberardo Pavesi. On the eve of his fine ride at the Giro del Piemonte in 1939 Coppi lodged with the Maino team although he finally signed on the dotted line for Legnano, for the 1940 season, only a few hours after his podium place. When Coppi was formally unveiled as a new Legnano rider in January 1940 Bartali did reportedly express the view that, with his slight build, the young man's form might not automatically transfer to Grand Tour racing, but that is a caveat you would apply to most callow riders no matter how talented. What was evident is that Coppi was a stunning prospect, one you would want riding for your team rather than the opposition.

The coupling with Legnano, for which Cavanna was handsomely rewarded, was a tad messy and not for the last time in his life – personal and professional – Coppi found himself in a complicated triangular battle for his affections. It is telling, however, that even at such a tender age Coppi found nothing unusual in this; in fact there was a finely tuned assumption of his own intrinsic worth. His slightly gawky persona disguised an uber-confident cyclist and athlete, a driven and at times quite ruthless individual. It is very easy to love Fausto Coppi. His cycling genius, his miraculous pedalling style and panache and human frailties were and remain very appealing. Equally, it is also possible to take an opposing view and rather resent his arrogance, naked ambition and occasional disdain for lesser mortals. He certainly divided the *tifosi* like a meat cleaver, as serial winners often do.

Coppi made a solid if unspectacular start to his first season as a professional with Legnano taking an encouraging eighth place in Milan–San Remo and a less impressive 12th at the Giro del Piemonte, but Pavesi had seen enough and included him in the Legnano Giro squad. As a debutant *gregario* he was to work for Bartali and lap up the experience. That scenario changed in an instant on stage two where a stray dog caused Bartali to crash badly while descending the Passo della Scoffera. Reports mention a dislocated elbow and a bruised knee and certainly that night the team doctor suggested Bartali should abandon. Bartali, though, had a score to settle with the Giro which had caused so much frustration despite his opening volley of consecutive wins in 1936 and 1937. Attended by *gregari* Mario Vicini and Bizzi he battled on during stage two to finish while Coppi, whether under instructions or not, stayed with the lead group, finishing in the same time as stage winner Pierino Favalli, thus establishing himself in second place in the GC. Very early days and, with Bartali's participation uncertain, it was important that Legnano still had a presence at the sharp end of the GC race.

The race marked time for a while holding its breath to see if Bartali could recover. Initially he leaked more time although Bartali insisted after the race had finished that he felt his strength coming back and he could still have won the GC with a strong final week. By stage 11, however, the Legnano DS Pavesi could wait no longer. A Bartali revival might or might not happen, but what was cast iron was that young Fausto Coppi was riding like a dream and the mountainous stage from Florence to Modena over the Abetone Pass awaited. It was time to give Coppi permission to attack and to order the team officially to work for the youngster.

Coppi needed no second invitation and despite biblically bad weather conditions – lightning, hail, freezing rain – eased his effortless way up the Abetone to take control of the stage. 'The Heron' took flight and, in his natural habitat, looked extraordinarily graceful. Bartali, who had in any case suffered a mechanical at the foot of the climb, now had no real option other than to ride for his young *gregario*. His inner turmoil can well be imagined. The king of all he surveyed in 1936 and 1937, he was then denied the chance to race in 1938, encountered a supercharged Valetti on his return and was now being upstaged by his own young *gregario*. Dark days for Bartali but he was a rider who prided himself in finishing races and if he was to ride all the way to Milan it was important that he be seen to achieve that with some dignity, serving a noble cause. 'Gino the pious' needed to show some humility – both in PR terms and for the good of his soul. So he gritted his teeth and largely kept his thoughts to himself, saving them for his autobiography. What is certain is that during the final stages, as Coppi did finally begin to falter a little in the Dolomites, Bartali offered stalwart support to Coppi and played no little part in the young man's triumph.

On stage 16, the first high mountain stage to Pieve di Cadore, Coppi was sick and weak after scoffing a chicken sandwich and paying the consequence when he tried to chase Vicini who saw the pink jersey faltering. Coppi collapsed in a ditch on the Passo della Mauria, vomiting profusely, in which condition Bartali found the young man after rejoining the head of the race after a puncture had delayed him. Bartali comforted the *maglia rosa*, passed him his spare bidon of water and laid him down on the grass to ease the stomach cramps before persuading him to continue. He then paced him back to the main group although Mario Vicini had escaped for the stage win. It had been touch and go but Coppi retained the jersey and was now just 59 seconds ahead of second-place Enrico Mollo in the GC.

The following day – a savage short mountainfest from Pieve di Cadore to Ortisei featuring the Falzarego Pass, the Pordoi and Sella – the two rode in tandem again. Sort of. Bartali twice waited for Coppi when he punctured but when Bartali himself punctured, Coppi, not recognising the need for support and teamwork at this stage of the race, started to attack before being called back by Pavesi. It was an uneasy truce but a powerful one while it lasted. The night before, the canny Pavesi had famously driven to the café at the top of the Falzarego Pass with two thermos flasks which he left with the café owner with a request that they be filled with hot tea in the morning and given to his two star riders when they passed. 'How will I know them?' asked the man, clearly neither one of the *tifosi* nor, indeed, a reader of *Gazzetta*. 'They will be the first two riders, one will be wearing pink and the other white and green' (the colours of Bartali, then the Italian national champion). And so they were.

Bartali took line honours on that stage which saw Coppi's lead over Mollo grow to in excess of 3 minutes, and with the race now virtually won also helped himself to the final mountain stage before bracing himself for Coppi's triumphant entrance into Milan. In *La Mia Storia* he later wrote: 'If I had been from another team he wouldn't have won the Giro. He was not experienced and he had his limits on the climbs, he would suddenly have nothing in the tank. When that happened in the Dolomites I was the one who saved him from disaster. I didn't do it for him I did it for Legnano who pay my wages.'

Although getting stronger by the day in the Dolomites, Bartali is over-egging the pudding in suggesting he could have won. He finished a full 45 minutes behind Coppi but, equally, there is no doubt that without his contribution in the latter stages, especially during the *maglia rosa*'s huge wobble on Pieve di Cadore, Coppi might not have won the 1940 Giro and Mollo could easily have sneaked in. That fact didn't sit easily with either Coppi or Bartali and compounded a sporting relationship that had already got off to a rocky start.

7
FAUSTO COPPI TAKES ON ALL COMERS (1946-53)

Within 24 hours of Coppi's great victory in 1940 Mussolini had taken Italy to war with England and France and the sporting landscape changed overnight. Although some of the smaller stage races and the big one-day races continued in Italy to a greater or lesser degree during the war, the Giro itself was shelved and it was six years before Gino Bartali and Fausto Coppi would renew their nascent rivalry, one that is still debated endlessly in Italian cycling circles.

But first they had to survive the war. For decades details of Bartali's war were unknown and the only war-related story that surfaced was a curious incident at Dachau concentration camp in 1943 when his name alone was credited with saving the lives of 21 Italian Jews, mainly from around Florence. A German officer, presumably a cycling fan, suddenly asked one of the inmates, Antonio Davitti, if he knew of Bartali, the great cyclist from Florence. Davitti said he did and even produced a faded press cutting of the star from inside his breast pocket. The German officer then instructed Davitti to draw up a list of 20 fellow prisoners who were to be spared the gas chamber and who were to work in the Dachau factory instead.

Initially, Bartali just got by. Bizarrely, when called up in October 1940 he failed the Italian Army medical with an irregular heartbeat. This would usually disqualify a man from duty but both the medical officer and Bartali realised that wasn't really an option given his reputation as one of the fittest men imaginable. Eventually a compromise was reached whereby he served as a messenger at an aeroplane factory near Lake Trasimeno, some 120km to the south-east of Florence. He could have used a motorbike to run his errands but persuaded a senior officer that it was nearly as quick on a pushbike, which also had the advantage of keeping him in training for the limited racing programme that was still being organised. The surrender of Italian forces to the Allies, closely followed by the occupation of Italy by the Nazis in 1943, changed all that. Bartali was demobbed and moved back to the Florence region where he was soon contacted by his good friend Archbishop Elia Dalla Costa who had become heavily involved with the Italian resistance movement, which was trying to save the lives of the many Jews in the area who were either being rounded up and sent to concentration camps or summarily shot. It was a personal plea for assistance from Dalla Costa and Bartali answered with action not words. His most regular duty was to tog up in training gear wearing a jersey emblazoned with his name just in case the Germans were in any doubt as to his identity: he was Gino Bartali, recent Giro and Tour de France champion, out on one of his famous long-distance training rides. While out for such a ride he would stop at a remote Franciscan friary, which was secretly housing many Jews, to collect the photographs of them that were needed for forged documents if they were to have any hope of escaping. These would be carefully rolled up and concealed in his bike frame and handlebars, and later that day he would ride back into Florence and pass them over to Giorgio Nissim, a Jewish accountant originally from Pisa, who coordinated the production of the forged documents. Bartali continued to act as a courier, on other occasions delivering the finished documents themselves. Lucca, Genoa and the Vatican – where the secret printing press was situated – were all regular destinations for Bartali. Dangerous work indeed, as was his decision to hide the Jewish family of his friend Giacomo Goldenberg in the cellar of his Florence apartment until the liberation of Florence in 1944. The true extent of his exploits only came to light after his death in 2000 when Nissim's sons were going through the diaries of their father who had also recently died. There in the diaries were neatly listed some of Bartali's trips and the tasks assigned to him. In September 2013 Bartali was posthumously awarded the honour Righteous Among the Nations by Yad Vashem, the Holocaust memorial and education centre in Jerusalem. His deeds certainly offer a searing insight into an elusive and seemingly dour individual.

Coppi, meanwhile, also endured an eventful war and, like Bartali, initially it was simply a case of muddling through. He was called up just two days after his Giro victory – Infantryman 7375 – but for two years or more he was spared combat with postings at Limone Piemonte and then Tortona, close to Novi Ligure. There was ample time to train, race and even to get his daily massage from Cavanna and for a while his was a comfortable enough war combining military duties with racing domestically. But eventually, in March 1943, his unit was shipped out to North Africa where he briefly experienced the heat of battle before he and many others were captured and made prisoners of war at Cap Bon on 13 April. Coppi was held captive at Majaz al Bab for the best part of two years where he was put to work as a lorry mechanic and occasional barber. The British cyclist Len Levesley serving at the camp was astonished to find Coppi giving him a haircut one morning as he recalled in *Fausto Coppi: The True Story*, by Jean-Paul Ollivier:

> I should think it took me all of a full second to realise who it was. He looked fine, he looked slim, and having been in the desert, he looked tanned. I'd only seen him in cycling magazines but I knew instantly who he was. So he cut away at my hair and I tried to have a conversation with him, but he didn't speak English and I don't speak Italian. But we managed one or two words and I got over to him that I did some club racing. And I gave him a bar of chocolate that I had with me and he was grateful for that and that was the end of it.

On 1 February 1945 Coppi was moved back to the Italian mainland to an RAF holding camp at Salerno just outside Naples. There he was briefly a batman for a British officer but the war was coming to an end and he was released in April, free to continue his cycling career. Within weeks he was racing again in the south, weak though he was, and picking up useful appearance money before he decided it was time to cycle home to Castellania regain his strength and continue his career in earnest. A truly remarkable career, rudely interrupted, was about to be relaunched.

In his pomp Coppi was perhaps the greatest natural talent the sport has ever seen, and his fortunes on and off the bike became the great soap opera of Italian sport, in fact of Italian life itself. Could anybody or anything beat the great man? He was always the one to beat, his stick-like body sometimes failed him, he was self-obsessed to a sometimes alarming degree, could be both vindictive and generous, suffered personal tragedy in the shape of his brother's death and was to embark on the most celebrated extramarital affair in sport. Yet by 1953 he had still amassed a record five Giro titles. And in two of those years he famously doubled up and took the Tour de France as well. The ageing Bartali resisted with some panache for a few years while Fiorenzo Magni, a great rider in his own right, was rarely cowed and was rewarded with his occasional hard-earned moments of glory. There was even a win for the stylish and charismatic Hugo Koblet who became the first overseas rider to win the Giro in 1950. But always it was Coppi who loomed largest, either dictating the race or the storyline, usually both.

Given their varied war experiences you might have thought that both Coppi and Bartali would have mellowed in their personal relationship when they started racing again in 1946. Life was manifestly too short for such bad humour and ill grace. But that is to ignore the inevitable rivalry when two of the greatest ever performers in a given sport find themselves competing in the same era. The media from

Gazzetta downwards stoked the fires, and their lifestyles and what they were perceived to stand for divided Italy so naturally that perhaps they were condemned to eternal enmity. Bartali would never refer to Coppi by name, he would always call him *l'altro*, the other one. They were also both as stubborn as mules and very difficult people in their own ways.

The great Alfredo Binda, called upon to manage the duo at the Tour de France and at various World Championships for the Italian team, summed it up best with his astute comment: 'It was like being asked to put a cat and a dog in the same sack. It was no good pretending they were friends. Their rivalry wasn't an attitude they adopted out of vanity, it was real and neverending.'

Clearly Bartali and Coppi could not race in the same team, so at the start of 1946 the latter had moved to Bianchi, taking his favourite mechanic Pinella di Grande with him and negotiating a place in the squad for his younger brother, the light-hearted but worldly Serse, who was in any case a strong, loyal *gregario* well worth his place in any team. The guru-like Cavanna was, of course, also omnipresent. Coppi is often described as a solitary figure, trapped in an unhappy marriage and at odds with the cycling establishment, but he certainly didn't lack for close confidants and soulmates in his corner.

The scene was set and the 1946 race optimistically dubbed the *Giro della Rinascita* (rebirth) although in reality there was very little new on offer. Even the venerable Cougnet was still in charge although his anointed successor, Vincenzo Torriani, was shadowing him and was poised to take over in 1948. War had raged through Europe and the wider world for six years but it was still Bartali racing against Coppi, the rest nowhere. The older Bartali had a couple of very good years left at best and was determined to make the most of them. He certainly looked strong and decided to make his move on stage nine, a mountainous day from Chieti to Naples. Reports differ as to whether Coppi was suffering illness or got delayed with a puncture and was unable to cover Bartali's attack but, whatever the reality, he lost 4 minutes to Bartali that day and, as it turned out, the race with it. Coppi rode strongly for the rest of the Giro, taking two of the mountain stages in the Dolomites but could never quite break Bartali who arrived back in Milan with a 47-second lead. It was a sweet moment of vindication but at nearly 32 the slim margin didn't augur well for the future; and, indeed, although he was to claim the runner-up spot three times in the coming years, Bartali's remaining Giros were to be a glorious raging against the dying of the light. He was never to stand atop the podium again.

Even in victory Bartali remained ever-suspicious of Coppi, as he revealed in an interview in *Miroir des Sports* that year. On the stage from Genoa to Montecatini Terme, Bartali observed Coppi drinking from a glass phial while rounding one of the hairpins on the Passo del Bracco and after the stage finished Bartali drove back to the spot in a team car to look for, and find, the phial:

With the meticulous care of a detective collecting evidence for fingerprinting I picked it up, dropped it into a white envelope and put it carefully in my pocket. The next day I rushed round to my personal doctor and asked him to send the phial to a lab for analysis. Disappointment: no drug, no magic potion. It was nothing more than an ordinary tonic, made in France that I could have bought without a prescription.

I realised that I should have to try to outsmart him and I devised my own investigation system. The first thing was to make sure I always stayed at the same hotel for a race, and to have the room next to his so I could mount a surveillance. I would watch him leave with his mates, then I would tiptoe into the room which ten seconds earlier had been his headquarters. I would rush to the waste bin and the bedside table, go through the bottles, flasks, phials, tubes, cartons, boxes, suppositories – I swept up everything. I had become so expert in interpreting all these pharmaceuticals that I could predict how Fausto would behave during the course of the stage. I would work out, according to the traces of the product I found, how and when he would attack me.

Extraordinary, paranoiac, and disturbingly obsessive behaviour from Bartali you might think although you might also argue it was the same hyper-alertness and attention to detail that probably saw him through his clandestine war activities.

Coppi's candid public confession later in his career of regularly using drugs more than confirmed Bartali's basic suspicions. Quite how much the crude use of amphetamines – *la bomba* – influenced a cyclist's performance is, however, a moot point as more often than not they would cause a rider to collapse and abandon the following day or to fall ill. It is also commonly accepted that many, perhaps the majority, of riders at the time resorted to using drugs in some form. Following the Second World War an estimated 90-million surplus amphetamine tablets appeared on the black market, originally shipped to Europe from the USA for use by American combat troops. They were not hard to obtain and at this stage doping in cycling was essentially the search for a magic potion or short-term tonic that would make the difference rather than anything we would recognise today as the systematic use of performance-enhancing drugs. Coppi, it should be added, was also genuinely interested in and at the cutting edge of nutrition, diet and hydration and at one stage even experimented with vegetarianism. Anything in the pursuit of victory.

The unfolding Bartali–Coppi rivalry was gripping enough but there was excitement elsewhere in this 1946 race when the organisers, full of patriotic fervour, decided to take the race into Trieste which was essentially still a war zone. The former Yugoslavia also claimed the city, which was occupied by Allied forces, and sporadic fighting was commonplace. On the day – stage 14 from Rovigo to Trieste – the Giro turned ugly when Yugoslav partisans stopped the race at Pieris, blocking the road and throwing stones and bottles at the peloton. Armed guards accompanying the race in turn fired over the protesters' heads by way of warning. Belatedly the organisers realised the possible error of their ways and declared the stage over there and then with all riders to receive the same time. A number of riders however, led by Trieste native Giordano Cottur and his Wilier Triestina squad, were determined to finish in the city itself where a considerable crowd had gathered. Which is exactly what they did, with reports indicating that Cottur was awarded the stage with 16 other riders crossing the line in Trieste itself. Although the finish passed off peacefully enough there was extensive rioting once the Giro left and headed for the Dolomites. It was a very volatile arena into which the race had strayed.

The following year featured another head-to-head between Bartali and Coppi, and the interest and excitement escalated further. Armed police were assigned to each rider to protect them from their fans and Bartali invested in earplugs in an attempt to get a decent night's sleep such was the noise of the crowd that gathered outside his hotel at night. In terms of time difference it was close in 1947 but there had been a shift in power. For much of the race Coppi seemed to toy with Bartali, waiting patiently for the moment to strike. From stage four, when he and Coppi were a class apart on the Abetone climb and bossed the stage from Reggio nell'Emilia to Prato, Bartali wore the *maglia rosa* and there was the illusion of an equal contest. At the end of stage 15 his lead in GC over Coppi was 2 minutes 41 seconds – a big deficit to make up on a rider of Bartali's class, but Coppi remained unflustered. He had done his homework and knew that nobody would be able to stay with him on stage 16 from Pieve di Cadore to Trento, a 194km ride which included the Falzarego and Pordoi passes. Coppi went initially on the Falzarego when Bartali's chain fouled but Coppi himself dropped a chain on the descent which allowed Bartali to regain contact, albeit only temporarily. Coppi was off again on the Pordoi and this time there was no stopping him as he rode into Trento 4 minutes 24 seconds ahead of the chasing pack that Bartali had gathered in an attempt to limit his losses. It might have been more but bad weather had seen a third climb planned for that day, the Sella, cancelled at the last moment. With no more mountain stages left, the race was his. Game, set and match Coppi.

Perhaps you can have too much of a good thing, however, and Fiorenzo Magni's win in 1948 was no bad thing for the Giro. Bartali and Coppi had arguably become a little complacent and made no attempt to animate the race in the first week, content no doubt to wait for the inevitable battle royal in the mountains in the final week. After stage eight they were both well over 7 minutes off the lead held by Giordano Cottur. But no stress: it would all be sorted in due course. The Giro was all about them and they would choose exactly when battle commenced. It was their show. At which point Magni, an emerging talent but at that point not really on the main contenders' radar, played his hand and set off with Vito Ortelli on an audacious break midway through the long stage to Naples taking in the Ariano Irpino ascent. The big hitters paid no attention which was a mistake because Magni moved into second place overall, well over 10 minutes ahead of Coppi and Bartali, and it transpired he was too good a rider to take liberties with.

Ezio Cecchi and Magni embedded themselves at the top of the GC but there was still stage 17, with the Falzarego and Pordoi to negotiate and Coppi, at 8 minutes 29 seconds with Bartali a little further back, was still capable of anything on such terrain. And Coppi in particular was beginning to hit his stride having won the short, sharp mountain stage from Auronzo to Cortina d'Ampezzo the previous day. He certainly rode beautifully again on stage 17 but was shocked at the end to see Magni roll in just 2 minutes 31 seconds later to regain the *maglia rosa* from Cecchi. Observers had Magni up to 5 minutes behind Coppi going into the Pordoi climb and everybody knew that Coppi was far superior going uphill. How did that happen? How indeed. That Magni benefited from fans pushing him up the ascent of the Pordoi is beyond dispute but that was hardly anything new, either at the Giro or the Tour de France. Some fans had always spontaneously rendered assistance. What is in doubt is whether Magni's sponsor Wilier Triestina – with an unexpected Giro win so close they could almost smell it – orchestrated the whole affair by bussing in supporters and placing them strategically up the mountain to lend a hand when their man was in trouble. Coppi and Bianchi suspected the latter and lodged an angry complaint but the judges had little hard evidence to go on and docked Magni just 2 minutes.

Far from mollified, Coppi stormed out of the race in disgust, taking his team with him. It's easy to understand their frustration but Coppi was in some ways the architect of his own downfall. It was he and his team who had snoozed on stage nine and let Magni get into that vital break and it was he who had banked on still being able to deliver the *coup de grâce* on the Pordoi. He was leaving it very late and such tactics can backfire. He could just as easily have had a mechanical or crashed on the Pordoi and lost his one chance to make good the time gap that way. And, finally, his decision to quit the race also rather ignores the fact that, regardless of any issues with Magni, his carelessness earlier in the race meant he still trailed the blameless Cecchi by 1 minute and 9 seconds with two flattish stages left. Magni eventually beat Cecchi by just 11 seconds, and Bartali, having long since accepted that the 1948 Giro was a lost cause, finished eighth overall.

Like many great winners, Coppi wasn't a very graceful loser. He didn't get much practice. Nor would his humour have improved a great deal later in the year when Bartali was reinstalled as the nation's hero with his stunning Tour de France victory ten years after his earlier triumph across the border. There was life in the old dog yet, and it was an angry and highly motivated Coppi who started preparing for the

1949 season. He decided to reduce the number of lucrative appearances he made on the track in the winter to start his road preparations early. He headed off to North Africa – Tunisia, Algeria and Egypt – with brother Serse to train in the winter sun and ride in a number of low-key races. He was determined to hit the 1949 season running and end all debate as to who was the greater rider. He intended to win the Giro and Tour de France back to back.

Coppi in his pomp as he takes Giro/Tour double

Mindful perhaps of his twin aims, Coppi rode within himself initially at the 1949 Giro but this was a course so loaded in his favour – huge mountain stage mid-race, the mother of all mountain stages towards the end and then a long time trial on the penultimate day – that there was more wriggle room if anything untoward happened. He was both relaxed and focused at the same time, a very dangerous combination. He went to work in earnest on stage 11, a forbidding mountain day from Bassano del Grappa which took in the Rolle, Pordoi and Gardena when he put 6 minutes into the field to move into second place behind Adolfo Leoni who he stalked all the way to stage 17. No slip-ups or loss of concentration this time.

And then the sporting world witnessed a genius at work. The new race director Torriani – perhaps wanting to make a name for himself and possibly also determined to ensure a win for either Coppi or Bartali after Magni had slipped through unannounced in 1948 – had designed the mother of all mountain stages from Cuneo to Pinerolo, 254km of undiluted pain taking in five major passes and climbs – the Maddalena, Vars, the Izoard, Montgenèvre and finally Sestriere. For Coppi it was payback time. Primo Volpi led the peloton onto the Maddalena but thereafter it was Coppi all the way as he took off into the murk and sleety blizzards on the high tops. There were still 190km to go but Coppi wasn't hanging around. For the best part of nine hours Italy came to a grinding halt as people crowded around radios to discuss the regular updates and marvel at Coppi's virtuosity. By the time he arrived in Pinerolo he was 11 minutes 52 seconds ahead of Bartali who was himself another 7 minutes 52 seconds ahead of the third man home, Alfredo Martini. With a generous 4-minute time bonus for the win, Coppi now led second-placed Bartali by 23 minutes 20 seconds. Coppi seemed almost to be from another planet.

Italian novelist Dino Buzatti best captured the moment and the wider significance of Coppi's *coup de grâce* at the 1949 Giro:

> There is nothing left to do but to accept the fact and assign to Coppi the position he is entitled to: numero uno in Italian cycling, or rather, in world cycling. Today there is a gap between him and Bartali but also a gap between Bartali and all the others; and both are the pride of Italian sport. Everybody envies us our two champions, starting with the French. We only hope that Bartali will hang in there, he is the necessary element of comparison for determining Coppi's class.

The Coppi–Bartali rivalry was now over, in the Grand Tours at least, as was demonstrated later that summer when Binda somehow managed to get the two protagonists to call a truce and for Bartali to ride at the Tour for Coppi. Coppi swept to yet another stunning victory, this time by nearly 11 minutes, with Bartali in second place – himself a further 15 minutes ahead of third-placed Jacques Marinelli. From this point onwards when they lined up in the same race the real threat to Coppi would come from elsewhere.

1950: first overseas winner

Switzerland's dashing Hugo Koblet, never knowingly seen with a hair out of place and with his sponsored comb and scented sponge always close to hand, was the next rider to step up to the plate. The music-hall artist Jacques Grello nicknamed him the *pedaleur du charme*, a moniker which stuck and became the title of a documentary film made in 2010 depicting his life. Koblet was a playboy but he had immense style on a bike and his warm-hearted personality made him popular with fans and opponents.

A lover of all things American, where he frequently holidayed, there was bizarrely more than a whiff of the all-American West Coast boy about the man from Zurich. Koblet was box office and for a couple of years he blazed a trail, an aesthetically pleasing but hard-as-nails roadman before he gradually lost the ability to climb effectively at high altitude. Some date this incipient weakness back to a trip to Mexico where he developed a respiratory problem; others are more cynical and believed that, as a notoriously overenthusiastic user of drugs and medication, his health was ruinously damaged. Certainly the Swiss documentary leaned towards the latter. It's difficult to be certain.

Koblet's story had the saddest of endings when he died in a car crash in 1964, aged just 39, an incident thought by some to be suicide, with one witness insisting Koblet deliberately drove his white Alfa Romeo sports car into a tree. It's possible. His marriage had broken up, a reconciliation had failed, he had squandered his money and the taxman was in hot pursuit. Life had certainly turned very sour for the man who once had the world at his feet. Back in 1950 he was a smiling, tanned, sporting god and a glorious, debonair antidote to the introspective Coppi, the moody, stern Bartali and the grimacing hard man Magni.

Before the 1950 Giro, although well regarded by Italian fans, Koblet hadn't really been considered among the main contenders. The three big beasts of Italian cycling were all in good form. The ever-versatile Coppi had enjoyed a profitable Classics season winning Paris–Roubaix and Flèche Wallonne and was the clear favourite; the granite-like Magni had won the second of his three Tour of Flanders titles and was going like a train, and even the old campaigner Bartali, enjoying an Indian summer of a season with the expectation of victory removed, had looked sprightly in winning Milan–San Remo.

Koblet kept his nose clean early on, avoided crashes, and made his first move on stage eight from Brescia to Venice when the climbers came alive on the Pian delle Fugazze climb. With Koblet and Pasquale Fornara escaping the select bunch at the end to nick 20 seconds, Koblet went into the *maglia rosa*. The following day Koblet repeated his excellent form in the mountains proper, finishing alongside the stage winner Bartali after a stage containing the Rolle, Pordoi and Gardena. That underscored his race-winning potential but the drama of the day concerned Coppi and a crash that caused him to abandon. Some way before the major climbs, near the village of Primolano, Coppi was manoeuvring his way to the front of the peloton when he collided with Armando Peverelli and fell to earth. Paverelli had lost the sight of his left eye after a crash in the 1949 Tour de France and might not have seen Coppi as he routinely went to pass on his left. The crash was neither high speed nor spectacular but Coppi immediately knew he was in trouble when he tried to remount. Something was definitely broken, and an X-ray revealed three distinct fractures to his pelvis. Not only was his Giro over but his season as well.

Racing accidents happen but as ever the circus quickly moved on. Koblet was still riding beautifully and cleverly crested the two major climbs on stage 13 ahead of the bunch to pick up further time bonuses and push his lead in the GC out beyond 7 minutes. Not that he and his Guerra colleagues particularly needed any help, but it was quite noticeable that Coppi's Bianchi team were now 'riding for' the new Swiss star rather than assisting Bartali. This started to cause quite a stir as it suddenly dawned on the *tifosi* that the Giro d'Italia was about to be won by an overseas rider. Bartali wasn't too pleased either, claiming that it was only his intervention with officialdom that had prevented a couple of the Bianchi team being asked to leave the race after they had missed the cut on the day Coppi crashed, when they had waited with their leader before he was taken to hospital. Bartali chipped a couple of minutes off Koblet's lead before they returned to Milan and in fact in terms of actual elapsed time got around the 3,981km course fractionally quicker than Koblet, but the *pedaleur du charme* had ridden a near-flawless race, tactically and physically, and hadn't missed a beat. With the aid of his cannily won time bonuses it was Koblet who stood atop the podium at the finish. And still not a hair out of place.

Coppi was up against it again in 1951. Not only had a mighty field assembled, with Louison Bobet leading the French charge and a team of hard nuts from Belgium spearheaded by Rik Van Steenbergen intent on mounting a challenge, but he was again struggling physically. He had broken his collarbone crashing at the finish of Milano–Torino on 11 March which torpedoed his preparations and saw him arrive at the start seriously undercooked. Everything needed to go Coppi's way if he was to have any chance. In the event it proved to be an entertaining tussle between Magni and Van Steenbergen who both found inspiration and rode above themselves along with Switzerland's other world-class star Ferdi Kübler who had won the 1950 Tour de France. Kübler was the complete opposite of the languid Koblet – unkempt, wild, hair everywhere and drenched in sweat. Coppi won a couple of stages and eventually finished fourth but could never quite get on terms. Bad weather in the Alps saw a couple of climbs cancelled, which also worked against him a little, but essentially it was that early season crash that did for the *campionissimo*.

Magni took the Giro without winning a stage and his victory, as well as being a triumph for consistency in mountains and in the two time trials, was down largely to a virtuoso display of descending on stage 17 from Trieste to Cortina d'Ampezzo. This was meant to be the crucial stage of the race – the Tappone – but the wintry weather prevented the peloton going up the Pordoi, Falzarego and Rolle, much to Coppi's dismay. The Mauria and Misurina were still testing enough climbs and Coppi and Bobet were out front all day but on the last descent Magni, although with no hope of winning the stage, decided it was now or never in terms of the GC and took his life in his hands in an attempt to put some time into Van Steenbergen. By cycling standards Magni was a muscular, thickset athlete and there is no reason why he should not have been an exceptional descender, but this was something out of the ordinary as he went for broke. Descending is very technical and a great skill but sometimes it also comes down to a state of mind and who wants it the most. On this occasion Magni was that man, as he put 3 minutes into the great Belgian to open up a lead of 1 minute 46 seconds. The Giro was his.

Coppi bounces back after personal tragedy

Fausto Coppi's life took a dramatic and tragic turn on Friday 29 June 1951 when his extrovert younger brother Serse died after a seemingly innocuous crash in Turin at the end of the one-day Giro del Piemonte. Serse was racing alongside his famous brother when his front wheel went into a tramline and he went to ground.

Serse had signed the finish sheet when he rolled in and was having a bath when he started to complain of a headache and quickly became unconscious. There was an agonising delay when he reached hospital; there was no suitable blood plasma available and Serse died before he could reach the operating table. A younger brother he may have been but Serse was much more than that to Fausto Coppi. He was the grounded, earthy, profane and worldlier member of the double act, a perfect foil to his complicated and fretting elder brother. He was a training partner, loyal *gregario* and room-mate. Serse was Fausto's sounding board and dispenser of common sense and arbiter of his wildly fluctuating emotions and passions. Now he was gone. In cycling terms it was touch and go for a while as to whether Fausto would continue but when he made the decision to ride on it was with a vengeance and anger. The cycling world needed to look out in 1952. As for his personal life, the shackles were off. He was unhappy at home and had already spotted Giulia Locatelli who, although married and often travelling with her doctor husband, made little attempt to disguise her passion for the unhappy Coppi.

Coppi was off the leash in all respects and 1952–3 saw the final great flowering of his extraordinary talent with two Giro wins, a second Tour de France title and the most crushing of wins in the World Championship.

The 1952 Giro was a controlled masterclass as Coppi looked to win well without emptying the tanks because he fully intended winning the Tour again shortly afterwards. He finished the race off in one fell swoop fairly early on in proceedings when, already in pink, he put 5 minutes into all his main rivals in winning the Venice–Bolzano stage which took in the familiar Falzarego, Pordoi and Sella passes. By this stage he was already over 8 minutes ahead of second-place Fiorenzo Magni. He was in cruise control and on stage 14 he effectively wrapped the race up by winning a long ITT and adding nearly 2 minutes to his lead over Magni. The last week was a virtual promenade to Milan, a gentle warm-down as he started planning and plotting for the Tour.

Sadly, the 1952 Giro will also be remembered for the Giro's first racing fatality when Orfeo Ponsin, a second-year professional with Frejus, was killed after a high-speed crash. It occurred on stage four, on Tuesday 20 May, some 30km from the finish in Rome when Ponsin was descending off the Merluzza climb and his front wheel hit a foot-high concrete block alongside the road. Ponsin was catapulted into a nearby tree and pronounced dead in hospital later that evening.

The 1953 race was a very different proposition for Coppi. Koblet was enjoying his last hurrah as a truly competitive Grand Tour rider and took the *maglia rosa* after stage eight, a very Koblet-friendly 48km time trial when he put 1 minute 20 seconds into Coppi. The 1950 winner retained the jersey without serious alarm all the way to the much-anticipated finale in the high mountains with stages 19 and 20 both monstrous affairs in their own way. The race proper would begin there.

Stage 19 incorporated four old friends – the Misurina, Falzarego, Pordoi and Sella – and Koblet went to the start line with a lead of 1 minute 59 seconds over Coppi which, although useful, was far from being decisive given the terrain that awaited. The duo rode alone together at the front of the race with Koblet setting a fierce pace on the Pordoi. Coppi then comfortably overtook him on the Sella only for Koblet to get back on terms with a brave descent. Koblet was the aggressor, wanting to close the race out there and then, although he was left hanging on at the end. Come the stage finish at the Bolzano velodrome, Coppi won an uncontested sprint and here the intrigue starts ahead of stage 20.

The accepted Giro story is that the two had spoken en route during stage 19 and that there was an understanding that Coppi would take the stage with Koblet now the Giro champion-elect. 'My compliments, the Giro is yours. You are the strongest,' Coppi reportedly said to Koblet at the finish. Very odd if true. It was only half-time so to speak in the epic mountain double-header that would decide the 1953 Giro and the toughest test by far was yet to come, on an incredible new climb, the Stelvio, which was making its long-awaited debut. Approaching from the north-east, from Ponte di Stelvio, the Stelvio is an epic cycling challenge by any criteria: 24.3km at an average of 7.4 per cent seeing an altitude gain of 1,808m topping out at 2,758m before the high-speed 22km descent to the finish in Bormio. The height was such that altitude – and the ability of a rider to cope with it – was a very real factor as much as the steepness of the climb and descent. The Stelvio – often featured in car adverts and named the 'greatest driving road in the world' – also takes in 48 hairpin bends. By way of comparison the Alpe d'Huez, one of the marquee climbs on the Tour de France, has 21 hairpins. The pass is normally closed from early October to the end of May so it's often touch and go whether it's in condition to race in the Giro.

Before the start of the epic stage 20 which traversed this visual treat came Act 2 of this favourite Giro mythology. Coppi had apparently settled for second place overall but his Bianchi team-mates were still convinced he could not only win the Stelvio stage but the Giro overall and started chivvying him up. Why wouldn't they? Their cut from the team pool would be considerably more if Coppi won rather than finished runner-up. At which point Coppi's grizzled *gregario* Ettore Milano decided to wander over and ask the ever-obliging Koblet to pose for a picture. With your sunglasses off please, Hugo. A quick comb of the hair first and the deed was done.

Having got Koblet to whisk off the shades, Milano was then apparently able to instantly divine, simply by looking into Koblet's eyes, that the race leader had overcooked the amphetamines the previous day. Dilated pupils were often a giveaway and Milano, also observing Koblet's red eyes and frequent yawning, also reported back that Koblet had not slept at all well. Koblet also appeared to be glugging water like it was going out of fashion, often the sign of dehydration which in turn was often a result of using amphetamines. In short, Milano felt Koblet was there for the taking. Come the stage itself Coppi, perhaps as motivated by the sight of an unaccompanied Giulia Locatelli standing on the mountain roadside in her distinctive white coat as much as anything, rode an inspired race, attacking finally and decisively some 11km from the summit of the extraordinary climb. The pictures of Coppi effortlessly climbing ever upwards – through what appears on occasions to be a tunnel of snow, so high are the banks of snowdrift – are among the most iconic in the sport and sealed his legendary status.

It should be noted, however, that Koblet looked strong for most of the day as well but rode a shocking race tactically. His sole objective should have been to shadow Coppi, instead he at one stage burned up valuable reserves of energy chasing down an utterly irrelevant break from the young Nino Defilippis who had possibly been encouraged to attack by Coppi. Koblet paid dearly for his profligacy when Coppi finally, gloriously, went on the attack but his was not a total collapse. Koblet finished the stage fourth, 3 minutes 28 seconds behind Coppi. Like the rest of the field, he had simply been beaten hollow by the manifestly superior man but Koblet had still ridden a half-decent stage for a man who was already beginning to exhibit problems riding at very high altitudes. That night, staying in the same hotel, they apparently bumped into each other in the lift and not a word was uttered. There was nothing left to be said.

That is the version of Coppi's final Giro win that has gone down in Giro legend but it would be staggering if 1 June 1953 hadn't loomed large in his mind for months beforehand. The greatest climber in Giro history – perhaps in cycling history – on the greatest climb the Giro has ever produced. On its race debut? Coppi was always going to give it his all and if he rode at his best nobody on the planet would live with him. At the age of 33 this might also be his last chance to take a Grand Tour. Already he had won two previous mountain stages on this 1953 Giro and, although Koblet had stayed with him the previous day, could the mercurial Swiss rider back it up? Coppi could 'go again' in the mountains, that was for sure. He had proved it time and time again. Coppi started the day just 1.59 behind Koblet, not a great deal when the world's best climber goes to work in his natural habitat. Do we really accept that Coppi was so intimidated by the challenge of Koblet and had given the race up before his Bianchi colleague Milano started his pep talk? As a canny champion he might talk his chances down a little, but he was on a roll, had made the world's best riders look as if they were going backwards the previous year at the Giro and Tour, and his confidence would have been high.

What is beyond doubt is the virtuosity of the ride and his form that year. Coppi circa 1952–3, in the Giro and elsewhere, was as good as it gets. He was riding in a state of grace en route to his final Giro title with a World Championship to follow later in the year when he soloed home by over 6 minutes, the rest of the world nowhere. After 1953, however, there were no more Grand Tour wins and just one more Monument, the 1954 Giro di Lombardia. He wasn't getting any younger and his personal life was becoming both complicated and distracting. He remained a sublime athlete who still enjoyed many great days on a bike but to a degree he was sated. The overwhelming hunger to win was ebbing away.

8

A RACE FOR ALL SHAPES, SIZES AND NATIONALITIES (1954-66)

Fausto Coppi wasn't gone yet, he was still a factor and continued to make the headlines one way or another, but his dominance had ended and as the shadow he cast receded a wonderfully rich variety of riders emerged blinking into the limelight: from Carlo Clerici and Arnaldo Pambianco to a rather unheralded star of track and road in Ercole Baldini and the perennially competitive and enduring hard man of Italian cycling, Fiorenzo Magni. In addition two quirky, occasionally downright odd, superstars of the sport in Charly Gaul and Jacques Anquetil stepped forward. Suddenly the Giro became a very eclectic race. During this fascinating period competitors from three nations other than Italy won the race – Clerici (Switzerland), Gaul (Luxembourg) and Anquetil (France) – while every style of rider had his day. Clerici was a very good *gregario* who enjoyed his day in the sun after which he tasted success just once more in his entire cycling career; Magni was a tank of a Classics rider who clung on heroically in the mountains; Baldini was an extraordinary hybrid of world-class track pursuiter and successful road racer; Gaul was one of the greatest climbers in cycling history, and finally Anquetil was virtually untouchable in time trials and had the ability to suffer in silence and survive in the highest mountains. Nobody could accuse the Giro of spawning stereotypical winners. It was a riot of diversity and character types.

Clerici's victory in 1954 was essentially an accident. Born in Italy to an Italian father and Swiss mother, his family moved to Zurich when he was young and as a result Clerici was dual qualified. It was, however, a time of plenty for Italian cycling and, having received little or no encouragement from the Italian Federation, he chose instead to become a naturalised Swiss citizen and completed the paperwork just a couple of months before the 1954 Giro. As a rider he was better than average but in no way a star. Going into the 1954 Giro his best result in a stage race of any substance was a third place at the 1952 Tour or Switzerland and a win in the GP de Suisse. Good-looking and easygoing, he was firm friends with Koblet and a natural ally for the 1950 champion as they lined up together in the Guerra team at the Giro start line in Palermo. Indeed, he had already rendered valuable and controversial assistance to Koblet the previous year when, although then riding for an Italian team, he helped pace Koblet back to the peloton after a crash. Clerici and his Welter team were much criticised for this supposedly unpatriotic act – despite the fact that the entire peloton up the road had slowed to allow the popular Koblet back – and eventually Welter reacted to a hail of criticism by withdrawing Clerici from the race.

Discontent was in the air at the start of the 1954 Giro. The riders and teams weren't happy at its 4,337km length, the longest in Giro history, with only two rest days being scheduled en route. Additionally, there were strong rumours – which subsequently proved to be true – that *Gazzetta* were paying Coppi appearance money which went against the concept of the race always being bigger than the rider. A rematch with Koblet and the possibility of a record-breaking sixth Giro success for Coppi had the potential to make the 1954 Giro a classic, but it was still an odd bowing of the knee by *Gazzetta*. Were they still so lacking in confidence about the intrinsic worth of their race? Having paid one dominant *campionissimo* – Binda – not to race the Giro in 1930, they were now paying Coppi to ensure his participation. Logic, consistency and the Giro are not always happy bedfellows.

Anyway, these best laid plans backfired. The opening stage, a 36km team time trial around the Monte Pellegrino circuit, went off as hoped with a crushing win for Coppi's Bianchi team and the *campionissimo* back in pink. That evening, however, he dined on oysters, seldom a wise move when involved in a sporting event, was violently sick during the night and only just made it to the start line in Palermo for the run to Taormina. An ailing Coppi lost 11 minutes to the stage winner Giuseppe Minardi that day and dropped to tenth in the GC, nearly 10 minutes behind. Still, he was being paid handsomely whatever the result, so it was no great personal disaster.

And so with the reigning champion already on the back foot, the peloton reached stage six, a rugged mountainous run from Naples to L'Aquila over difficult Abruzzi countryside. Arbos team rider Nino Assirelli had embarked on a long, seemingly irrelevant solo break, when Clerici broke away from the peloton to bridge the gap, at which point they started working hard together. Coppi might still have been suffering from food poisoning or simply resigned to the fact that 1954 wasn't to be his year. Also his affair with Giulia Locatelli was coming to a head with both parties on the verge of leaving their respective spouses, and it's not unfair to suggest that Coppi's mind might have been elsewhere. Koblet, meanwhile, was very sanguine about the break. Firstly he was wholly supportive of anything that could further damage Coppi but, more importantly, he acknowledged that he was in Clerici's debt from the previous year. All these factors were playing out on the road as Assirelli and Clerici put the hammer down and a becalmed peloton failed to respond. By Naples the duo were over 11 minutes ahead of the next chaser – Edward Peeters – and had put a jaw-dropping 35 minutes into the main contenders. In terms of GC, Clerici, who had started the day handily placed in sixth, was now 34 minutes ahead of Magni in tenth with Coppi and Koblet languishing even further behind.

In one fell swoop Clerici's coup sucked the life out of this mystifying race with nobody either willing or able to raise a head of steam and challenge the young rider whose Swiss status now rather mocked the Italian fans. Interest in the race began to wane although the appearance of Locatelli, following Coppi in the Bianchi team car, in the individual time trial around Lake Garda, stoked up reports of their now open affair which was gripping Italy. There was a thought – or, rather, a desperate hope – that perhaps Clerici would crack on stage 20 when the ride from San Martino di Castrozza to Bolzano crested the Rolle, Pordoi and Gardena but, although Coppi rode strongly that day to take line honours, Clerici rode comfortably enough with Koblet to finish just under 2 minutes behind. He was too competent a rider not to make the best of this once-in-a-lifetime opportunity.

The disgruntled peloton, meanwhile, was still miffed at their general treatment and the nadir came the following day on the penultimate stage when the peloton staged a go-slow taking well over 9 hours to negotiate the 222km from Bolzano to St Moritz which traversed the Bernina Pass. Koblet was allowed to slip away to take the line honours in his homeland while the veteran Bartali, riding his last Giro, also went up the road at the end to acknowledge the applause of the crowd, but generally there was huge dissatisfaction on a day that was quickly dubbed the Bernina Strike. Just under 24 hours later the peloton were greeted with jeers as it rode into the Vigorelli Velodrome in Milan. Clerici was the victor and no blame attached to him but what on earth had been going on with the rest of them? The Italian Cycling Federation were not happy and refused to allow an Italian team to ride at the Tour de France that year while initially it announced a two-month ban for Coppi although that was later quashed. The glory was Clerici's but it wasn't the Giro's finest moment – or indeed Coppi's.

The 1955 Giro was a much more satisfying affair. Gastone Nencini was the talented and much-hyped new kid on the block – the first of many to be dubbed 'the next Coppi' – and Coppi himself at 36 had set his sights on one last glorious swansong win. In the event both were upstaged by Magni. Like Bartali and Coppi he also tended to polarise the Italian fans on the roadside mainly on account of his self-confessed Fascist sympathies which came out during a war-crimes trial in 1946 when he was among those accused of being responsible for the killing of Italian partisans at the 'Massacre of Valibona'. Magni was acquitted of any part in the killings but not before he had admitted to being a former member of the Fascist militia. Prematurely bald, stern-looking and with an authoritarian manner, he was not a man to be messed with. Strangely one of his claims to fame is that he was the first big-name rider to cajole a big sponsor from outside the cycling industry to support a team: rather incongruously Nivea, the skin product company, decided to align themselves with this beast of a rider and alpha male.

In 1955 Magni acquired the *maglia rosa* early on without particularly seeking it and was happy enough to pass it on to Nencini when the young tyro stormed to victory on stage nine. Magni knew that quality survival was the priority in the big mountain days ahead if he was to stay competitive, and that was best achieved without the distractions and strains of being the race leader. By pushing himself to the limit on every descent Magni managed to keep in touch on big mountain days. In fact he was one of the first specialist descenders who made a real virtue of the additional speed their extra weight could generate and were skilful and brave enough to pick the optimum line. And Magni had a plan. If he could stay in contact with the *maglia rosa* until stage 20 – which he achieved being just 1 minute 29 seconds behind Nencini – he and his team had spotted a 15km stretch of road just outside Thiene that was rough and rutted even by Italian standards and akin to the terrain on which he was so successful at the Tour of Flanders, which he had won for three years in succession from 1949 to 1951. This was a rare opportunity to use those Classics skills on the Giro and an unexpected gift from the organisers. How to make best use of this good fortune? Firstly the Nivea mechanics installed wider, heavier tyres on Magni's bike and that of the team to guard against punctures because it was clearly going to be chaos. Then he and his team put feelers out among members of the peloton they felt might be 'friendly', notably Koblet who was well out of contention in the GC but was capable of thwarting Magni's best-laid plans if he led a chase in the hope of a face-saving stage win after a disappointing Giro. If he backed off, Koblet could expect every assistance in winning the final stage.

The scene was set. Just as expected it was chaos at Thiene and Magni, as one of the few riders not to suffer a puncture, took flight with Coppi. The two big beasts of the peloton were away in a glorious break dripping in nostalgia for their fans. Nencini tried to give chase but flatted and then waited for the fractured peloton in the hope that it would regroup and chase down the leaders. The *maglia rosa* was to be sorely disappointed in that respect. Up front the two legends rode hard together for the best part of 160km. They both knew this was the decisive moment and there was no stopping them. On the roadside fans, listening to radio coverage of the approaching race, quietly put away their 'Forza Nencini' and 'Viva Nencini' signs and hurriedly scribbled new words of encouragement on pieces of cardboard. Forza Magni and Viva Coppi. It was a wonderfully poignant dash for glory by the past masters. On the day, Magni was manifestly the stronger rider taking the longer turns but Coppi, in good spirits after a fine stage win in the Tappone or Queen stage the day before, was going nicely as well and Magni would be unlikely to consolidate such a long break without the five-time champion's considerable assistance. Both men of the world, the deal was quickly done. There was never the angst between Coppi and Magni that there was between Coppi and Bartali; they were much more able to coexist. In return for services rendered Coppi would, of course, be allowed to take the stage win and indeed there at the stage finish you can see Magni applying his brakes before the line to ensure the deal was honoured. The duo finished 5 minutes 37 seconds ahead of the next group home which included a tearful Nencini. Magni was now 13 seconds ahead of Coppi in GC but with only the final flat stage into Milan remaining Nencini was marooned some 4 minutes back. Theoretically it was close between the two front-runners but effectively the day was done, the race was lost and won. Coppi knew that and made no effort to animate the final stage which Koblet, with Magni's Nivea team lending a well-moisturised hand, duly won.

Glory in defeat as Magni defies serious injury

Magni's stock was high after such a dramatic win but his finest moment was to come the following year, in 1956, when he finished runner-up to Gaul. This was the race when he simply refused to quit despite not one but two serious injuries. It was on stage 12 – Grosseto to Livorno – that Magni crashed and broke his left collarbone. He still managed to finish but was taken to hospital and his retirement from the race seemed imminent. In hospital, however, he refused the offer of a plaster cast and opted instead for an elastic bandage arrangement, believing he could race on. To an extent he could but he was inevitably short on power on the left-hand side of his body – a particular problem when going uphill and in time trials – so his chief mechanic Faliero Masi cut out and fashioned a piece of inner tube so that one end could be attached to the handlebars. The other end was then free for Magni to bite into when the going got tough to provide the extra purchase needed to bring his back muscles and glutes fully into action. It was odd-looking but ingenious and extremely effective. Magni kept riding, literally through gritted teeth, although applying the left brake was still extremely painful; but it really did look all over on stage 18 – Lecco to Sondrio – when the cycling gods again toyed with him. Not only did Magni crash again but he landed heavily in a ditch on his left side and this time manage to break his humerus, basically the upper left arm. Unsurprisingly, Magni temporarily passed out with the pain and only came around in an ambulance which was called to the scene, at which point he angrily demanded to be let out, remounted his bike and pedalled gingerly back to the peloton which had slowed. The Giro was going through a more gentlemanly phase.

Magni made it to the finish but surely had to call it quits; but, no, he insisted on going on. 'The Lion of Flanders' was roaring defiance. Magni knew full well that he had broken another bone but refused to undergo X-rays when taken to hospital to assess the damage. With confirmation of a second break, the team doctor would be almost duty-bound to order his withdrawal from the race. It is difficult to fathom quite what was driving him on because at this juncture – before the historic events of stage 20 – Magni was outside the top ten and in no way a podium contender. But when pride and obstinacy combine with the inherent obsessiveness of a top cyclist the result can be extreme and often inspiring.

This was the case in the racing deciding stage 20, a full-blown mountain epic from the spa town of Merano to a summit finish on Monte Bondone, a remarkable day in which Gaul displayed his genius to come from nowhere to win and Magni demonstrated his courage to finish an incredible third on the day and move into second place overall. Suffering horribly both climbing and descending, he gave chase to Gaul over the Costalunga, Rolle and Brocon before the finish at 1,660m on the Bondone. The one thing perhaps in his favour was the bitterly cold and snowy conditions and high winds which saw the stage reduced to a battle of survival because Magni had already been in survival mode for a while. There had been calls for the stage to be cancelled on account of the weather but after a race in which Magni's injury had been just about the only point of interest – Coppi had crashed out and abandoned during stage six – race director Torriani found the prospect of an epic showpiece stage irresistible. In one way Torriani was totally wrong. There were 44 abandons on a frozen, snowy day when riders were pushed beyond what is acceptable and were left fighting for their lives rather than merely finishing a race. But in another way he was thoroughly vindicated: Gaul waged war with the mountains while Magni's dogged resistance in the face of impossible odds sealed the stage's legendary status. Monte Bondone 1956 lives for ever more in cycling's history.

Even for Gaul, who climbed from 11th and over 16 minutes behind overall to first place overall, it was a close run thing as René de Latour wrote in *Sporting Cyclist*:

> A search was going on for a missing man. The searcher-in-chief was former world champion Learco Guerra, now manager of the Faema team. The man he was looking for was Charly Gaul, who had not been seen for the last twenty minutes. Guerra was driving his car up the mountain pass, peering through the clogged-up windscreen when, by sheer chance, he saw a bike leaning against the wall of a shabby mountain trattoria. 'That's Charly's bike!' he exclaimed to his mechanic.
>
> They rushed into the bar and there, sitting on a chair sipping hot coffee, was Charly Gaul, exhausted, so dead to the world that he could hardly speak. Guerra knows bike riders. He talked gently to Gaul. 'Take your time, Charly,' he said. 'We're going to take care of you.' While a masseur was ripping off Gaul's wet jersey, Guerra had some water warmed and poured it over the rider's body. Then, rubbed down from head to toes, Gaul's body gradually came back to life. He lost that glassy look and in a few minutes he was a new man again.

Extraordinary stuff. Later, just over the finishing line, Gaul had to be helped from his bike and his frozen jersey cut off his shivering body as the medics sought to treat his hypothermia. Tour de France director Jacques Goddet, a guest of the Giro that day, insisted that Gaul's ride 'passed anything seen before in terms of pain, suffering and difficulty'. But at least Gaul was one of cycling's greatest ever climbers and operating in his element. Magni was a non-climbing specialist riding for well over 9 hours with a broken collarbone and arm. The victory and honour were Gaul's but the glory belonged in equal measure to Magni.

Monte Bondone featured the following year – 1957– but this time it was a much less happy experience for Gaul who was leading Nencini by 56 seconds at the start of stage 18 from Como to the summit finish. The weather was set fair and the day was largely rolling rather than mountainous, with just the one set-piece climb to the finish. The margin of victory seemed the only matter of debate and Gaul was possibly off his guard a little. Nobody could match him on the mountain he had conquered just 12 months earlier.

Early in the day Gaul stopped for a 'natural break' during which time proper race etiquette insisted that he should not be attacked. Having climbed off the bike and found a suitable hedge, Gaul's bitter rival Louison Bobet, who had started the day in third place just over 1 minute behind, and Nencini rode past and according to Bobet's faithful *gregario* Raphaël Géminiani some fairly profane language ensued. Bobet, his French team and Nencini had themselves stopped for a natural break a few kilometres earlier when Gaul decided against stopping but kept riding tempo.

When Gaul stopped, however, Bobet decided to dispense with etiquette and put the hammer down along with the talented Géminiani, Nencini, Baldini, Miguel Poblet and Lino Grassi – a mighty sextet to be up front and off the leash. Suddenly Gaul was in serious trouble so early in the day and he gave chase in vain. By the end of the day he trailed the stage winner Poblet by 10 minutes and had plummeted to fourth in GC over 7 minutes behind Nencini who now had a slim 19 seconds lead over Bobet. Gaul fumed. Barring an act of God he now had no chance of winning a race he had been controlling comfortably.

The following day was the final mountain stage from Trento to Levico Terme and although the San Lugano, Rolle and Brocon offered plenty of potential for Gaul he held out no hope, especially as Bobet was supported by a climber of Géminiani's ability. At best he could try and make mischief, which is precisely what he did when the opportunity arose. All the main contenders found themselves in an elite group of six climbing the San Lugano and Rolle, but coming down the latter Nencini suffered a puncture. Bobet and Géminiani went for the jugular and increased the pace but Gaul decided to wait for Nencini and render what assistance he could. Anything to irritate Bobet and possibly deny him the Giro.

Together they started riding hard in tandem, there was just a chance Nencini could still salvage this Giro. Up front the French team, although going well, were getting no assistance from Baldini who had effectively downed tools and was hanging off the back, unwilling to ride against fellow Italian Nencini. The odds still strongly favoured Bobet who was going well with Géminiani in close attendance, but as they powered up the Brocon to 'victory' they glanced back and there was the *maglia rosa*, tucked in behind Gaul, closing at a rate of knots, so much so that Gaul swept by to win the stage and Nencini dropped into Bobet's wheel to finish on the same time. Nencini, with a massive assist from Gaul, had preserved his lead and effectively won the Giro. Gaul had taken his revenge and denied Bobet and although that could not compare with victory itself it was sweet enough. He was much less happy, though, with the change of nickname he underwent as a result of this stage. Before he started he was 'the Angel of the Mountains'. After the race, for evermore, or at least in France, he was 'Cheri Pipi' or 'Monsieur Pipi'. Much less flattering and a permanent reminder of a race that went badly wrong.

Gaul was some way short of his best the following year when Ercole Baldini, who had finished third overall in 1957, managed to claim an underrated win against all the big hitters. Baldini was a thoroughly modern rider and 1958 was his *annus mirabilis* with an Italian National championship and later in the year a World Road race title in Reims. His versatility was always his strength, as he had demonstrated from the start of his career with a World Pursuit title on the track in Copenhagen in 1956, which he followed up with an Olympic road-race title in Melbourne later that year. Nicknamed 'the Forlì train', he also relieved

Jacques Anquetil of the world Hour record in 1956, logging a distance of 46,394m at the Vigorelli Velodrome. Unsurprisingly, stage victories in the two longer time trials kept Baldini well in contention in the 1958 Giro, but it was in the mountains that he unexpectedly shone, taking the leadership on stage 15 when he won the Apennines stage from Ceserna to Verona which negotiated the Bosco Chiesanuova ascent. Baldini was unstoppable as he powered his way uphill and finished 46 seconds ahead of Gaul and more than 2 minutes ahead of a group containing defending champion Nencini, Bobet and Géminiani. What's more he also took a tightly contested Dolomites stage two days later to complete a job well done.

For a few short years Baldini was a class act on the road and, with two podium finishes in the Giro in his first two years as a professional, he quickly superseded Nencini as 'the next Coppi' but his road career tailed off quite sharply from 1959 onwards. As a pursuiter on the track he kept going for a few years with World Championship bronze medals in 1960 and 1964 but his was a curious career possibly not helped by a lucrative and indulgent contract with Ignis from 1959 onwards which allowed him to choose his racing schedule. A big man and always prone to weight problems, Baldini needed to race regularly and his physical condition became an issue, but in fairness combining elite track and road careers is a fiendishly difficult act to pull off. His 1958 Giro win, however, was a consummate performance against a very strong field.

That year, an ageing Coppi limped home nearly 1 hour behind the leader in 32nd position, not so much a lap of honour as a sad farewell to old haunts, and 1958 was the last time he competed in the Giro. His racing career was spluttering to a close and by the end of the following year he was gravely ill after contracting a particularly lethal strain of malaria while on a joint cycling/hunting trip to Burkina Faso, western Africa. There was a delay in diagnosing Coppi on his return and he died on 2 January 1960. He was just 40.

Baldini had shown that riders with a strong time trial who can hang tough in the mountains could win the Giro and the following year there was nearly a repeat performance from Jacques Anquetil in the 1959 race. The enigmatic but stylish Frenchman had contested the *maglia rosa* with Gaul right from the start, but had seemed to take control of the race in the latter stages after a strong ride on a mountainous stage 15 projected him back into the lead which he reinforced in the 51km TT from Torino to Susa when he put over 2 minutes into Gaul. Anquetil was one of the first exponents of 'big gear' riding, and wasn't notably aerodynamic in his style although his feet were always pointed down in the style of his great hero Coppi. The final showdown was to be on the penultimate stage from Aosta to Courmayeur, a whopping 296km mountainfest taking in Gran San Bernardo, the Forclaz and the Piccolo San Bernardo. Gaul, nearly 4 minutes down, was nonetheless in gung-ho mood and was predicting a 5-minute victory over Anquetil. Much to the latter's chagrin, the margin was nearly double that but in many ways he only had himself to blame after neglecting to eat properly and suffering a calamitous bonk on the final climb. Even though Gaul flatted twice climbing to the summit, he won the stage and finished 9 minutes 48 seconds ahead of Anquetil to claim his second Giro. The Frenchman, who had been well and truly routed, just about hung on to second place overall.

Anquetil becomes the first French winner of the Giro

Not everybody had enjoyed watching a battle so heavily loaded in favour of the pure climbers. Anquetil was a great champion and popular 'box office' rider and his continued presence in the race helped the Giro's prestige. So in 1960 an attempt was made to balance things up with two time trials, the second a lengthy 68km affair from Seregno to Lecco on stage 14, which clearly had the potential to significantly affect the GC battle. To deflect possible criticism of the *corsa rosa* being too 'Anquetil friendly', however, a massive new climb was introduced on the penultimate stage, the Passo di Gavia, which at 2,621m was slightly lower than the Stelvio but which included passages that were steeper. At the time an inferior road surface added further to the challenge. It also 'boasted' a fearsome descent into Bormio made even more dangerous by the condition of the rutted and sometimes muddy road, so much so that it was decided in advance that no team vehicles would be allowed down in support of their riders. Instead competitors would have to carry spare inner tubes and tools if they wanted to guard against inevitable punctures. Old-style. In future editions of the Giro the Gavia was to gain a reputation for epically bad weather but on its debut it was unusually benign; indeed, the rather underwhelmed *La Stampa* correspondent thought the Gavia 'did not live up to expectations although beautiful and majestic'. The climb itself, though, was murderous and it was a stage deliberately set up to encourage a drama or two and it succeeded wonderfully in that aim.

After duly destroying the field in the long time trial on stage 14 – over half the field would have been eliminated had the cut been enforced – Anquetil was in the driving seat but not quite home and hosed as they prepared for the Queen stage. Second-placed Gastone Nencini was at 3 minutes 40 seconds and was a good climber and descender while Gaul was in fifth place at 7 minutes 32 seconds. Who knows what he might be capable of on the Gavia if the mood took him?

The race was far from won. Firstly, Imerio Massignan, an outrageously gifted young climber who had finished second to Gaul in the decisive penultimate stage the year before, went on the attack, helped initially by Rik Van Looy. Dubbed *gamba secca*, skinny legs, when racing the year before, Massignan was 1 minute 25 seconds ahead of the chasing group of lead riders at which point the youthful-looking Italian took off in search of the stage win. Riding brilliantly, he piled on the pressure while further back it was chaos as quality riders struggled in his wake. Gaul was chugging along but not looking a world beater and Nencini had slipped to more than 5 minutes behind the stage leader despite numerous pushes from Italian fans. Further back still, Anquetil was fighting for his Giro life. Help came in the unexpected form of Angelo Coletto, a good quality rider who had endured a poor race, but who was going well that day. Coletto decided to ride with Anquetil and offer him a little support. Anquetil was an enigmatic but generally popular member of the peloton and although he could be difficult he also had a reputation for not forgetting favours and services rendered. It was a decisive moment as Anquetil rallied just a little but just enough.

Meanwhile, up front Massignan was dominant but enduring wretched luck on the much-hyped and feared descent, suffering not one, not two but three punctures, all of which delayed him considerably. His misfortune certainly cost him a crushing stage win and possibly even a remarkable charge at the overall title. Agonisingly, right at the end he was slowed again by a flat for Gaul to deny him even the stage win. Nencini was next over the line at 1 minute 7 seconds and then Coletto and Anquetil hoved into view at 3 minutes 41 seconds. Anquetil had defended the *maglia rosa* with 28 seconds to spare and France had its first winner of the Giro d'Italia. As for Massignan, a nation had been captivated by his courage and appalled at his bad luck. His nickname was quickly upgraded to '*il Ragno delle Dolomiti*', 'the spider of the Dolomites', which could hardly be bettered.

Finishing an unremarked seventh in the 1960 Giro was Arnoldo Pambianco who had been a member of Italy's 1956 Olympic squad with Ercole Baldini when he finished seventh behind his team leader. He was a former Italian amateur road-race champion and also finished second in the World Amateur championships so he was a rider of some repute, and on turning professional he immediately established himself as a *gregario di lusso* variously for Baldini, Nencini and Massignan. Busy helping others, the professional cycling world had not really seen him at full throttle but this was a man who in the space of three months in 1960 finished seventh as an unprotected rider at the Giro and seventh again at the Tour de France riding in support of Nencini, the winner. Pambianco was a seriously underrated talent but that was to change at the 1961 Giro, one of those glorious occasions when the underdog has its day.

The returning champion Anquetil started as favourite but with just one TT, a 53km run from Castellana Grotte to Bari, the race was by no means loaded in his favour and after publicly declaring his intention of repeating Coppi's Giro/Tour double he was hoping to expend as little energy as possible in the process. Everything seemed on course when he moved up to second place in GC after the time trial on stage eight, at which point Pambianco was over 5 minutes adrift in ninth place, seemingly out of sight and out of mind. He was, however, competing as a protected rider on this occasion for his new team Fides and was biding his time. By stage 14 Pambianco had stealthily moved up to third place, 78 seconds behind Anquetil who had now assumed the lead. Still the alarm bells were not ringing for the reigning champion, however, and, remarkably, he and his Fynsec team happily allowed Pambianco to join an otherwise anonymous seven-man escape consisting of Silvano Ciampi, Dino Liviero, Armando Pellegrini, Renato Giusti, Mario Bampi and Marino Fontana on the seemingly innocuous stage from Ancona to Florence. That septet enjoyed themselves hugely while the peloton dozed, and eventually finished nearly 2 minutes ahead of the bunch, a result which saw Pambianco take the *maglia rosa*. Anquetil, for whatever reason, had been caught napping.

Pambianco's lead of 28 seconds was a slender one but he then confounded the sceptics by improving that advantage by a further 16 seconds during the first big Dolomites stage. This was getting interesting and the excitement was building. There was still a sting in the tail to the 1961 route with the penultimate stage negotiating the Pennes and Giovo climbs before its denouement on the Stelvio again. There was still scope for almost anything to happen. Rik Van Looy took off in search of glory but tore a calf muscle on the early slope of the snow-

Huge crowds gathered at the Arena Civica in Milan for the finish of the first Giro d'Italia in 1909.
© AF Fotografie/Alamy Stock Photo

Five-time winner Alfredo Binda was so dominant that the Giro organisers paid him to stay away in 1930. © Offside/Farabolafoto

Alfonsina Strada, still the only woman to complete a Grand Tour. © Offside/Farabolafoto

Gino Bartali and his younger brother Guilio, whose death in 1936 affected Gino profoundly.
© Offside/Farabolafoto

What glories awaited the coltish Fausto Coppi, pictured here on the eve of the 1940 Giro. © Offside/Farabolafoto

After a distinguished war, Bartali tastes victory again in the 1946 Giro. © Keystone/Stringer/Getty Images

Three Corsa Rosa legends and the Pope: Bartali, Costante Girardengo and Fausto Coppi meet His Eminence ahead of the 1950 race. © Offside/Farabolafoto

Coppi in his pomp on the Stelvio
in 1953. © Offside/Farabolafoto

1950 winner Hugo Koblet
alone in the mountains.
© Keystone-France/Getty Images

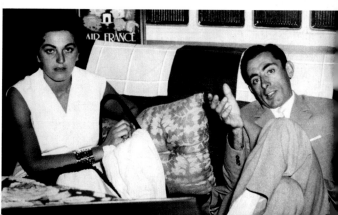

Coppi and Giulia Occhini –
the 'Dama Bianca' – go public
with their romance in 1954.
© Mondadori Portfolio/Getty Images

Domestique Carlo Clerici was a surprise winner in 1954. He is seen here with his friend and compatriot Koblet, with Rolf Graf in the background. © Offside/L'Equipe

The extraordinary Fiorenzo Magni completed the 1956 Giro through gritted teeth. Literally. © Offside/L'Equipe

Nothing left: Charly Gaul is helped off his bike after his epic win on Monte Bondone in 1956. © Keystone-France/Getty Images

A penny for their thoughts: Bartali and Coppi mellowed a little in their later years. © Offside/ Farabolafoto

Giuseppe Fallarini and Pierino Baffi attend mass before a stage in 1959. © Offside/L'Equipe

Hanging tough on the wintry mountain climbs was always the key for Jacques Anquetil. © Offside/L'Equipe

Arnaldo Pambianco was the surprise but popular winner in 1961. © Keystone Features/Stringer/Getty Images

Not even a small avalanche stopped the race on the Stelvio in 1965. Here, Egidio Cornale picks his way to the finishing line. © Mondadori Portfolio/Getty Images

Vin Denson after claiming Britain's first ever Giro stage win, at Campobasso in 1966. © Offside/L'Equipe

An army marches on its stomach, as do Grand Tour riders. Felice Gimondi is pictured here with his daily intake on a typical Giro day. © Mondadori Portfolio/Getty Images

Eddy Merckx wrapped in a blanket atop Tre Cime di Lavaredo. This was his best ever day on a mountain according to the man himself. © Offside/Pressesports

On the attack, as always: Merckx in 1973.
© Offside/L'Equipe

The Pope has the honour of meeting Merckx in 1974. © Keystone/Stringer/Getty Images

Catania 1976: Kas riders in a state of shock after hearing of the death of their colleague Juan Manuel Santisteban in a crash earlier that day. © Bride Lane Library/Popperfoto/Getty Images

Untouchable: Bernard Hinault on the attack on the Stelvio in 1980.
© Offside/L'Equipe

The Badger bares his teeth: Hinault en route to another Giro win in 1985. © Offside/L'Equipe

Where did it all go wrong? A dejected Laurent Fignon ponders the possible chicanery that thwarted his best efforts in 1984. © Offside/L'Equipe

Francesco Moser finally wins the Giro, in 1984 – and doesn't it feel good. © Offside/L'Equipe

You can feel the tension: Roberto Visentini and Stephen Roche eye each other as Robert Millar looks on in 1987.

© Offside/L'Equipe

Last hurrah: Marco Pantani in stage-winning form the day before being kicked off the 1999 race.

© Pascal Pavani/Getty Images

The glorious Passo Gardena has featured prominently in many Giri. © Lars Ronbog/Getty Images

Supermario – Mario Cipollini – was a serial winner of the sprints, and holds a Giro record of 42 stage wins.
© Tim de Waele/Getty Images

Number 108: fans hold up Wouter Weylandt's race number the day after his death from a crash at the 2011 Giro.
© Offside/IPP

Winter can strike at any time on the Stelvio: Ryder Hesjedal, Michele Scarponi and Alberto Rodríguez Oliver riding into the storm. © Tim de Waele/Getty Images

The sinuous Stelvio hairpins and corners. © Tim de Waele/Getty Images

Britain's Mark Cavendish took the points jersey in 2013, when he also won five stages.
© AFP/Stringer/Getty Images

Cruising, on a lazy Sunday afternoon: winner Nairo Quintana leads the peloton home on the final stage in 2014. © Bryn Lennon/Getty Images

Alberto Contador pointedly insists his 2015 Giro triumph was his third, not second, GC win.

© Luk Benies/Stringer/Getty Images

No, not a scene from the trenches but a heavy crash on the Colle dell'Agnello for Ilnur Zakarin at the 2015 Giro. Happily, despite appearances, he suffered no serious injuries.

© Luk Benies/Stringer/Getty Images

Day of redemption: Vincenzo Nibali roared back into contention in the 2016 Giro with a memorable win on stage 19. © Luk Benies/Stringer/Getty Images

plastered Stelvio which left Gaul chasing the stage win, the last major triumph of his career. Pambianco, though, was well used to pacing himself on these big mountain days and judged his effort well, finishing in second place just 2 minutes behind Gaul. Anquetil had been beaten fair and square.

Pambianco never soared to those heights again but one so-called lesser light who did build on a first unexpected Giro success was Franco Balmamion – 'the Eagle of Canavese' – who followed up a shock win the following year in 1962 with a repeat triumph twelve months later. Balmamion had finished 20th behind Pambianco riding as a *gregario* for Bianchi in 1961 so at least had that experience under his belt when he was hired by Carpano to ride in the 1962 Giro with a slightly nebulous role but basically in support of Nino Defilippis who would play it by ear. Defilippis was the bigger name and a fine one-day racer well capable of bagging a few stage wins but had flattered to deceive in big stage races. Meanwhile, the Giro organisers had temporarily fallen out of love with time trials – there were none and therefore Anquetil absented himself – but no fewer than seven hilltop or mountain finishes were scheduled. It was a climber's delight.

Balmamion's race started with a seemingly disastrous bonk on stage two, as he failed to eat properly on a spitefully cold and wet day, and after losing the best part of 12 minutes to the leader his support role now seemed set in stone. Which is how it continued until a catastrophic stage 14 which had seven significant climbs lined up – the Duran, Aurine, Forcella Staulanza, Cereda, Rolle, Valles and San Pellegrino passes. The weather forecast for the eastern Dolomites was dire, initially cold and wet with the snow starting in earnest on the Staulanza. There had been talk of a cancellation earlier in the morning but these are the conditions that make the Giro special and different, and the organisers were loath to give up on their Queen stage. The riders, of course, had almost no say in the matter. They were just expected to perform. The stage went ahead but the weather was off the scale. No fewer than 57 of the 109 riders remaining abandoned, including the normally indomitable Gaul. Belgian hard man Rik Van Looy also decided enough was enough, a pretty good litmus test as to the severity of the conditions. Eventually, as the blizzard intensified, Torriani relented and ended the race on the Rolle, some 40km short of the planned finish. The surviving riders were stopped and helped off their bikes, they were to be spared the Passo Valles and San Pellegrino. Vincenzo Meco was the hero who took the stage with Baldini having one of his inspired days in second place and Imerio Massignan third.

The race leader before the stage start had been Armand Desmet, another tough Belgian rider, but he suffered terribly in the cold and his team had forgotten to pack any change of kit and warm clothing in their car to dispense at one of the earlier summits. He dragged himself over the line in 29th having lost 18 minutes, but on such a day simply finishing was worthy of praise. Earlier in the day Defilippis had climbed off his bike at one stage and looked set to abandon but Balmamion – going very well – and the team's other *gregari* insisted he continued. There was a race to win and money to earn. Defilippis remounted and prevailed to such an extent that he came fourth to move into a handy fifth place overall.

This was also the day of a little sideshow that has gone down in Giro folklore featuring Nencini, one of the best descenders in the peloton, and Henry Anglade, one of his few equals in that respect. As Anglade – who rejoiced in the nickname 'Napoleon' – recalled it in the Belgian cycling magazine *Coup de pedals*:

> I couldn't tolerate the idea that Nencini was the best descender of the peloton. I said to him, call the blackboard man, we'll do the descent together and whoever comes second pays for the aperitifs this evening. So he called the ardoisier and asked him to follow us. The road was of compressed earth. We attacked the drop flat out. I let Nencini take the lead so that I could see how

he negotiated the bends before attacking him. In the end I dropped as though I was alone. At the bottom, I had taken 32 seconds out of him, written on the blackboard. I was really tickled. I had beaten Nencini. The next time I saw him was that evening in the hotel I was staying at. He had just bought me an aperitif.

Two relatively uneventful Dolomite stages followed as the survivors licked their wounds, at the end of which Balmamion, the talented *gregario*, had moved into seventh position behind Graziano Battistini. In touch but still flying nicely under the radar. Stage 17 was where Balmamion won the Giro in remarkable style. Defilippis had burned his matches early in the stage with an audacious break, which had been followed by GC contenders Massignan and Battistini and when the peloton regrouped Balmamion had no hesitation in joining another break that sprinted off down the road. His 'leader' Defilippis had made his play and been found wanting; now it was his turn to have some fun and so strong was the attack that the breakaways raced into Monferrato nearly 7 minutes ahead of the pack, giving Balmamion the overall lead by more than 2 minutes. A staggering ride. By the time he reached Milan that was nearer 4 minutes with Massignan in second place and Balmamion's disgruntled team leader Defilippis in third. Balmamion, the *gregario* who lost 12 minutes on stage two and who never actually got around to winning a stage, had only gone and walked off with his first Giro d'Italia.

Balmamion's second Giro title the following year was fashioned on exactly the same terrain as the infamous stage 14 just 12 months earlier except this time the weather was kinder and all six classified climbs were completed as planned. It was a matter of honour for Torriani that this be the case. On this occasion Balmamion tracked the *maglia rosa* Vittorio Adorni for the best part of a long day as Adorni panicked and chased down a breakaway by Vito Taccone – who was no threat to the lead – and then struck on the final climb to put 3 minutes into Adorni and assume a Giro winning lead. It was an exemplary ride and Balmamion's back-to-back Giri stirred the Italian nation. The last rider to achieve successive Giri wins was, of course, Coppi and there was a natural desire to anoint a successor. Balmamion was never that – he was not quite so enduring on the flat and had none of Coppi's time-trialling excellence – but he was a charismatic crowd-pleasing climber who claimed another five top ten finishes in the years to follow, including a runners-up spot in 1967. A rider to be reckoned with.

Although entertaining and eventful, the 1962 and 1963 Giri had felt a little in-house and parochial and to tempt Anquetil back therefore it was decided to plan a flattish 50km TT on stage five in 1964 which should, barring accidents, see him take the *maglia rosa* early in proceedings. The generosity would end there but the fireworks in the mountains were saved for the end, giving Anquetil time to consolidate his lead and prepare for the battles ahead. All this was very timely because Anquetil was now at the very height of his considerable powers and wanted to mount a final serious attempt on that elusive Giro/Tour double. He had demonstrated when winning the 1963 Tour de France, when he had ridden brilliantly in the mountains to limit his losses to his strongest rival Federico Bahamontes, that through sheer willpower and aerobic capacity he could handle the big mountains in his own idiosyncratic way. It was now or never for the double.

Anquetil's 1964 Giro went like clockwork. He headed the GC after winning the 50km Parma to Busetto TT and defended it for 17 days all the way back to Milan. The attacks came from all quarters and various riders came within sniffing range of the jersey – Renzo Fontona got to within 33 seconds, Renato Pelizzoni 19 and Guido De Rosso 17, but Anquetil repelled all boarders not least on the climactic stage 20 which included five huge climbs – Maddalena, Vars, Izoard, Montgenèvre and Sestriere – in nearly 8 and a half hours of toil from Cuneo to Pinerolo. It was difficult that day to try and anticipate where the biggest threat would come. On paper Italo Zilioli at 1.22 and Balmamion lurking at 3 minutes 3 seconds would have caused concern but Anquetil's real challenge was to pace himself perfectly all day so that he arrived at the finish completely spent. As a non-specialist climber, if he reacted too aggressively to attacks he could quickly put himself in the red. It would involve a huge amount of stoical suffering as he dug deep but he always knew that. Zilioli was the most active of the main contenders and came very close to putting Anquetil out the back on the Vars climb although ultimately he overcooked it slightly himself and couldn't ram home the advantage. Balmamion missed his chance on the Izoard which he had pinpointed as his battleground when he had to answer an ill-timed call of nature and eventually it was Franco Bitossi, a fine climber but no threat to GC, who put the hammer down. Anquetil just ploughed on in the elite chase group with one of the gutsiest rides of his career, finishing just 2 minutes down alongside Vittorio Adorni and Zilioli with Balmamion a further 3 minutes back. The worst was over and he preserved his 1.22 advantage over Zilioli in the final two stages. Victory in the 1964 Giro, if not quite the ultimate – that was to follow later in the year when he completed the double at the Tour – was one of Anquetil's finest moments. As his colleague Raphaël Géminiani said in interview in 2003: 'People said he was cold, a calculator, a dilettante. The truth is that Jacques was a monster of courage. In the mountains, he suffered as though he was damned. He wasn't a climber. But with bluffing, with guts, he tore them to shreds.'

Vittorio Adorni was a very fine rider who had been knocking on the door of a Grand Tour success and his moment came the following year when he was a dominant winner of the 1965 Giro. In fact, an excited *Gazzetta* declared him 'The best *maglia rosa* since Coppi.' In terms of winning margin – 11 minutes 26 seconds ahead of Italo Zilioli – it is difficult to argue with that assessment. It was a career-best performance from a very good rider. Young tyro Felice Gimondi, riding as a *gregario di lusso* for Adorni, claimed afterwards, however, that if his Salvarani team had let him off the leash he could have won the race but that's a big claim. Not only did Adorni win by a distance, he seemed to be riding well within himself most of the time.

Adorni took the jersey on a very lumpy stage six but was happy enough to hand it over to Bruno Mealli for a while after a *fuga di bidone* – an innocuous looking break that actually contains a potential GC winner – on stage eight saw a low-key and unheralded break finish nearly 15 minutes ahead of the bunch in Catanzaro. That gave Adorni a breather before he really went to work winning the 58km time trial in Sicily between Catania and Taormina while virtually closing out the race by putting over 3 minutes into his rivals on stage 19, a testing day in the mountains. It meant Adorni had plenty of leeway on the Stelvio the following day when he rode comfortably with the podium contenders behind Battistini and Ugo Colombo. Battistini took the stage and in so doing became the first winner of the newly introduced Cima Coppi, a prize which henceforth was to be presented to the first rider over the highest point of any Giro. The drama of the day – and a memorable set of images – came in the final 350m when a snowslide blocked the road. The riders had no option but to dismount and carry their bikes over and through the snow to reach the finish.

Vin Denson claims a first British stage win

The following year, 1966, was a curious affair indeed, won by Gianni Motta from Zilioli but featuring a strong-looking Jacques Anquetil who nonetheless appeared to make little or no effort to contest the race. His Ford France team had become involved in an acrimonious rivalry with Ford Italy. They shared the same parent company as Ford Italy but were in fact bitter commercial rivals as Ford Italy looked to ruthlessly undercut their French neighbours. Another triumphant Giro for Anquetil would be massively beneficial for Ford Italy in terms of reflected glory but in fact make little impact back across the border in France. Anquetil did lose 3 minutes on stage one – from Monaco to Diano Marina – after a crash but he was unhurt and stage one is a little early for such a classy rider to decide the race was unwinnable. What is beyond doubt, though, is that fairly early in proceedings he abandoned aspirations to win the Giro and started riding for team-mate Julio Jiménez and indeed occasionally offered help to Gianni Motta from the Molteni squad. High among his priorities appeared to be stopping Gimondi. After the glory and purity of Adorni's win the previous year this 1966 Giro appeared a tainted affair.

The politics and machinations were not edifying and further evidence that the Giro was still a pretty raw sporting event come from Vin Denson, Anquetil's popular British *gregario* and the first British rider on the Giro since Freddie Grubb in 1914, the hardest race in history. Writing in his memoirs *The Full Cycle*, Denson recalled trying to defend Jiménez's *maglia rosa* riding into Naples at the end of stage eight:

> We got into Napoli and were going down through the old dock area, where the streets are really narrow, and the Italian spectators were standing on their Romeo and Juliet balconies and pelting us with the contents of their rubbish bins. We held on to the pink jersey but I ended up covered with old damp spaghetti, tomato juice and banana skins. I must have stunk. We stayed in a really high-class hotel that night and I'll never forget the look on the doorman's face when he went up in the lift with me. I was standing there gently humming with all this rotten food on me, and he kept trying to hold his breath or tilting his head upwards to get some fresh air.

The following day brought a much happier memory and Britain's first-ever stage win at the Giro when, with the race becalmed, he, Antonio Bailetti and André Messelis were allowed to take off on a break between Naples and Campobasso. Denson might have been fairly inexperienced in Grand Tour racing but pulled off a nice trick when, at the crux of the race, he dropped back behind the duo and then deliberately dropped his bidon to distract them. This was his cue to attack just below a short climb and, having crested that in the lead, he descended like a demon to claim a famous victory, winning by 44 seconds.

The novelty of a British stage winner struck a chord with the Italian media and the always chatty Denson provided good copy. A sturdily built rider who enjoyed his food, Denson had begged permission for another bowl of pasta the previous evening with the apparently tongue-in-cheek promise that he would win the forthcoming stage by way of thank you. *La droga di Denson e un piatto di ravioli* (Denson's drug is a plate of ravioli) read the *Gazzetta* headline the following day. In his book Denson also records the odd goings-on with the two Ford teams. On one occasion all the Ford France *gregari* were told in advance when Motta would attack and that they were not to react to protect Anquetil's position. Much to his surprise Denson records later that he and other team members received a surprise bonus payment for their 'efforts' – or lack of them – at the Giro, a lump sum he used to help finance a bar he was opening up in Ghent. The Giro, even as it matured, still had that Wild West feel about it. Anything could and did happen, which clearly included receiving a generous bonus from your team leader who, for whatever reason, had decided not to contest the race that year.

9

EDDY MERCKX REWRITES THE RECORD BOOKS (1967-76)

Until 1967 the Giro d'Italia had born witness to three truly great champions – Girardengo, Binda and Coppi. All were homegrown and, of course, all three were anointed with the moniker *campionissimo*, the only Italian riders to this day to be so honoured although the exact 'qualification' for such status is not clear. In terms of achievements and palmares, Bartali, for example, would probably rank above Girardengo. Style, panache and public popularity are definitely factors as well and have to be factored in. There had been worthy if sporadic raids from abroad, most notably Koblet, Gaul and Anquetil, but no overseas rider had truly stamped his dominance on the race in the style of a *campionissimo* … until Eddy Merckx arrived on the scene. A youthful, charismatic Merckx, looking like a young Elvis Presley, made his Giro debut in 1967 and immediately made his presence known with two stage wins before fading to ninth place overall in his first stage race of over a week. In the seven incident-packed and occasionally controversial years that followed he was to win five Giri to take his place alongside Coppi and Binda in the pantheon. There might have been a sixth in 1969 had he not been chucked off the race and banned for a month after failing a drugs test – the ban was later overturned – and in 1971 he didn't enter at all.

The litany of Merckx triumphs seems so comprehensive and inevitable that you could be forgiven for thinking his march to glory was effortless, routine almost. Far from it. Early in his Giro career Merckx was diagnosed with a potentially serious heart condition yet raced on regardless, trusting in fate while from 1970 onwards he was always riding in pain following a serious track accident the previous autumn which left him with a displaced pelvis for the rest of his career. Then there was the deep rage and resentment of being chucked off the 1969 race for the doping offence which he refutes to this day. Contrary to what many assume it wasn't all plain sailing against an outclassed peloton. There was plenty of angst and suffering along the way.

In many ways Merckx considered Italy his cycling home. He cut his Grand Tour teeth at the Giro and had raced in three Giri before he went anywhere near the Tour de France. Over the years there were a record-breaking 78 days in the *maglia rosa*, 24 stage wins and that from a non-specialist sprinter, and three Giro/Tour doubles. All this was achieved in the colours of two of Italy's top teams, firstly Faema and then Molteni, and when you then factor in his record-breaking seven Milan–San Remo victories and strangely Mediterranean good looks for a Belgian, there was no more identifiable sporting figure in Italy. He wasn't always popular – there was a fair degree of love–hate about his relationship with the *tifosi* – but Merckx was always overwhelmingly the story. For the first time since Coppi the race had a central figure around which everybody else danced. The splendid Felice Gimondi was his fiercest rival and fought valiantly on behalf of the rest of the cycling world against this almost extra-terrestrial figure to claim three Giri himself during this period, but objectively you would have to add the caveats that one of those, 1967, was against the callow youth who finished ninth and another, 1976, came when the Merckx hurricane had completely blown itself out and he scrambled home in eighth.

Merckx was always precociously gifted and ambitious but it wasn't a given that he would make an immediate impact when he made his Grand Tour debut at the 1967 Giro. The Belgian was undoubtedly a major one-day talent. He had demonstrated that back in 1964 when he took the World Amateur road title on the hilly Sallanches course, and by the time he lined up for the start of the 1967 Giro in Treviglio he had also won the first two of his seven Milan–San Remo titles. As a stage racer, though, he was still relatively unknown and inexperienced although he had played a strong hand in helping Britain's Tom Simpson win the 1967 Paris–Nice. He had showed loads of potential but the Giro would be his testing ground. Generally speaking, he exceeded expectations and, at the age of 21 in his first Grand Tour, he was handily placed in third, 50 seconds off the lead, after two encouraging victories on stages 12 and 14. Stage 12 in particular, a mountain day from Caserta to Blockhaus, showcased his talents but the young tyro was eventually found wanting in the 45km time trial from Mantua to Verona when he slipped out of the reckoning and Jacques Anquetil assumed the race lead. Not that Anquetil won the stage – that went to the young Dane Ole Ritter.

Ritter averaged an impressive 47.3km per hour to win. Such a performance wasn't far off the Hour record pace, remarked Anquetil, just 6 seconds back in fourth place on the day, and indeed five years later Ritter did go on to break the Hour. Following the time trial Anquetil had a 53-second lead over Gimondi and was probably marginal favourite to win but before the denouement of the race came one of the most notorious incidents in Giro history, a collective outbreak of cheating on stage 19 which finished atop the Tre Cime di Lavaredo climb. In filthy conditions Wladimiro Panizza, a specialist climber, had headed up the mountain 3 minutes to the good and with the commissaries in close attendance tried everything he could to dissuade fans from giving him a push. Panizza appeared to be going very strongly but a couple of hundred metres short of the line was passed by a bunch of riders who had been trailing by a long distance just over two kilometres from the finish. Gimondi, Merckx, Motta, Adorni, Silvano Schiavon, Italo Zilioli, Aurelio González Puente, Michele Dancelli and Francisco Gabica all steamed past Panizza who had gone from a nailed-on stage winner to tenth. The truth soon emerged. In foul, foggy weather the group to a man had benefited from multiple pushes from fans and taken tows from their team cars where the incline steepened to 14 or 15 per cent just under two kilometres from home. It was a blatant outbreak of cynical mass cheating.

An outraged Torriani annulled the result of the stage although it is noticeable that, with a good proportion of top Italian riders in the group, no further disciplinary action was taken when clearly expulsion or at the very least a punitive time penalty was strongly indicated. As ever the disciplinary code on the Giro d'Italia was an infinitely flexible document. *Gazzetta* writer Bruno Raschi promptly renamed Tre Cime di Lavaredo 'le montagne de dishonore'.

There was possibly more chicanery afoot on the final stage that mattered, stage 21, when Anquetil looked to defend a 34-second lead on a stage that took in the Tonale climb in testing wintry conditions. Gimondi struck with great decisiveness and Anquetil, with just two of his *gregari* left, could not follow. Nor, more surprisingly, could Franco Balmamion or Vittorio Adorni who both normally excelled on such a climb and who had both started the day with a strong opportunity at GC. There seemed absolutely no attempt to organise a chase group. Gimondi, as if by mutual consent, was being allowed to ride way with the race by his fellow Italians who finished the day 4 minutes back with Anquetil. The 1967 Giro had its winner.

By 1968 Merckx was ready to go the full distance although there was an alarming health scare on the evening of the third stage from Narvona to Saint Vincent. Merckx was relaxing after a fine stage win when Enrico Peracino, team doctor at Merckx's Faema squad, invited Italy's leading cardiologist, Professor Giancarlo Lavezzaro, their guest for the night, to test the Belgian and another top rider, Adorni, using a then state-of-the-art cardiogram. Lavezzaro was shocked to find that, according to the results, Merckx was in the throes of a heart attack although outwardly the rider appeared to be well enough, though noticeably fatigued following a tough stage. Lavezzaro asked Merckx to repeat the test first thing the next morning. The result again appeared to confirm a clear case of non-obstructive hypertrophic cardiomyopathy, a condition closely related to that which has caused high-profile sportsmen to collapse in modern times, notably Fabrice Muamba when playing for Bolton against Tottenham Hotspur in the FA Cup in 2012. Merckx's team and Lavezzaro faced a dilemma. Did they tell Merckx – who to all intents and purposes appeared to be a super-fit and healthy 24-year-old – about his condition. Should they pull him from the race? When informed of the readings Merckx appeared unfazed and opted to ride on.

In Daniel Friebe's biography of Merckx, *Eddy Merckx: The Cannibal*, Lavezzaro remembers Merckx 'making vague noises about his cardio-grams always being funny' but also recalls the Belgian insisting that he would race on whatever the diagnosis. Lavezzaro returned to his home in Turin and fully expected to hear news every day over the next fortnight of a Merckx collapse during the race. In fact, despite his condition, the Belgian proceeded without alarm to his first Grand Tour triumph and the first of his five Giro titles, a figure he matched at the Tour de France. He was also three times the victor in the Vuelta a España, won three World Championships and on 19 occasions claimed victory in one of cycling's five Monuments – the one-day classics Milan–San Remo, Tour of Flanders, Paris–Roubaix, Liège–Bastogne–Liège and the Giro di Lombardia.

Notwithstanding his possible heart problem, Merckx made impressive progress in 1968. He had moved to Faema from Peugeot having never really settled fully in the French squad who were also notoriously poor payers at the time. He had signed for his new Italian team on 2 September 1967, the day before he went out and won the World Professional Road race championship, meaning he could wear the rainbow jersey the following year whenever he wasn't in pink. After a couple of days in the *maglia rosa* early on he took a firm grip onthe jersey after a superb ride on stage 12 which ended with a climb up Tre

Cime di Lavaredo in filthy conditions. The scene of ignominy just 12 months earlier, this time it was the scene of possibly Merckx's best ever day in the mountains. A 12-man break had ridden hard to earn a 9-minute lead and the bunch were on the point of letting them go when Merckx sparked up and set off in pursuit, meaning that anybody with any hope of contesting the race lead had to try and go with him. No chance. As he charged up the 2,320m Tre Cime di Lavaredo he both reeled in the break and pulled away from the lead group. By the top he had taken the stage by 40 seconds from Giancarlo Polidori, the sole survivor of the original break, while he had put more than 4 minutes into Motta and Zilioli and 6 minutes 25 seconds into Gimondi who had been thoroughly routed. A stunning performance which always ranked high in his own personal recollections.

'I won almost effortlessly, I seemed to be flying,' recalled Merckx in a biography written by Rik Vanwalleghem.

> The crowning glory was that memorable stage over the Lavaredo where I made mincemeat of everybody. Although I had enjoyed success in my career I was still a rough diamond when I joined Faema and there was an immediate benefit when I started eating properly and attending training camps. Italy polished me. I attended a winter road racing camp Reggio di Calabria rather than the Six Days I used to love and the results were there to see in my Giro win.

It was in 1968 that the Giro introduced dope testing for the first time and, although not particularly sophisticated, it bore fruit immediately with eight positives including two of the big names. Gimondi tested positive for amphetamine triggered apparently by his ingestion of Reactivan, a trade name for fencamfamine. Although the test clearly indicated the presence of Reactivan, it was not on the proscribed list at this stage and Gimondi was therefore exonerated and his third place in

GC stood. Franco Balmamion also tested positive although later cleared, but a positive from Gianni Motta, the 1966 winner, was upheld and his fifth place scrubbed from the record books. The other riders who tested positive were Raymond Delisle, Peter Abt, Franco Bodrero, Victor Van Schil and Mariano Díaz, while Mariano di Toro refused a test. All of which constituted an early shot across the riders' bows. The 1969 Giro would see an even bigger name implicated and a huge scandal. That of Merckx himself.

Merckx arrived at the 1969 Giro in the form of his life having reeled off impressive one-day wins at Milan–San Remo, Tour of Flanders and Liège–Bastogne–Liège. He and his team were ready to take on the fabled Giro/Tour double and to that end was intent on riding a conservative race doing no more than absolutely necessary. All seemed to be going to plan after stage 15 when he moved into a comfortable 1.41 lead over Gimondi after the 49.3km TT around San Marino, after which the race paused for a rest day before a none too demanding stage from Parma to Savona. All was quiet during that stage as the peloton barely raised a sweat as an unofficial day off was called and the race soft-pedalled into Savona. As the race leader, Merckx gave a urine sample and disappeared to his hotel for an early night, unaware of the firestorm that was about to break. Later Dr Cavalli, overseeing the testing, was alerted to one positive for fencamfamine, the drug for which Gimondi had tested positive the previous year. It was the sample of Eddy Merckx and somehow news of the positive spread far and wide, so much so that by breakfast time the following morning Merckx was just about the only person unaware of the situation as the media started laying siege to the Excelsior Hotel where he was staying. Professor Alexandro Genovese had been summoned overnight from the University of Milan and at 7 a.m. undertook a second careful analysis of the sample which confirmed the positive, at which point the head of the race jury informed the Faema boss Vincenzo Giacotto.

At 10 a.m., accompanied by Torriani, Genovese and Giacotto went to Room 11 together, asked for Martin Van den Bossche to leave the room and broke the news to Merkcx who had just been pulling on the *maglia rosa* to begin another day's racing. Soon a clutch of journalists, photographers and even one camera crew were in his bedroom as well recording events. Photographer Tommy Strouken captured virtually the entire episode in a remarkably candid set of photographs which were later widely circulated.

Merckx protested his innocence and circumstantially at least had the makings of strong case. He had already been tested on eight occasions on this Giro and been negative on every one of them. Why would he resort to drugs on such an innocuous stage and on a day when there was no threat of him losing the *maglia rosa*? He knew absolutely for certain that, as the race leader, he would be required for a urine test at the end of the stage. Of all the days a cyclist might be tempted to use amphetamines on the 1969 Giro d'Italia this was the least likely. It wasn't proof of innocence but there was a degree of logic in his defence. Giacotto, meanwhile, had been warning him throughout the race to be ultra-cautious about drinks being offered to him and food in the hotels. Although most of the *tifosi* has taken him to their hearts there were others who deeply resented his brash foreign presence.

It was an unholy mess. Torriani wanted to delay the start of stage 17 and get permission from the UCI to let Merckx ride on but the clock was ticking and they couldn't make contact. Merckx offered to give a new sample, which he did, and which later that day was pronounced as negative. The Giro had to move on, though, and when the peloton rolled out Merckx was not among them. Gimondi was the new leader although he refused to wear the jersey for the duration of that stage. The whole drama continued to escalate. The Swiss newspaper *Blick* reported exclusively that 'Belgian paratroopers are preparing to free Merckx from Italy' although the truth was rather more prosaic. The aeroplane of the Belgian royal family had in fact been despatched in an orderly fashion to bring a distraught Merckx home. Diplomatic relations were tense, however, and there was the inevitable talk of an Italian plot to disgrace a Belgian rider who was simply too good for them. Had the samples been switched? Were they properly monitored in the rather primitive lab accompanying the Giro? Had one of his water bottles been tampered with? Merckx also mentioned an alleged approach to him earlier in the race from an individual connected to Gimondi's team who offered a 'suitcase full of money' to throw the race. Merckx rejected the idea outright. Throwing races was not his style.

Given the furore, things died down remarkably quickly. Merckx's month-long ban was lifted which at least enabled him to start the Tour de France on 28 June. With Merckx gone Gimondi eased his way to a second Giro although the poignancy was not lost on most. Exactly 12 months earlier he, Gimondi, had tested positive for the same drug. Then it was not on the banned list; in 1969 it was. Merckx fumed for a couple of weeks; his attempt at the double had been thwarted and somebody was going to pay. At the Tour he went on the rampage, dominating the GC, winning the Mountains jersey and the Points competition in an extraordinary display of all-round strength. The Giro/Tour double would have to wait another year but, rest assured, it would be his sooner rather than later.

In the weeks after his ejection from the race, and before the start of the Tour, Merckx received more than 7,000 letters of support and sympathy from his fans. Unable to contemplate answering them all personally he printed up a postcard with a short message and picture which his team posted back to the fans: 'Your moral support and sympathy have consoled me and fortified me in the most painful hours of my career. I am very grateful to you and will do everything I can to keep your faith in me. Eddy Merckx.'

Despite his continued outrage over this incident it should be stated that this was not the last time Merckx was to become embroiled in doping controversies. At the 1973 Giro di Lombardia he tested positive for norephedrine for which he was suspended for a month, fined 150,000 lire and stripped of his race victory. Meanwhile, in his final competitive season in 1977 he tested positive for pemoline at the Flèche Wallonne and was suspended for a month as well as having his eighth-place finish discarded.

When Merckx reluctantly returned to the Giro in 1970, it was with the strict proviso that any doping tests be completed in a high-tech laboratory in Rome and not onsite at the Giro itself in some remote location with little security. In fact, Merckx was initially determined not to race at all but, as the lavishly paid team leader of Italy's top team, that was never really an option. The Merckx who again set his sights on the double in 1970 was, however, a very different rider and athlete from the one who had raced in 1969. And, indeed, that remained the case for the rest of his career. Soon after claiming that extraordinary, angry, victory at the Tour de France in 1969, on 9 September Merckx was involved in a horrific crash at the Pierre Tessier outdoor velodrome at Blois, riding in a lucrative 'earner' after the Tour de France. It was his 36th Criterium race since the Tour had ended on 20 July and his third event of that evening. The weather was bad but a big crowd had stayed on to watch the final of the Derny race which was rolling along when, out of nowhere, a fatal accident occurred. The Derny riding as pacemaker for Czechoslovakian rider Jiří Daler lost control after a pedal broke off and crashed to the bottom of the track. Merckx swerved up the track to avoid the falling motorbike and collided with Daler and both smashed into the concrete rim around the top of the track. Merckx catapulted into the air and landed on a grass bank some metres above the track where he lay unconscious, covered in blood. Meanwhile, the Derny driver riding for Merckx, Fernand Wambast, considered the best in the business, steered towards the bottom of the track, thus avoiding taking out more riders but sealing his fate, as he smashed into the sliding Derny. Merckx suffered a bad concussion – observers say he was out cold for nearly 45 minutes – cracked a vertebra low in his back and his pelvis shifted horribly. For the second time that year King Baudoin's royal aircraft was despatched to foreign parts to bring Merckx home. For months his career hung in the balance and, although ultimately he recovered, the physical damage plagued him throughout the rest of his career.

'I was only young and the injuries were to trouble me for the rest of my career but I got through,' Merckx told me when I interviewed him once on the subject.

I noticed the difference straight away in 1970 when I raced the Giro. I had won Paris–Roubaix and Paris–Nice in the spring and felt OK but I hadn't really been tested in the mountains. As soon as that happened on the Giro I noticed I didn't have the acceleration on a mountain climb that I once had. Climbing was no longer the waltz it had been for me. From now on I had to grind it out, I needed to drain the life out of my opponents rather than despatch them with one blow. I needed to adjust my position on the saddle and I was always needing massages and manipulation. Before Blois riding my bike was a pleasure, after Blois it was a cross to bear although just occasionally there were days when I felt free of pain like I was before September 1969. In the end I grew philosophical. I could still turn the pedals, the bike still went quick. Not as quick, but still very quick. The only difference between me and my opponents was that I started most races in pain, they hit the wall three-quarters through or at the top of a big climb.

I began to use it to my advantage. Being in pain from the start made me sharp and on edge and well-motivated. I had no fear of what lay ahead. I was already suffering. My opponents had all that to look forward to but they didn't know when it would ambush them in the race. Sometimes, also, it was very bad and it was as if I raced so fast just to get the race over so I could stretch out on the floor or the bed to get comfortable. The mind can overcome great setbacks and make a person very strong. Cyclists live with pain, if you can't handle it you will win nothing. If you don't want to suffer, take up another sport. Winning Grand Tours and stage races is often about pain management. When the terrible accident occurred at least I escaped with my life. I was the lucky one that was my reaction.

So with that in mind just consider that in the next five seasons (1970–74) Merckx achieved three Giro/Tour doubles and another Giro win in isolation in 1973. And the one year that he did not win the Giro was when he didn't enter. For a man with a bad back, fighting through the pain, it was a remarkable achievement.

Perhaps it was the pain from his back or the memory of his ignominy 12 months earlier, but Merckx was in a detached, businesslike mood in 1970 with very few of the extravagant flourishes of his early successes. He was there simply to set the record straight, in his own mind at least. He also needed to win the Giro by expending the minimum amount of energy and he achieved that mainly by putting time into his main rivals in the long time trial and resolutely defending his lead all the way to Milan. The TT, a 56km affair from Bassano del Grappa to Treviso, suited him well and he took full advantage, with second-placed Ole Ritter 1 minute 46 seconds behind and Gimondi over 2 minutes behind. Merckx rode the 56km at an average speed of 47.4kmh. In the words of Bruno Raschi, he rode like 'one of the horsemen of the Apocalypse'. The daylight Merckx put between himself and the other main contenders was enough although there was a minor scare on the final day, a mountain stage from Dobbiaco to Bolzano, where on the third consecutive mountainous day his back started to seize up on the Pordoi and he required a few discreet pushes from his *gregari* to crest the summit. That apart, it was a trouble-free return to the scene of his personal low the previous summer and he came out of the Giro in superb form. A few weeks later he routed all comers at the Tour, finishing nearly 13 minutes ahead of second-placed Joop Zoetemelk.

The 1971 Giro saw a brief and perhaps welcome break from the Merckx hegemony with the Belgian, having completed the double the year before, deciding that for the time being he had plundered enough and that he would content himself with the Tour de France and World Championship. That opened the way for others and that brief window provided a timely opportunity for Sweden's Gösta Pettersson to record a notable triumph. Pettersson was something of a novelty, coming from the amateur Olympic tradition. Indeed, he didn't turn professional until he was 29 in 1970 with one of the reasons he gave being that it wasn't until then that he felt the still new anti-doping procedures gave him a chance of competing on a level playing field, rather indicative of how prevalent some felt doping had been in the peloton.

As an amateur Pettersson was extremely accomplished and successful, anchoring Sweden to three consecutive World Championship gold medals in the team time trial (100km) in the company of his brothers Erik, Sture and Tomas. Together they were known as the Faglum brothers after the small village in which they grew up and they also took the silver medal in that event at the 1968 Olympics in Mexico. While still an amateur he won the 1968 Milk Race in the UK, leading from start to finish, and when Ferretti team manager Alfredo Martini finally persuaded him to turn professional in 1970 he met with immediate success, winning the Tour of Romandie and posting a remarkable third place in the Tour which came after a solid sixth in his Grand Tour debut at the Giro.

Pettersson was a major talent, a charming man and rode with a cool Nordic detachment that contrasted well with some of the more volatile Latin temperaments on view. His victory was also a notable tactical success as he tracked five different Italian wearers of the *maglia rosa* – Marino Basso, Enrico Paolini, Ugo Colombo, Aldo Moser and Claudio Michelotto – before he struck with deadly effect in the mountains on stage 18 which saw the race go from Linz in Austria to Falcade via the Tre Croci, Falzarego, Pordoi and Valles passes. Everybody found it hard going but the Swede animated the decisive move with Gimondi, Herman Van Springel and Francisco Galdós and was rewarded with the leader's jersey which he defended comfortably in the remaining mountain stage and improved slightly in the final time trial. Pettersson was a popular and seemingly unhurried winner, a rider who rarely appeared at the limit. Winning the 1971 Giro was the highlight of his professional career although he competed with honour in three subsequent editions before retiring from the sport in 1974. It's interesting to speculate what he might have achieved had he turned professional five or six years earlier.

Merckx was back riding for a different Italian team, Molteni, at the 1972 Giro and it was time to reassert his authority. Although his back problem never cleared entirely, he had spent much of 1971 having intensive osteopathy and physiotherapy sessions and was learning to manage the problem. There was no bigger star in sport, let alone cycling, but relentless winning can be a double-edged sword, and during this phase of its history the Giro was struggling a little in terms of profile. A low-key, unobtrusive Swede – Pettersson – had won in 1971 and now the unbeatable Belgian was back in 1972. This was the stuff of nightmares for Italian TV executives, and in 1972 live TV coverage of the final hour of each stage ceased, replaced by a nightly highlights package. With no dominant Italian rider or personality around which to base the drama its appeal was limited to the cognoscenti. Gimondi was always spirited but he was no Merckx. Barring injury or an act of God, 'the Cannibal' was going to win, which stripped the race of any dynamic tension.

Merckx again had the double in mind and was so superior, so consummate, that he only rode hard when it was necessary. Riders who are simply 'very good' can come undone utilising such tactics which leave little wriggle room if anything goes wrong; only the great champions can play with the opposition like that. It doesn't make you popular but again the great champions don't seem overly bothered about that. In fact, that attitude almost defines them.

Merckx chose his moment and struck on stage seven in the Sila mountains of Calabria with ascents of Monte Scuro and Agnara to take the jersey and defended it without alarm all the way to the finish. On the decisive stage he attacked with the previous year's winner Pettersson to put 4 minutes into most of his major rivals. For a while Pettersson was tucked in just behind him in GC but the Swede fell away during a curious stage 12 which was essentially a 40km time trial at Forte dei Marmi, the novelty being that the TT was divided into two 20km events with a gap of two hours between the two races. Times in both races were added together to give one consolidated time and at the end of the process both Merckx and Roger Swerts were credited with 49 minutes and 54 seconds although Merckx was awarded the stage because the electronic timing separated them by 0.26 of a second. Events were enlivened a couple of days later when big-name but struggling riders such as Motta and Zilioli, along with Willy De Geest and Giovanni Varini, were thrown off the race after blatantly accepting tows up the Jafferau. Their guilt was beyond doubt although quite how their crime differed from other cases in Giro history, when such behaviour was either tolerated or lightly punished, is not clear.

Merckx went on to win the 1972 Tour to complete his second double, which equalled the record of Coppi, and he followed this with a 1973 Giro win that was routine in one way but extraordinary in another. In the Giro he took the lead on stage one to dominate from start to finish, repeating the 'sunrise to sunset' triumphs of Binda in 1927 and Girardengo in 1919 and helping himself to six stage wins in the process, but what was truly remarkable was his preparation for the Giro. Just five days before the 1973 Giro started in Verviers in Belgium on 18 May, he had won the Vuelta a España in San Sebastián, holding off Luis Ocaña and Bernard Thévenet in a hard-fought race of over 3000km. Merckx effectively rode – and won – two Grand Tours back-to-back. In the purely athletic sense it was wondrous but Merckx, who took the Points competition as well as the GC at the 1973 Giro, was reducing the Giro to a monotonous procession and the national TV station RAI stood by its decision to broadcast only highlights in the evening. In fact on some days there would be no highlights at all, just a short report on the national news. What the race badly needed was a new Italian star to contest the issue, and in 1974 that individual finally presented himself in the form of Gianbattista Baronchelli.

Baronchelli's career was singular to say the least. Born in Ceresara, he was a prodigious young talent who hinted at a significant future career in the Grand Tours – a man to challenge and perhaps even beat Merckx – before that dream was shattered and he became merely a stalwart of the peloton. Once or twice a season, though, he would rouse himself and record a startling one-day win – there were triumphs at the Giro di Lombardia in 1977 and as late as 1986 – and he took a silver medal behind Bernard Hinault in the 1980 World Championships on the particularly gruelling climbers circuit around Sallanches. In 1974 he was just 20 and, although gifted, it seemed laughable to suggest that he might be a serious contender for a podium place at the Giro, yet perhaps we shouldn't have been surprised. In 1973, still riding as an amateur, he had won both the Tour de l'Avenir – often dubbed the amateur's Tour – and the Girobio, its equivalent in Italy. He then signed for the SCIC team where Franco Bitossi was the team leader and initially in his first Giro the aim was simply to gain experience while Merckx did battle with that very fine climber José Manuel Fuente at the top of the GC rankings.

For the first half of the race Baronchelli hovered around the top ten until stage 11A, when, riding alongside Merckx and Bitossi, he produced an outstanding performance between Modena and Il Ciocco which took in the Radici and Il Ciocco ascents. Fuente was just under 1 minute up the road but Baronchelli's strong effort propelled him to fourth in GC which he improved to third the following day after he finished seventh in a 40km time trial won by Merckx. Fuente still led the race, by a slender 18 seconds, and with the biggest mountains yet to come he was talking confidently of holding off the champion. Meanwhile, 2.30 behind Fuente, Baronchelli was becoming a factor in the race, a definite contender for third position.

Fuente's hopes were dashed on stage 14, seemingly a testing rather than epic run along the Ligurian coast taking in much of the latter stages of the Milan–San Remo route. Torrential freezing rain, however, immediately upped the degree of difficulty and Fuente, as Anquetil and others had done before him, made the elementary mistake of missing a feed or forgetting to eat. When Merckx and Gimondi took off on the Ghimbegna climb Fuente was nowhere to be seen and in no time the *maglia rosa* was off the back of the chasing bunch. Nothing could revive him and he eventually struggled home over 10 minutes behind the stage winner Giuseppe Perletto and 8 minutes behind the Merckx group. As 'cracks' went, it was one of the more impressive in Giro history. Baronchelli, meanwhile, beginning to flex his muscles, had broken away from the Merckx group to take over 1 minute out of them and as the peloton dried out at the finish in San Remo, he found himself in second place overall, just 35 seconds behind Merckx. He couldn't win, could he?

Well, no, in the end he couldn't but by the time the race reached Milan he had reduced the lead to just 12 seconds, the narrowest Grand Tour win of Merckx's career. It was a bravura performance which hinted at glories ahead, perhaps when Merckx retired. They never quite materialised although there was another runners-up spot at the 1978 Giro and a third position in 1977. For Merckx it was a narrow escape. His body was beginning to rebel after being driven to the limit for the best part of a decade but there was still just enough left in his tank for one final historic season before a sharp decline set in. He had to marshall his resources, though. Ever ambitious, he had wanted to 'top' Coppi in claiming a third Giro/Tour double but to achieve that he needed to ride a measured Giro in 1974 although there were other contributing circumstances. Back in the winter he had picked up a nasty case of bronchitis at the Six Days of Antwerp and become quite ill and, playing catch-up, had endured a poor Classics season. In many ways he had to ride himself fit in the 1974 Giro and as such was vulnerable. An exceptional world-class climber, like Fuente, could now cause him much grief in the mountains and although sport is full of 'ifs' it is clear that if Fuente had not forgotten to eat and suffered so badly on stage 14, he may well have had the beating of Merckx in 1974. It wasn't to be.

Merckx went on to win a then record-breaking fifth Tour in dominating fashion even if he did have to undergo surgery to lance a saddle sore just before the race and the wound wept unpleasantly all the way around France. So much for the glamour of cycling. Merckx was a man on a mission, his insatiable appetite and need to win was as great as ever, but he was also an athlete who was beginning to hit the wall. His genius flared periodically in the next two years but, alas, the Giro, where he had forged his reputation as a Grand Tour rider, was never to see Merckx in all his glory again.

After the final great winning burst of his career that spring, winning Milan–San Remo, the Tour of Flanders, Liège–Bastogne–Liège and the Amstel Gold, Merckx missed the 1975 Giro with what was initially diagnosed as tonsillitis although as he admitted himself it was probably just plain exhaustion. In his absence the 1975 Giro was, to put it mildly, an anonymous affair. Two stalwarts of the peloton – Italy's Fausto Bertoglio and Spain's Francisco Galdós – seized their moment to contest the GC but Felice Gimondi rather missed his cue and came home a distant third in a race that didn't live long in the memory. Bertoglio did became the first Italian winner since Gimondi in 1969, and Belgium's Roger De Vlaeminck accumulated seven stage wins, but the Giro impatiently awaited the return of Merckx the following year to see if he could surpass Coppi and Binda and claim a sixth title.

Merckx did reappear for the 1976 Giro which started in tragic circumstances in Sicily when, for the second time in its history, the race witnessed a rider fatality as Juan Manuel Santisteban of the KAS team lost control of his bike on a sharp right-hand bend on stage one and crashed head first into an iron railing. Santisteban, an experienced six-year professional with stage wins on the Vuelta a España on his palmares, had been riding hard to help his KAS colleague José Linares González rejoin the peloton after puncturing midway through the high-speed 64km Criterium around Catania. Agonisingly it was a split stage that day and the peloton, shocked as the news of Santisteban's death spread, was still required to ride another short 80km stage to Syracuse that afternoon. The mood was subdued throughout the race's three days in Sicily and not even Merckx could lift the spirits. In fact he was struggling as rarely before. Run-down and again suffering from a saddle sore, he was a pale shadow of his former self as he trailed home a disconsolate eighth, at no stage really threatening to contest the issue. This time Gimondi seized his opportunity to claim his third Giro, clinching it on the penultimate stage, a 28km time trial.

The end was nigh. It was a second Gimondi win over Merckx at the Giro but the real Merckx had left the arena. In later years the Italian spoke interestingly about their 'rivalry' at the Giro:

> His rise really affected me mentally. In 1967 and 1968 it was starting to become very clear that the time would come when he would enjoy an unprecedented dominance. My own rise to prominence had been rapid but suddenly, mainly due to Merckx, I had to settle for much less. I had to take my chances as and when they came. Merckx taught me that you don't have to be a leader or the absolute number one figure to reach personal goals in life.

Gimondi's no-nonsense approach served him wonderfully well. It was his rotten luck to be a Grand Tour rider at the same time Merckx was at his zenith but, by refusing to be crushed by Merckx's presence and by setting his own standards, he carved out his own illustrious career. Not only did he win three Giri but no rider in the race's history can match his nine podium places. Reliable in the extreme, Gimondi completed all 14 Giri he entered and only twice did he finish outside the top ten.

10
NOTHING AND NOBODY CAN OUTFOX 'THE BADGER' (1977-86)

The departure of Merckx from the scene allowed others to breathe and alternative storylines and characters to develop, for a while anyway, before the arrival of another dominating rider in Bernard Hinault who was to produce some of his greatest rides at the Giro d'Italia. The mix in 1977 was eclectic to say the least. The reigning world champion Freddy Maertens was the 'foreign raider' and, although known primarily as the world's best sprinter and a serial stage winner, he possessed the all-round ability to contest GC races as well. In 1976 he had finished eighth at the Tour de France and just before he arrived in Italy Maertens claimed the best stage win of his career by taking the GC at the Vuelta a España. Admittedly it was the flattest Vuelta in history as Maertens helped himself to a remarkable 12 stage wins but he always possessed unusually good endurance for a sprinter. He would clearly dominate the early flat stages in the Giro a few weeks later but could he hang tough in the mountains as well? A rugged, volatile Flandrian, Maertens had a history of doping although he insisted never in Grand Tours – and there were also admissions of heavy drinking. He was box office, though, a character and a flamboyant but consistent stage winner. Indeed, he always claims his 54 wins in 1976 should be considered the biggest annual haul in road-racing history, arguing it was superior to the 54 Merckx also claimed for 1971 which included three track events.

Lined up against Maertens was the stylish Francesco Moser, the latest big Italian hope who was coming into the form of his life; indeed, he was to win the World Championship a few months later at San Cristóbal, Venezuela. Moser was to become a big 'player'; in the Giro, in the ten seasons from 1977 to 1986 he claimed six podium places, including a win in 1984, but he was generally riding slightly against the odds. A superlative time-trial rider, Moser was a big, hefty man by cycling standards and, although he could often channel that power successfully on the climbs, the possibility of a bad day in the mountains was never far away. He was generally walking a tightrope but the prospect of the brilliant natural sprinter and the exceptional natural time-trial rider having to effectively fight out the *maglia rosa* in the mountains was intriguing and full of potential for the spectator.

The rider nobody had really factored in was Belgium's Michel Pollentier, Maertens's *gregario di lusso*, who had twice finished seventh at the Tour de France, in 1974 and 1976. Pollentier was to achieve lifelong notoriety in 1978 when he was thrown off the Tour de France when taking the yellow jersey at the top of the Alpe d'Huez climb for attempting to supply a false urine sample. The Belgian filled a condom with an untainted sample and concealed it under his armpit where it was attached to a tube from which he intended to provide the sample. Unsurprisingly he was rumbled and ejected from the race.

That lay in the future. Back in 1977 he was seen mainly as Maertens' sidekick and initially the race progressed as predicted with seven early stage wins for the insatiable Maertens before he crashed and broke his wrist on a seemingly innocuous half-stage at the motor-racing track in Mugello when he tangled with Rik Van Linden at the finish, gunning for his eighth win of the Giro. In an instant his race was over and although the consistent Pollentier was well placed in second, 55 seconds behind Moser, Maertens's crash seemed to herald an all-Italian clash between Moser and Giambattista Baronchelli. The high mountains beckoned. Could Moser perform well enough to hold off Baronchelli, the more natural climber?

Instead, it was Pollentier who proved to be the strongest in the mountains where he also cleverly used Baronchelli's enmity with Moser to his advantage. On stage 18, a long mountainous run from Cortina d'Ampezzo to Pinzolo, he made a temporary pact with Baronchelli to distance Moser by 85 seconds, with Baronchelli winning the stage and Pollentier finishing by his side. The following day, meanwhile, Pollentier earned extra valuable seconds and went into the final stage – a 29km time trial – with a lead of 2 minutes 2 seconds. It was too short a distance even for a superlative TT rider like Moser to mount a proper challenge, and indeed he seemed to lose heart and suffered the indignity of coming second by 30 seconds to the Belgian. In view of what happened the following year it's impossible not to view Pollentier's performances at the 1977 Giro with a degree of scepticism although, equally, if he was doping he almost certainly wasn't the only one.

Belgium was to claim its seventh Giro win in 11 seasons – from three riders – in 1978 when Johan De Muynck sneaked away from the slumbering peloton on stage three and defended the jersey all the way back to Milan in a fairly nondescript race that had started two weeks earlier than usual to avoid clashing with the 1978 Football World Cup which began in Argentina on 1 June. The chief interest probably came in seeing the veteran Gimondi, the three-time winner but no longer a GC candidate, riding strongly and intelligently in support of his Bianchi colleague De Muynck who took his chance on the final climb and descent into Cascina on stage three. It was one of those moments that can only really be explained by a momentary loss in concentration as the main contenders seemed content to let a man who had finished second overall in 1976 to nick a 52-second lead. As it happened he won the race nearly three weeks later by 59 seconds. A strong climber, and with Gimondi watching his back, the Belgian rarely seemed under pressure despite the narrow margin, but it wasn't a Giro to live in the memory. The race did not match its grand setting and not for the first time the

Giro started looking round for a star or for ways of manufacturing a greater level of excitement.

By 1979 there had only been two Italian winners in the preceding nine years and back-to-back wins by two relatively low-key Belgians particularly stuck in the craw. At least when Merckx won his presence and place atop the podium conferred status and majesty on the Giro. There was reflected glory but it was difficult to find much glory in wins by Pollentier and De Muynck. Torriani was well aware of this and came up with the none too subtle ruse of including no fewer than five time trial stages totalling 136km for the 1979 Giro. In a decidedly flat first half of the race it was stage 11 before it was even to poke its head above the humble 1,000m mark. This was clearly a course designed with the popular Moser in mind but with the added advantage that it also suited a new Italian star – Giuseppe Saronni – and their bitter rivalry very much appealed to the *tifosi*. It wasn't quite Girardengo versus Binda or Bartali against Coppi but there was a real animosity between the two that provided a compelling subplot and frisson whenever they rode.

Saronni, from Novara in Piedmont, had competed as an 18-year-old in the Team Pursuit at the Montreal Olympics and confirmed his promise two years later the 1978 Giro when he won three stages and competed gamely to the end to finish an excellent fifth. The new French superstar Bernard Hinault, sensational winner of the 1978 Tour de France, didn't yet fancy doubling up with an early season Giro so the 1979 Giro field was relatively clear for the domestic riders to take centre stage. So clearly was it a time-trialler's Giro that the Magniflex–Famcucine team, home of those fine climbers and Grand Tour veterans Baronchelli and Alfio Vandi, immediately handed over the team leadership to Swedish time-trial specialist Bernt Johansson who was to eventually finish third behind the Italian duo.

The race made a curious start with many members of the peloton suffering badly from conjunctivitis, as in indeed were many fans after an outbreak of the infection in northern Italy. Some medical experts even suggested that the race be cancelled or postponed to avert the possibility of spreading it unnecessarily around the country. That was probably never a serious option but certainly the Inoxeran team was so badly affected that five of their riders, including their GC man Giovanni Battaglin, were forced to withdraw the day before the race.

The 28km time trial from Rimini to San Marino on stage eight, taking in the Monte Titano (739m) climb was an early game-changer with Saronni proving a strong TT rider when the road went uphill and the 84 seconds he gained on Moser put him in the box seat for the rest of the race, wearing pink all the way to the finish. Although he closed out the victory with another prestigious win over Moser in the long 44km TT on the final day from Cesano Moderno into Milan, it was never quite as simple as that because, although the mountainous stages in the final week were modest by normal Giro standards, they were still testing enough for two useful but by no means stellar climbers to be wary. One bad day and they could not only lose out to each other but a third rider might become a factor. It made for a compelling spectacle with both Saronni and Moser close to their limits and wary of any unexpected challengers.

Saronni was off the mark with a popular Giro win but in truth the race was marking time until the Giro debut of cycling's next big superstar, the volatile Bernard Hinault. By the start of the 1980 season the aggressive and indomitable Breton, aged 25, had already won the Tour de France twice and also had a GC win at the Vuelta on his palmares. He had conquered both Grand Tours on his first attempt and saw no reason why he shouldn't repeat the hat-trick at the Giro, something no rider had ever achieved, not even the remarkable Merckx. Hinault had big plans for 1980 generally, wanting to equal the Merckx achievement of winning the Giro, Tour and World Championships in the same season. He might have arrived in Italy as a debutant but he was a strong favourite and a marked man right from the off.

Hinault and that canniest of all *directeurs sportifs* Cyrille Guimard knew that *in extremis* the entire Italian peloton was likely to ride against him rather than let a Giro debutant from France walk off with the honours. Emotions would be running high so together they embarked on a minor charm offensive with the media ahead of the race. Guimard embarked on a crash course in Italian so he could both talk to the media and understand, to a certain extent, what was being said to and about his star rider. Meanwhile, Hinault banked much goodwill and credit from the fans for taking time out after a gentle Prologue opener in Genoa to visit the grave of Coppi in Castellania and visiting the *campionissimo*'s brother Livio who still lived in the village. The *Gazzetta* photographer was, of course, on hand to record and publicise this 'private' visit.

It was a good, diplomatic start by Hinault but the gloves soon came off when he claimed the *maglia rosa* in fine style after a longish time trial on stage four, finishing just 14 seconds behind Jörgen Marcussen but a full minute ahead of TT specialist Moser and 2 minutes ahead of Saronni who was also normally so reliable in time trials. The die was cast. If the highly touted Italian duo couldn't match Hinault on such a favourable stage, what hope was there for them come the high mountains where Hinault was unlikely to crack? It was with that thought in mind that Moser made the unlikely suggestion via the media that he and Saronni – and their teams – unite in common cause against Hinault. Anything but a French win. This potentially was quite serious because Hinault's Renault team were comparatively young and inexperienced and defending the jersey against such a twin-pronged attack would be a massive task. Instead, in an absolute masterstroke, Hinault essentially gifted the *maglia rosa* two days later to a talented and very ambitious young Italian, Roberto Visentini, who was allowed to animate a break on the road to Orvieto and take the overall lead. Hinault slipped quietly down to eighth in GC at 2.58 and Renault made no attempt to regain that time the following week; indeed, he subtly rode in support of Visentini which well and truly called Moser and Saronni's bluff. For that duo there was only one scenario that could possibly be worse than a thumping Hinault win and that would be a surprise and glorious victory by a thrusting young Italian who would then threaten the domestic duopoly they enjoyed. Suddenly they had to look after their own interests again and the united front against Hinault quickly cracked.

Hinault and Guimard continued to play a tactical blinder. A mighty Stelvio day had been planned for stage 20 and such was his dominance that Hinault could almost certainly have recouped all of his time in one fell swoop there but it was leaving things a little late. Things could go wrong. The weather could intervene and see the Stelvio ascent cancelled while Torriani had added a twist to the normal Stelvio tale by situating the finish at Sondrio, some 80m from the summit, which theoretically would allow inferior climbers like Moser and Saronni the opportunity to chase Hinault down and limit their losses. This was a Giro when all concerned had to keep their wits about them. Ideally what Hinault needed was a pre-emptive strike to recoup most of the time before the race's denouement on the Stelvio.

Stage 14 presented the ideal opportunity, a typically rugged run across the Abruzzo Mountains from Foggia to Roccaraso taking in three or four stiff climbs. Throughout the race Renault's sprinter Pierre-Raymond Villemiane had been having a dart at the intermediate sprints so no alarm bells rang when Hinualt, never afraid to help deserving and devoted workers, led out his *gregario* at Isernia where Villemiane claimed the modest daily prize in the Fiat Panda competitions. Everything seemed *tranquillo* except this time, as the peloton relaxed, as they habitually do after an intermediate sprint, Hinault attacked viciously and headed for the hills of the Rionero Sannitico and the Roccaraso. It was classic Hinault. When in doubt attack and yet again he had outfoxed his main rivals. Only Wladimiro Panizza, a very fine climber and an underrated performer generally, could stay with Hinault who was basically taking on an entire Italian peloton single-handed minus his Renault team-mates who were either soft pedalling at the back or blocking for all they were worth at the front of the bunch. Hinault took the stage and better still his planned attack had projected Panizza into the pink jersey which gave Moser and Saronni yet another headache. The young Visentini meanwhile cracked altogether but was to feature prominently in future Giri.

And so to stage 20 – the Stelvio – and another classic ride straight from the coaching manual from Hinault, with Guimard, of course, in the background, planning and plotting. On the morning of the stage Panizza led GC by 1 minute 8 seconds with Hinault in second place and Giovanni Battaglin another 17 seconds back. These were the only three realistic contenders. One way or another Moser, Saronni and Visentini had been routed but the race still needed to be closed out. Panizza was very strong in the high mountains and Battaglin was a remorseless stayer who would have to be broken. Unless Hinault could put a considerable distance between himself and that duo at the top of the Stelvio he could yet be in trouble because the Italian peloton, when push came to shove, would undoubtedly put domestic rivalries and squabbles behind them and unite and ride eyeballs out over that final 80km to try and rescue a win for either Panizza or Battaglin. What Hinault ideally needed was a Renault team-mate up the road in a break who could then unite with Hinault for that long, testing final stretch into Sondrio. That would even things up a little but how to execute such a plan?

Jean-René Bernardeau was the key, a talented if mercurial young French rider who had entered the 1980 Giro with a heavy heart. His brother had died just before the start of the race and he had wanted to withdraw but Hinault had cajoled his young compatriot into staying on. Bernardeau on a good day was one of the stronger Renault riders. Hinault would definitely need his assistance and now, right at the end of the race, came an opportunity to produce a ride that would honour his brother's memory. The plan was for Bernardeau to get into a break well ahead of the Stelvio itself but to keep just a little in reserve – not at all easy on a climb that intrinsically demands so much – so that when Hinault launched his own attack lower down the mountain, he would be on hand to ride when Hinault bridged the gap. If that could be accomplished Bernardeau would then hopefully have enough left in the tank to ride into Sondrio with his team leader.

Such plans can be fraught but on this occasion it worked perfectly. Bernardeau, enjoying his best ever day on a bike, not only managed to animate the six-man break, which reached the bottom of the Stelvio climb 6 minutes ahead of the pack, but he then moved smoothly to the front and distanced his fellow escapees. Meanwhile, lower down the mountain Hinault went to work with possibly the most savage, concerted attack of his extraordinary career. Three times he put the hammer down and eventually the elite group cracked, even a hardened climber like Panizza. Bernardeau reached the summit first with Hinault not far behind and the chasing bunch nearly 4 minutes down the mountain. Soon Bernardeau was joined by Hinault and, resisting the temptation to look back, they took their relentless turns all the way down to the finish where Hinault gratefully gifted the stage win to his deserving helper. Somewhat clutching at straws the Italian media thought this rather condescending and arrogant on Hinault's part but it was a well-established tradition in all the Grand Tours when a great service had been rendered by a *gregario*, and if anybody deserved the glory it was the grieving Bernardeau.

The 1980 Giro had been won in masterful fashion by one of the most complete riders – physically, tactically and temperamentally – in cycling history. Indeed, there are some who bracket Hinault with Merckx himself at the top of the pantheon and his 1980 Giro victory is one of the races they cite in support of that claim. Hinault was in extraordinary form that year and although a knee injury forced him to quit the Tour de France mid-race, while in yellow, he returned to win the World

Championship at Sallanches. Hinault was in his pomp and the Giro had seen the very best of him.

With Hinault absenting himself from the Giro the following year, 1981, there was an opportunity for other riders to have their own shot at glory, none more so than the persevering Giovanni Battaglin who probably realised that, as he approached 30, it was now or never. Battaglin had been there or thereabouts for a while and had finished third in the Giro as far back as 1973, a feat he repeated in 1980 behind the imperious Hinault. He was a man who could ride hard in the mountains and stay competitive in the time trial but objectively, compared with the greats of the sport, he was unexceptional. Yet suddenly, almost from nowhere, he enjoyed his *annus mirabilis* in 1981 winning both the Vuelta and Giro, a double only ever achieved previously by Eddy Merckx. For 47 days that year, from the start of the Vuelta on 21 April and the end of Giro on 7 June, Battaglin reigned supreme, albeit Hinault was also missing from the Vuelta. Sensing a Giro course that had been designed with Saronni specifically in mind, with 30-second time bonuses for stage winners, Battaglin and his Inoxpran team had initially targeted just the Vuelta but despite the shortest of turnarounds found himself in good form at the Giro. Riding conservatively to start with, and with nothing to lose, he then produced two powerhouse displays in the two Dolomites stages to go into the decisive 42km TT in Verona with a 50-second lead over Tommy Prim and a 59-second advantage over Saronni. The latter was still the marginal favourite but it was going to be close and Inoxpran DS Davide Boifava was wary of possible sabotage by the *tifosi* and, indeed, interfering race officials. With that in mind he informed Torriani that an Inoxpran team car would follow Saronni at a discreet distance on the course and film his ride to ensure fair play. Distrust or paranoia? Who knows, but this was the atmosphere in which Giro races were often conducted. As it happened the stage went off without controversy and a third place on the day from Battaglin, 1 second ahead of Saronni, was more than enough to secure overall victory.

Hinault, with the Giro/Tour double very much on his mind, returned the following year and the 1982 route, generously laden with time trials plus a potentially decisive Dolomites stage late in the final week, suited him nicely. He had no weaknesses, nothing to fear, but he also made clear at the pre-race press conferences that the double that had eluded him in 1980 was his priority and that he was looking to win without alarm or undue exertion. For the best part of the race the Giro, with many of the peloton cowed by the presence of Hinault, proceeded without too much excitement or intrigue but that all changed on stage 17, a rugged but hardly epic 235km day from Fiera di Primiero to Boario Terme with just one really significant climb at the end, the Croce Domini. Whether Hinault and Guimard underestimated this final climb as they looked to conserve energy or Hinault simply suffered a *giornata no* – a day without energy – is up for debate, but what happened on the road is that an elite group including Prim, Lucien Van Impe and Silvano Contini escaped and Hinault, lacking a really strong support team that year, was unable to go with them. Contini won the stage and went into pink over 2 minutes ahead of Hinault and the peloton waited to see what retribution would be wreaked. Badgers can be ferocious when disturbed or threatened. The defeat and partial humiliation festered overnight and Hinault had his revenge the following day which presented a stage that ordinarily would seem to offer no opportunities to strike back. But Hinault was no ordinary rider.

Stage 18 was a modest 85km run from Piamborno to Monte Campione finishing with a fierce climb and a grim-faced Hinault went to work from the gun, with the express aim of destroying Prim and Contini, a task he executed with ruthless efficiency. By the end of a short but exhausting day, under 2 and a half hours of full-on riding, order had been fully restored and Hinault was back in pink. He defended the jersey with some ease on the big Cuneo to Pinerolo stage which, as can happen with big, much-anticipated set pieces, rather fizzled out and disappointed with none of Hinault's main rivals building a head of steam. Hinault finished the job in the final time trial and immediately set his sights on the Tour which he virtually reduced to a routine promenade around France. During the early 1980s Hinault was simply a different class. Avoiding injuries and crashes was his only real concern.

Diving in and out of the Giro narrative during this era was Giuseppe Saronni and in 1983, with Hinault again pursuing other challenges and one of the flattest Giro courses in history beckoning, he took his opportunity well to win an Italian-dominated race from Roberto Visentini. The latter would actually have won the race on accumulated time by 48 seconds but, in an effort to ensure a victory for either Saronni or his perennially popular rival Moser, generous time bonuses had been included in the race, even for the time trials which was unusual to say the least. Saronni obliged with three stage wins, including the main time trial on stage 13 but again it wasn't a Giro that gripped the imagination.

Moser finally bags a Giro in controversial circumstances

By any criteria the 1984 Giro d'Italia was one of the most controversial Grand Tours in history, with Laurent Fignon seemingly having to take on the race organisers as well as Italy's finest home-grown riders as he attempted to claim another Giro title for France. With 140km of time-trialling and a minimum of high mountains, it was unashamedly set up to make a GC win possible for the veteran Francesco Moser who was coming to the end of a long and distinguished career without a Giro win on his palmares. After Saronni's second overall win in 1983 the attention was focused firmly on Moser and from an early stage the media started talking of 1984 being Moser's Giro. Begging to differ in that respect, however, was Fignon, who had ridden in support of Hinault in 1982 when he finished 15th. In a career badly disrupted by serious injury Fignon sometimes struggled for consistency but in May

1984 he was in his pomp and arrived in Italy as the reigning Tour de France champion. With Hinault back in France resting a knee injury, and with Guimard calling the shots as DS, Fignon clearly had an outstanding chance of victory.

The race started badly for Fignon with a careless hunger knock on stage five, the Blockhaus climb, seeing him finish over 1 minute behind Moser on terrain that should have massively favoured the Frenchman. Fignon ceded the pink jersey to Moser and immediately Moser fever took over. Already he was in front and there were two long time trials beckoning later down the line and just one really testing day in the high mountains, on the Stelvio. Much work to do obviously but everything was falling into place nicely for the Italian. Finally, after all these years. For two weeks he pulled the jersey on every morning and a nation started to believe. It was Moser's Giro after all.

For Fignon the reverse on the Blockhaus was an unexpected blow in a race he had already calculated would be touch and go given its Moser-friendly terrain. Rather than be deterred, though, he and the wily Guimard set about devising a strategy for what they called guerrilla warfare. They were under no illusions that, with a Moser victory seemingly preordained, they would effectively be riding against the entire Italian peloton. The duo were relaxed, though; the Stelvio was the key, their chosen battleground. That is where Fignon would strike and win the Giro.

Ahead of stage 18 and the Stelvio, Moser was still in pink and over 2 minutes ahead of Fignon but the latter was confident of taking all of that back, and much more, to give himself a cushion against Moser's expected late charge in the final time trial. Throughout the race encouraging reports had been coming in of the Stelvio road being clear of snow but on the night before stage 18 they suddenly changed to bulletins warning of bad weather at the summit. Sudden changes of weather can, of course, always happen in the mountains. The following morning, however, a number of media, supporters and camp followers were up early and drove the route and reported no particular difficulties. There was old snow, of course, on the high slopes but the road was completely clear and conditions better than most previous years the Giro has been through. The race organisers, however, quoted the National Roads authority and the local Trento authorities, insisting there was an avalanche risk and at short notice cancelled the ascent of the Stelvio. The race was rerouted to climb the 1,884m Tonale and the Palade (1,518m) but, frankly, they were small fry compared to the Stelvio where Fignon would have expected to turn the screw. Fignon was dumbfounded and disheartened by the strange turn of events and, although he tried to attack on the Tonale, he eventually settled for simply riding tempo with the lead group on the Palade. His version of events was: 'Our plan for a huge offensive had been wrecked by the duplicity of the organisation who had little regard for the rules of sport.'

That evening Fignon and Guimard, having vented their spleen, looked at the route map and thought there was still a possibility of salvaging the race on stage 20 which included a good deal of climbing over Pordoi, Sella, Gardena and Campolongo. Fignon rode with indignant rage and destroyed all the class climbers. More importantly, he finished 2 minutes 19 seconds ahead of Moser and was now in pink again, albeit narrowly.

Fignon, however, really did feel he was taking on a nation and that Moser's win was predetermined. Moser simply had to win. In reality, with only a Moser-friendly time trial left, the race was already won and lost but the intrigue and bitterness continued to the end with Fignon complaining that the Italian TV helicopter flew ahead of him with the downforce threatening to blow him back while the same helicopter flew behind Moser, effectively creating a tailwind. Fignon, no mean TT rider himself, did well to finish 2.24 behind Moser but that left him just over 1 minute behind in second place.

Defeat didn't sit at all well for Fignon – 'my chest burned with pain, the pain you feel at injustice' – and it gnawed away at him for five years before he worked it out of his system and won the Giro the next time he contested the race, in 1989. To illustrate the form he was in during the 1984 season, and why he was so confident he could have cracked Moser on the Stelvio, he romped to victory over his former team leader Hinault, now riding for La Vie Claire, at the Tour de France. In 1984, Fignon remained forever convinced that, given a level playing field, he should have joined the pantheon of those with a Giro/Tour double on their palmares.

Hinault's falling out with Guimard – the two had parted company when the latter switched his allegiance to Fignon – and move to La Vie Claire, not to mention recurring knee problems, had caused a considerable mid-career blip. By 1985, however, it was Fignon, after his mighty efforts in 1984, who was beginning to struggle with injury and he was forced to miss the Giro and indeed the Tour with an Achilles issue that eventually required surgery. Moser was still riding strongly, his Giro title had inspired an Indian summer to the end of his career, and although the course wasn't so blatantly designed in his favour it was still pretty benign by Giro standards. The talented Roberto Visentini was challenging as well but Hinault rode himself nicely into form in the opening fortnight and La Vie Claire also benefited by having two cards to play if necessary with a credible Plan B in the young American Greg LeMond. The key moment came on stage 12, a long time trial which Moser really needed to win if he was to stand any realistic chance of defending his title. Passions were running high among the crowd and Moser rode well but Hinault had the bit between his teeth and roared to victory to take control of the GC. It was a rough day at the office, though: Hinault was covered in spittle when he crossed the line while journalists observed that La Vie Claire's support car, in close attendance behind Hinault, rode with the mechanic holding the back door permanently open on the more remote sections of the course. The team explained that this was an attempt to provide some kind of protection from overenthusiastic fans who perhaps didn't have Hinault's best interests at heart.

Moser continued to ride strongly, however, and Hinault had to stay alert right to the finish. Stage 19 witnessed another piece of alleged duplicity on the part of the race organisers. At the unveiling of the route the previous autumn the stage was definitely listed as finishing at the summit of the Gran San Bernardo Pass yet the night before the stage Torriani suddenly announced that the finish was now to be six kilometres lower down, taking the steepest part out of the climb, where Hinault would expect to cause most damage. Hinault was not amused and was none too pleased either in the final time trial to see the Italian TV helicopter again hovering behind Moser, seeming to blow him along a little, but he stayed focused, limited his loss on the stage to 7 seconds and was home and dry. This was Hinault's farewell to the Giro. Three races, three wins to go alongside his two wins in two starts at the Vuelta. Indeed, he was to win ten of the 12 Grand Tours he completed, winning five Tours and finishing second twice. Later in 1985 he completed his second Giro/Tour double. The Giro witnessed some of the best, most controlled and astute racing of his career and if the *tifosi* occasionally grew tired of his dominance and ability to trump their home-grown stars, his Breton grit always struck a chord. His passion more than matched theirs and as a rider he dealt with anything the Italians could throw at him. Literally on some occasions.

In 1986, with the race starting in Palermo, the Giro suffered a third rider fatality and the second on Sicilian soil with Emilio Ravasio crashing heavily during stage one from Palermo to Sciacca. In an incident horribly reminiscent of the accident which had claimed Fausto Coppi's brother Serse, Ravasio remounted after his crash and, apart from bumps and bruises, all seemed well when he rolled across the finish line 7 minutes behind race winner, Sergio Santimaria. But soon after he complained of feeling unwell and lapsed into a coma. The young team Atala rider died 16 days later, having never regained consciousness.

Visentini, riding in his ninth Giro, emerged as the winner, producing powerful and spirited performances on two of the more demanding days, the hilltop finish at Sauze d'Oulx and then the summit finish at the ski resort of Foppolo. Visentini possibly had rival Greg LeMond to thank for the latter because Torriani was all for cancelling the ascent of the San Marco Pass en route to Foppolo, the major climb of the day and the crux of the stage where Visentini and LeMond would be looking to put time into Saronni and Moser. The race director again argued that weather and road conditions were dangerous but LeMond immediately made his displeasure at that prospect known and the travelling English-speaking media corp dutifully kicked up a fuss on his behalf. For once Torriani backed down and the stage duly went off without incident or alarm with there seemingly nothing unusually hazardous or wintry on the San Marco Pass. Moser in particular suffered but he recovered well in the final time trial to put 1 minute 41 seconds into LeMond – normally a very good time-trial rider himself – and claim third place overall. Moser's victory in 1984 might have been contentious and slightly tainted, but he had been a consistently top-level performer in the Giro for a decade or more and the race was going to miss his stylish presence.

11

STEPHEN ROCHE SURVIVES 'CIVIL WAR' TO WIN THE TOUR AND GIRO (1987-91)

Some races take on an importance and mythology out of all proportion to what actually happened and many would argue that the 1987 Giro falls into that category. Riders within the same team clashing as they ruthlessly pursue personal ambition and glory is almost a cliché within cycling. Yet there remains something undeniably special about Stephen Roche's victory in 1987 when at times he was not only taking on his leader Roberto Visentini but also the majority of his own Carrera team, their sponsors and tens of thousands of fans on the roadside. It's a deliciously nuanced story, one very evocative of the Wild West days of the Giro, and can be viewed as both an act of betrayal and a career-defining moment when a competitor refused to be artificially constrained. The events of May and June 1987 also quickly took on a greater significance retrospectively in that Roche's victory in the Giro was the first leg of a stunning season that also saw him emulate Eddy Merckx in winning the Giro/Tour double and the World Championship. At the time of writing they are the only two cyclists to achieve this.

The first thing to state, categorically, is that Roche never saw himself as anything other than a joint team leader with Visentini and therein lies the nub of the entire story. At the end of the 1985 season Roche was signed by Carrera's DS Davide Boifava specifically to win big races and that included Grand Tours. Roche had always shown potential as a road racer and already had a Paris–Nice victory and two Tours of Romandie titles on his palmares in 1985 when he finished third in the Tour de France, an outstanding performance that definitely hinted at even greater glories. The dapper Irishman was on a steep upward trajectory and Carrera were determined to get their man, eventually signing him on the eve of the 1985 World Championship. In an ideal world Roche would probably race the Tour and the World Championships – he was already a bronze-medal winner from 1983 – while Visentini contested his beloved Giro, invariably his only major target of the season. But make no mistake, Roche was already a big-name rider, well capable of leading a team, when he moved to Italy. He was never a foot soldier and was not being paid one of the biggest basic salaries in cycling to ride as a *gregario* or even a *gregario di lusso*.

In that first winter the move went spectacularly pear-shaped after Roche crashed heavily at the Paris Six Days and damaged a knee cartilage, an injury that was to plague him on and off for the rest of his career. It was only diagnosed a couple of months later and, although Roche underwent an operation, the surgery wasn't entirely successful. Short of fitness and form and still in discomfort, Roche struggled through his debut season with Carrera, nobly trying to contribute to the team effort in the Giro before being forced to withdraw a couple of days before the finish. Unable to climb with any intensity he also struggled around the Tour de France in 48th position, a remarkable performance given his condition. Visentini's triumph at the 1986 Giro, at the eighth attempt, was seen by many, not least Visentini himself, as underlining his pre-eminence in the team but others saw it as a one-off triumph, a career peak that would never be repeated. Roche, meanwhile, never viewed himself as anything other than a potential Grand Tour winner. He had been at barely 50 per cent in 1986, but as soon as he got the knee fixed properly he would be competitive again. No question. That winter Roche underwent another knee operation which, temporarily at least, seem to solve the cartilage issue. Certainly he didn't have to contend with swelling after every day's racing, as he had throughout most of 1986. Fortified by a much better winter of training, Roche started afresh for Carrera in 1987 and immediately hit his straps, with wins at the Tour of Valencia and Tour of Romandie and a second place at Liège–Bastogne–Liège where he rode powerfully all day, only to be caught napping on the line by Moreno Argentin.

Roche was named in the Carrera squad for the 1987 Giro and it was that decision by the management that is fundamental to what followed. Did they assume he was riding simply to get fit for the Tour or were the team tactics even discussed in any detail? Or perhaps it was deliberately left a little open-ended. A little dynamic tension can be a wonderful thing but it can also get very ugly. From the outside looking in there was a widespread assumption that his efforts would be directed in the defence of Visentini's title but again Roche begged to differ. He now considered himself well and truly back to the fitness and condition that saw him claim that third place in the 1985 Tour de France, a performance that in athletic terms could probably be considered at least the equal of, if not better than, Visentini's win over a far from epic Giro course in 1986. Roche was in sparkling early season form in 1987, while Visentini had made his usual slow start. But he was the reigning champion and an Italian riding in an Italian team in his home Tour.

The cat was immediately set among the pigeons when Roche defeated Visentini in a curious quick-fire eight-kilometre time trial that was advertised as a descent from the well-known Poggio climb, which always takes centre stage in Milan–San Remo – but in fact featured equal measures of flat and uphill riding as well as fast downhill sections. The Carerra team, and indeed the vast majority of the peloton, opted for their aerodynamic TT bikes with solid wheels but Roche felt his normal road bike was better suited to such a varied test of man and machine. Roche's subsequent surprise stage win – Visentini was the strong favourite for the stage – might only have been by 7 seconds but it had a massive knock-on effect. Two days later the strong Carrera line-up dominated a 43km TTT and that win projected Roche into the *maglia rosa*, 15 seconds ahead of Visentini.

For the next ten days Roche wore the leader's jersey which established the legitimacy of his challenge for the GC in his own eyes if not in those of his team. The internal tension was palpable though. Tellingly, Visentini shadowed his team-mate rather than opposition riders and most experienced observers could sense trouble brewing. The vast majority of the Carrera team were solidly behind Visentini but one rider at least – Belgium's Eddy Schepers – was firmly in the Roche camp. Schepers had loyally ridden for both Visentini and Roche the previous season but when the team hinted strongly that they would not be keeping Schepers on for the 1987 season only Roche argued the case for his *gregario*. Carrera relented and Schepers was a devoted Roche man thereafter.

Schepers was also a very fine and practical racer. On a very quiet short stage – stage six from Terni to Terminillo – Schepers and Jean-Claude Bagot were allowed to slip away on a break that could have no possible influence on the eventual GC rankings. Bagot, of the Fagor team, was a very decent climber but couldn't shake Schepers off over the three minor climbs that presented themselves and, come the final run-in, Schepers, who possessed a punchy finish, was the clear favourite to win. At which point Schepers started negotiating on behalf of his master. If they agreed that the stage was Bagot's could Roche rely on a little support from Bagot and his Fagor colleagues in the high mountains if Roche found himself isolated? The deal was done and after Schepers led the finish out for the sake of appearances, Bagot came past to take line honours.

Roche's fortunes nosedived on stage 13 when he suffered a very bad day at the office in the Rimini–San Marino TT. Visentini, always good and sometimes exceptional in time trials, was rightly favourite for the stage and duly won in impressive style but Roche was very poor by his own standards, finishing 2.47 back in 12th position. The reigning champion now led by 2.47. Roche has always insisted that his poor ride was down to Visentini distracting him on the day of the TT accompanying him on his practice ride, constantly quizzing him over which gear to use where and when on the course, and pestering him with more questions as he tried to get his head together over a light lunch. That might be true but a top rider is totally responsible for his own routines and preparations. Blaming his poor TT ride on Visentini doesn't really wash as a valid explanation. What is interesting, though, is his reaction to his team's excessive joy in seeing Visentini back in the lead. Roche, having worn the jersey for the team for ten days, was disappointed but not surprised. He knew which way the wind was blowing.

Roche still had the support of his room-mate Schepers, however, and that evening they studied the route book long and hard. How could they get back at Visentini without being seen to overtly attack the team's pink jersey? It wouldn't be easy. Eventually they drew a ring around Sappada, two days later on stage 15, a mixed day starting with 100km of flattish terrain and ending with three lumpy hills finishing with the Cima Sappada, topping out at just under 1,300m. It was basically a leg-stretching exercise before the Dolomites and most of the peloton would be hoping for a relatively uneventful day. It was, however, exactly the sort of stage when a relatively harmless break might go up the road.

Just such an opportunity presented itself as the peloton went over the first climb – Forcella di Monte Rest – when Bagot and Ennio Salvador attacked. Roche used the supposed need to cover that move – there was in fact no need whatsoever, the duo were not factors in the GC – as a fairly flimsy excuse to launch his own attack. What was clever is that he launched his bid to bridge the gap on the descent where, to use his own vivid phrase, 'I cut the brake cables.' Attacking on a climb is blatant and there for all to see but sometimes, going downhill, you can just have one of those magic-carpet days when you are in synch with the descent and can pull ahead without touching a pedal, without obviously forcing the pace and animating the race. That's what Roche did and he soon bridged the gap to Bagot and Salvador, but now what to do? Roche was having fun, the devil was in him for sure, but he also assumed the Bianchi and Panasonic teams would be organising the chase and he was on borrowed time. In fact, a furious Visentini had put the Carrera team to the front of the bunch to chase Roche down and everybody else was being towed along. When Roche received this news from his perplexed DS Boifava who had driven up to Roche to order him back, it was like a red rag to a bull: 'I was riding eyeballs out so pumped up with anger by the fact that my team were "riding" behind me that I didn't feel any fatigue at all. Rage drove me on for almost 40km.'

This was war. Civil war. Roche was almost caught at the foot of the second climb but as the bunch came back together another break went off, including Schepers, and Roche just about managed to tag on. Carrera, meanwhile, had buried themselves over those 40 flat kilometres chasing their erstwhile colleague and nobody had anything in reserve. At one point Biofava drove up and ordered Schepers back to help the struggling Visentini but the experienced and brave Schepers declined, arguing that the best and logical tactics now were to ride for Stephen Roche. Johan van der Velde took the stage and Roche came home in an 11-man group 46 seconds behind, while a broken Visentini limped home in 58th position at 6.50. The team 'leader' did not have a single *gregario* by his side such had been the damage of a dramatic day. Afterwards it was chaos and the media went into meltdown. Italy's reigning champion and the pink jersey, who started the day nearly 3 minutes to the good, had been ridden ragged and humiliated by his own Carrera team-mate. As Roche was accepting the jersey a fuming Visentini was doing a TV interview alongside the makeshift podium with Italy's RAI. 'Tonight somebody is going home,' he fumed ominously.

Roche didn't go home. The fact that he had regained the *maglia rosa* and Carrera could still win the Giro ensured that; it was his get-out-of-gaol-free card. All the time he was in pink how could anybody seriously argue against him? The next week, however, was to be the most uncomfortable of his career. The gloves were well and truly off as he later recalled:

From that point onwards Visentini didn't talk to me at all. And he kept on attacking me, the day after Sappada, the next day and the next day. It was mayhem on the road that first day back in pink. Everybody wanted my blood. I would never in my wildest dreams have imagined it was going to be as difficult as it was with the fans. They had been whipped up into a frenzy because there was all this stuff in the press about me being a traitor, cheating on my team-mate. People were waving banners daubed with pictures of raw meat dripping blood and saying Roche Bastardo, Roche va a casa – but seeing that hardened my determination. On the climbs fans were shouting all kind of abuse and trying to punch me. Some had rice in their mouths and then, as I approached, they were taking a mouthful of red wine and spitting it all over me.

The very next stage was a classic Dolomites day – Croce Comelico, Gardena, Sella, Pordoi, Marmolada – and not at all pleasant for Roche as he ran the gauntlet of the fans. For most of the time he rode with the ever-loyal Schepers on one side and a good friend and former Renault colleague Robert Millar on the other. Millar, an English-speaking ally in a very foreign peloton, had also served the same cycling apprenticeship at the ACBB amateur club in Paris as Roche and was always an individual who would make up his own mind on any given issue and react accordingly. As a GC contender himself, riding with the *maglia rosa* was an obvious tactic for the day in any case. A couple of Fagor riders also rode with Roche to form a protective bubble as they worked off the team's debt to Schepers for allowing Bagot the stage win much earlier in the race. And it wasn't only the enraged fans that Roche had to be wary of.

> Visentini did everything he could to get clear that day and that wasn't all he was up to. As we were coming over the top of one of the big climbs Eddy [Schepers] and I had fallen back a bit and Roberto [Visentini] dropped back towards us. I thought for a moment that he was coming back to help. But when we reached him he kind of swerved. We didn't know why but we managed to avoid him. Then he veered again as if to force me off the cliff. I avoided him again but he almost put Eddy over the cliff. I rode alongside him and put my hands on his bars and made it clear that if he tried that again he would be coming over the edge with me.

In the end it began to calm down a little although Roche spent the rest of the Giro eating meals in his room at night with the food prepared by his masseur Silvano Davo to avoid the possibility of some outside agent – or team-mate – trying to poison the leader. His personal mechanic Patrick also ensured that Roche's bike didn't leave his sight during the night. Roche kept cool and closed out the most controversial Giro in modern-day history with an emphatic win in the final TT, Visentini having gone home the previous night after breaking a wrist in a fall on the penultimate stage. A loquacious Irishman, Roche also seemed to win the PR battle. At one stage, when quizzed by *Gazzetta* about the situation and Visentini's complaints of treachery he replied: 'Roberto fell off in the Tour of the Basque country and hit his head. He sometimes gets hold of the wrong end of the stick.'

Roche had worn the pink jersey for 18 days during the race and finished 3.40 ahead of Robert Millar. By any criteria he was the strongest rider in the 1987 Giro and a worthy winner but still the controversy rages. Afterwards he and Schepers didn't hang around but drove to Paris through the night with two friends who had come down for the final stage. After a quick celebratory glass of champagne and a croissant they went on a training ride. The Tour de France awaited.

Andy Hampsten becomes the first North American to win a Grand Tour

After the dramas of 1987 the tantalising prospect of a rematch loomed the following spring but Roche, having moved to the Fagor MBK team, suffered a recurrence of his knee problems and never made it to the start line, while Visentini was never really a factor, finishing a dispirited 13th. Given the failure of a much-anticipated rematch to materialise, 1988 could have been a massive anticlimax but in this golden mini-period for the Giro another compelling story developed, namely the emergence of the American team 7-Eleven and ultimately the dramatic victory of Andy Hampsten who became the second North American to win a Grand Tour and first to win the Giro.

The genesis of 7-Eleven away from the European mainstream was a remarkable story in itself, the brainchild of Jim Ochowicz, a former Olympic team pursuit rider who was also a huge ice-skating fan. His wife was Olympic ice-skating gold medallist Sheila Young and the couple were firm friends with Olympic ice-skating legend Eric Heiden who had won five Olympic gold medals at the 1980 Games at Lake Placid. Heiden was in turn a massive cycling fan who spent hours on his bike for training and had always been intrigued by the possibility of switching to cycling. After Lake Placid they got together to form a cycling team to race in North America with the presence of Heiden helping to secure a strong sponsorship with 7-Eleven. The team, based on North American and Mexican riders, proved very successful domestically and in 1985 tried its luck in Europe, competing in that year's Giro when Ron Kiefel and Hampsten both made an immediate splash with stage wins. The following year Hampsten, riding that season for La Vie Claire, won the Tour of Switzerland and the Young riders jersey when finishing fourth at the Tour de France, while the 7-Eleven team claimed three stage winners at the Tour in Davis Phinney, Jeff Pierce and Dag Otto Lauritzen.

Hampsten was back on board with 7-Eleven at the 1988 Giro, which had plenty of scope for climbers, with the consensus being that the short but downright nasty 120km stage from Chiesa in Valmalenco to Bormio, taking in the Aprica and Gavia, would be a major battleground. And as is often the case with the Gavia, the high-speed and at times dangerous descent into Bormio was likely to be as big a factor as the ascent itself. All this was widely anticipated before the peloton pulled into Chiesa in Valmalenco on the night of Saturday 4 June. After what had been a sun-kissed Giro up to that point, the weather suddenly turned very nasty overnight and by Sunday morning sleet and icy rain was falling at the start which was situated at about 600m. You didn't need to be a meteorologist to guess what conditions would be like 2,000m higher up the mountain. There were discontented rumbles from some teams but the race organisation, always a law unto itself, appeared unconcerned on this occasion despite the conditions which, even at the start, appeared to be infinitely worse than anything experienced on the Stelvio four years earlier when that climb had been inexplicably cut from the stage.

What transpired was remarkable and, although it's difficult to compare epic bad weather in the Giro, it is doubtful if the peloton have ever been asked to race in worse conditions, certainly in modern times. The 7-Eleven team, despite accusations of being a bit wet behind the ears in terms of European racing and general Grand Tour experience, were among the least concerned by the worsening weather reports. Most of the team were based in the high mountains in Boulder, Colorado, where extreme winter weather was a fact of life. Hampsten was their main GC hope and riding well, handily placed in fifth, and he was particularly at home in such conditions. He, too, was based in Boulder but had also been brought up in North Dakota which specialises in huge winter snows and freezing, almost Arctic conditions. The Giro was his big target for the year and, slight of build, he had decided to try and toughen up and improve his strength and endurance during the winter. For weeks at a time, at the urging of the 7-Eleven coach, Mike Neel, he had climbed off his bike and had gone for gruelling eight-hour hikes in the Rockies in the depths of winter. It was as much a mental toughening-up exercise as anything and on the Gavia that day it paid off handsomely. 7-Eleven were well organised and had been plotting long-range satellite weather forecasts for a week ahead, and had spotted the possibility of extreme weather on the Gavia ahead of many teams. Three days before the stage Ochowicz had gone into a sports shop en route and bought every pair of ski gloves and thermal vests they had along with a dozen thermos flasks.

On the day itself Ochowicz rose before dawn, filled the thermoses with scalding hot sweet tea and filled the team musettes with piles of substantial sustaining food rather than light energy bars and gels. He then drove behind a snowplough to the top of the Gavia to await the arrival of the peloton. This was a day on which simply surviving would ensure a good finish. On the climb up, a relay of 7-Eleven domestiques brought hot tea up to Hampsten every five minutes or so to ward off hypothermia for their lead man who was tapping away quite nicely in his natural element. It might have been cold but he had known much worse on the almost tundra-like conditions of a wintry North Dakota. And the worst bit of the day was going to be the descent. He was saving his physical and emotional energy for that. First to crest the summit was the excellent Dutch climber Johan van der Velde and, although strictly speaking he was the opposition, Ochowicz relented and poured a steaming hot mug of tea from a 7-Eleven thermos and stuck it in his hand. Van der Velde was frozen like a statue, such was his physical condition, and lost nearly 1 hour of time on the descent.

Hampsten chugged into view just over 1 minute behind, going remarkably well. Already wearing a woollen ski hat and neck warmer, he also added a jacket to try and offer some protection against the wind and cold as the race headed downhill. Staying upright was the only thing that really mattered on the descent. There were virtually no spectators, and the team cars, at this point, were struggling miles behind. In the swirling mists and spindrift, you could have gone off over the side and nobody would have noticed. Hampsten also recognised that another big danger was getting your gear set and sprockets encased with frozen snow and ice, rendering them unusable. The worst possible thing you could do was freewheel as you usually would on sections of such a long descent: 'I knew I had to keep one gear working,' Hampsten recalled. 'I kept it in the 53x14 and pedalled the whole way down. I never stopped pedalling so it never stopped working.'

Hampsten kept rolling steadily along and eventually finished second behind Dutchman Erik Breukink who had produced an equally heroic and resourceful ride. The American was now in pink but shortly after the finish the pent-up emotions and tension of the hardest and most testing day he had ever spent on a bike hit Hampsten like a ton of bricks. First he became very angry and started shouting at everybody, then he climbed into a car with a heater on and asked to be left alone while he cried his eyes out. The stragglers were still a long way off, making their way down the slopes, and there were press reports of many riders, not caring whether they were disqualified or not, simply climbing into their team cars when they finally came into view and driving most of the way before remounting their bikes with a few kilometres to go. In the event there were no disqualifications.

Recovering from such a day was 7-Eleven's biggest task because they now had a pink jersey to defend, but recover they did and after riding defensively through the rest of the mountains Hampsten applied the *coup de grâce* on the stage 18 time trial, an 18km uphill run from Levico Terme to Valico del Vetriolo. The resilient American won that in convincing style to give himself the best part of a 2-minute lead over Breukink, which he sustained without alarm all the way to the finish. It was a career highlight for Hampsten who enjoyed some more fine days back at the Giro, not least a third place the following year, but he was never quite able to match what he achieved in 1988. And perhaps it's no wonder. On that day on the Gavia he and others pushed their bodies to the limit and beyond.

Nineteen eighty-nine was Laurent Fignon's long-awaited year of retribution although initially he played hardball with the race organiser Torriani who he still held responsible for his controversial defeat in 1984. There was probably never any danger of Fignon not competing but he and his System U team made Torriani sweat a little bit. They were in no mood to be messed around.

Torriani, coming to the end of his reign, had in fact produced a superb course, demanding in every respect, and Fignon was now back to full fitness after his serious injury problems. The route suited him, there was a score to be settled and he felt in great shape. Hampsten was also back to defend his crown and, although he was making noises about targeting the Tour, there was no doubt that if the cards fell his way the American would mount a fierce defence of his title. Alongside them, Greg LeMond was a dangerous floater, Breukink was always lively and Roche was also at the start line although with little fitness and form after his injury-ravaged 1988. It was an interesting, high-quality line-up.

The Tappone, the Queen Stage, came on stage 14 with five major passes to negotiate – the Giau, Santa Lucia, Marmolada, Pordoi and the Campolongo – and the weather was again foul alternating wildly between freezing fog, icy rain and snow flurries. Fignon was not normally a great lover of such conditions but this was a notable exception and his preparations were unusual to say the least. He got his masseur to massage him from head to foot with his strongest lotion – the equivalent of Ralgex by the sound of it – and despite the Arctic conditions Fignon insists he didn't feel the cold all day; in fact he described it as a day from Dante's *Inferno*.

Fignon went into pink but the race was far from won and Fignon woke up the following morning feeling fatigued and in pain with an old shoulder injury – the result of a skiing accident in his teenage years – flaring up under the stress of the previous day's effort. Flavio Giupponi, who had actually won the epic stage the previous day to go into second place overall, was going well, as was Hampsten, and at this point delicious sporting irony kicks in. Fignon got through stage 15 – split stages based around Trento – but was filled with a sense of foreboding the following day when the weather again turned nasty and he was faced with another monstrous stage taking in the Tonale and Gavia passes. Five years earlier Fignon had raged when Torriani altered the Stelvio stage at short notice but on this occasion he was only too glad to see the stage cancelled altogether. An extra rest day was proclaimed. Was Torriani seeking to quietly make amends for 1984, as the Italian press suggested? Possibly but bear in mind this came just 12 months after the race director had been bitterly criticised for allowing the Gavia stage to proceed. To a certain extent Torriani was damned if he did and damned if he didn't, the fate of all race directors.

Fignon was spared but was still suffering the following day when he underperformed on a mountain time trial, which reduced his lead to just over 1 minute on Giupponi and Hampsten, but then the fine weather returned in the mixed-terrain stages of Liguria and Tuscany and his old war wound settled down. Fignon had weathered the storm and he showed his class on a tough mountain day on the penultimate stage when he resisted attacks from Giupponi and Hampsten after Gianni Bugno had taken off to claim the stage. Revenge was almost his and, although he had to hang tough in a final marathon 53.8km TT, Fignon was good value for one of the sweetest wins of his career. His form had been rock-solid which he demonstrated a few months later when he finished second at the Tour just 8 seconds behind LeMond.

The Giro of this era was never boring but nobody, with the notable exception of Laurent Fignon who sang his praises in advance, anticipated the extent to which Gianni Bugno would dominate the 1990 edition, leading the race from start to finish. Nor would anybody have suspected that Wolfgang Amadeus Mozart, dead for nearly 200 years, was to play a part in that victory. Most tipsters made Fignon the favourite but, after his Herculean efforts in 1989, he was lacking motivation and form and was in any case eventually to crash out. Greg LeMond was also present with his new Z team but it soon became apparent that he had made a late start to the season and was riding mainly for fitness while Charly Mottet, a rising French star, and the recent Vuelta winner Marco Giovannetti were also likely contenders. In the event, of those named only Mottet raised a gallop and Bugno won easily. The 26-year-old was clearly a talent and had won Milan–San Remo in fine style earlier in the season but only Fignon among the riders, and indeed the press, tipped him as a winner before the start in Bari. Although the race itself may have lacked drama, Bugno's win was a good story. Riding for the Chateau d'Ax-Salotti team, he imposed his authority right from the start by comfortably winning the opening-day 13km time trial and he continued to dominate proceedings for the next three weeks, appearing to be the strongest TT rider and rock-solid in the mountains. At no point did his victory appear anything other than inevitable and yet it wasn't quite that simple.

A gifted, natural athlete, Bugno's Achilles heel had been his descending and sense of balance on technical sections which was well below what you would expect from a top professional and, recognising this, he had sought and found a remedy: music. He and his team turned first to a psychologist in an attempt to improve his descending and it was he who suggested listening systematically to all the great works of Mozart for half an hour a day for an extended period and to 'replay' those tunes in his head when he was descending or negotiating difficult roads. This is exactly what he did in the spring of 1990 with immediate results at Milan–San Remo and then again at the Giro. He believed it helped transform his descending while his time-trialling morphed from good to very good. So dominant was Bugno that, having defended his lead through the mountains without apparent difficulty, he could even afford to make a bad mistake on the final long TT from Gallarate to Varese and still win the stage to increase his lead. On a day when the weather deteriorated quickly, Bugno had started the time trial with front and back disc wheels, which proved very tricky to handle as the wind blew. Prevaricating as to whether to stop and change to his normal road bike with regular wheels he flatted, which made his mind up for him. Despite that mid-race delay, Bugno won the TT from Marino Lejarreta by 1 minute 20 seconds which rather summed up his dominance.

Such was Bugno's dominance that many were predicting a long reign at the Giro, but this exciting and unpredictable period in the race's history continued with the most unexpected but equally impressive win for Franco Chioccioli who had been competing in the Giro since 1982. It would be damning Chioccoli with faint praise to call him a Giro stalwart; he was better than that, completing all 13 Giri he entered and claiming seven top-ten finishes in his career. But nobody saw this triumph coming. Chioccoli rode a textbook race and effectively clinched his victory on the Tappone, the second Dolomites stage, when he attacked on 'Coppi's climb', the Pordoi, to pull decisively ahead of his nearest rival, Claudio Chiappucci. He then underlined that with a commanding performance in the marathon 66km time trial at Casteggio. In many ways it was a heart-warming story although not without controversy given Chioccioli's sudden improvement in performance later in his career. French competitor Erwann Menthéour accused Chioccioli directly of doping but there was nothing to back his claims up and the result stood. The era of suspicion of every exceptional performance was upon us, with some accusations fully justified and proven while others were left hanging unsatisfactorily in the air.

12

'BIG MIG' AND THE RISE OF MARCO PANTANI (1992-8)

Miguel Indurain had been a professional for eight years and was a veteran of 15 Grand Tours before he first entered the Giro d'Italia in 1992 when he lined up as the reigning Tour de France winner. There are many good reasons for this absence from Italy's premier race. As a top Spanish rider competing for Spanish teams he was naturally expected to compete in his national tour, the Vuelta a España, while in the earlier part of his career he was required to ride in the service of Pedro Delgado whose main target every year was the Tour de France. That left little or no scope to contest the Giro, but the excessively mountainous nature of the *corsa rosa* some years was also a deterrent. 'Big Mig' in his full maturity, when he took over the team leadership, was the latest, and arguably the best, in a long line of supreme time-trial riders who found a way of winning Grand Tours by hanging tough in the mountains and then destroying opponents in the time trials. If the course was too obviously a mountainfest from the off he was likely not to enter.

Come 1992 and after a long apprenticeship he was suddenly the biggest name in the sport. In 1990 he had sacrificed himself one final time for the fading Delgado at the Tour and could have finished much higher than tenth if he had ridden for himself. The following season, as team leader, he hit his straps and claimed the first of five consecutive Tour de France wins and finished runner-up at the Vuelta a España.

Indurain could no longer, in all consciousness, delay his Giro debut and the 1992 route didn't look particularly horrendous with a reassuring 66km time trial on the final stage if he needed any further encouragement. If the worst came to the worst and he struggled, he could claim with some truth that he was using it as preparation for the Tour de France – as Greg LeMond had done on occasions – while if he got off to a flying start and felt good he could chase the General Classification.

To the surprise of nobody Indurain did start well and simply kept improving, which left the opposition powerless to resist. Stage nine with its summit finish at Terminillo looked fraught indeed but so strongly did he climb that Laurent Fignon, making his final appearance at the Giro, and Claudio Chiappucci both ceded time to him while other climbing specialists had to dig very deep to stay with Indurain. The big Basque repeated that bravura performance in the Dolomites when stage 12 traversed the Staulanza, Giau and Falzarego passes and there seemed no chink in his armour, and it was exactly the same the following day when he dealt comfortably with the Campolongo, Pordoi and Bondone. Indurain in his pomp was a very tough man to counter and throughout the 1992 Giro he had the luxury of knowing that the race this year ended with that long time trial into Milan. Naturally he won that with some ease, making the catch on Chiapucci just before the finishing line. Indurain might not have won the Giro without breaking sweat but he certainly hadn't overexerted himself. There was plenty left in reserve for the Tour de France, which he duly won six weeks later. Low-key and modest, authorative without being demonstrative, polite without being fawning, Indurain was difficult for Italian fans and media to get a handle on. He sucked the drama and excitement out of a race that thrived on both, but he was in no way a hate figure. There was very little to dislike about 'Big Mig' unless you were one of the poor souls being spat out the back when he put the hammer down.

It all seemed ridiculously straightforward and routine, which invariably aroused suspicion. Cycling had entered the EPO era and now the consensus seems to be that from the early 1990s onwards its use was commonplace but its detection rare, with the authorities unable to identify the worst of the dopers until the late nineties and early noughties. Indurain frequently had to fend off questions about his remarkable performances and did so with as much dignity as you can on these occasions while also pointing to his never failing a drugs test – although that is a statistic which rather lost its relevance in light of Lance Armstrong also claiming he never failed a drugs test. His collaboration at times with the now disgraced Italian doctor Francesco Conconi, a pioneer in the use of EPO, adds fuel to the fire for some conspiracy theorists, but what can be said with some certainty is that Indurain was an exceptional athlete with a fairly unique physiological make-up. A resting heartbeat of 28 is about as low as the medical profession has ever encountered in a fit athlete, while his lung capacity was measured at 7.8 litres, which was reckoned to be at least 20 per cent above most other members of the peloton who would themselves be considered exceptional in that respect. From 1985, when he turned professional, to the Grand Tour-winning days (1991–5), he shed the 10kg or 22lb which was key to him being able to compete in the mountains. In 2012, at the age of 46, and 14 years since he had ridden in earnest, his power output was recorded at 450W, which compared favourably with current professionals half his age.

Away from the GC duel, in 1992 the flamboyant Mario Cipollini was beginning to make his mark on the Giro with four stage wins and the first of three Points titles. A muscular, larger-than-life sprinter from Lucca, Cipollini had enjoyed a stellar amateur career and had been steadily making his mark on the Giro with the Del Tongo team, winning a stage on debut in 1989, two stages the following year before his successes of 1992 with the GB-MG team. An outrageous showman nicknamed '*il Re Leon*' or 'Super Mario', Cipollini provided a counterpoint to the grim suffering and introverted nature of many of the GC contenders, appearing to enjoy a life of wine, women and song as he blasted his way to endless sprint victories. In an extraordinarily long career Cipollini was to notch up at least one stage win in 13 separate Giri and ended up beating Alfredo Binda's record number of stage wins of 41. As an out-and-out sprinter he sometimes offended the purists by making no attempt to actually finish the three-week race, but he added massively to the spectacle and was a firm crowd favourite. For much of that time, particularly with Seaco team, he surrounded himself with a highly trained sprint train which sometimes seemed to reduce his wins to a formality.

Much encouraged by his superb Giro/Tour double in 1992, Indurain decided not to tinker with a winning formula and opted to race the Giro again the following season, turning his back on the Vuelta, a race which strangely he was destined never to win. 'Big Mig' was in a rich vein of form and again it was difficult to see where the serious opposition might come from once he distanced himself from other potential contenders in the 28km TT at Senigallia. It was impressive stuff although as a spectacle the race desperately needed somebody to put up a fight and at least land a few blows. In the end Latvia's Piotr Ugrumov, a gritty and resourceful climber, was that man. The aggressive Ugrumov never stopped attacking but got little joy until the penultimate stage. Indeed, the gap between him and Indurain had widened to 1 minute 34 seconds after stage 19, a 55km TT predictably won by Indurain (although with long uphill stretches, not as commandingly as some might have predicted). The Latvian sensed that perhaps Indurain was weakening and summoned one final effort the following day which ended with a ten-kilometre climb into the town of Oropa. This time he finally put a little daylight between himself and Indurain but the defending champion, going deeper than at any time in his two Giri to date, kept churning away and limited his loss to 36 seconds, giving him his second title by just under 1 minute.

It was closer than the previous year but the three weeks of tough racing had again put him in fantastic shape for the Tour which he duly won again to complete the double-double.

The 1993 race was notable in one other respect. Riding in support of Claudio Chiappucci was a 23-year-old specialist climber named Marco Pantani, who was ultimately forced to quit on stage 18 with tendonitis of the knee. Pantani, from Cesena in Emilia-Romagna, had caused much excitement and discussion as an amateur with three consecutive podium finishes in the Girobio, culminating in victory in 1992 after which he turned professional with Carrera Jeans-Vagabond. A product of the Fausto Coppi cycling club of Cesenatico, Pantani was lean but athletic and was clearly destined for the Grand Tours. There the only question was whether he could handle the rough and tumble of the peloton on the flatter days and limit his losses sufficiently in the time trials where his fluid style meant he could be surprisingly competitive although his lack of horsepower was clearly going to be a disadvantage on certain stages.

By 1994 Pantani was in great form and enjoying his first flush of success. Warming up with fourth-place finishes at both the Giro del Trentino and Giro della Toscana, he was nonetheless again expected to ride as support for Chiappucci at the Giro but it soon became obvious that the apprentice was fast overtaking the master. Pantani needed to be let loose in what was to prove an unpredictable race when for once Indurain's calculated, almost metronomic approach ran into difficulties. A young Russian, Evgeni Berzin from Vyborg close to the Finnish border, torpedoed Indurain's tried and tested tactics by beating the Spaniard in the two individual time trials with his barely believable triumph in stage eight in particular signalling a changing of the guard, covering the 44km course fully 2 minutes 34 seconds ahead of Indurain. Where did that come from? Berzin also demonstrated an ability to compete well in the mountains and the Russian defended the jersey with a great deal of panache all the way to Milan to win by just under 3 minutes from Pantani with Indurain third at 3.33.

Berzin was that comparative rarity, a Grand Tour winner whose talent was initially forged on the track. A former World Amateur Individual and Team Pursuit champion, he was a second-year professional with the Italian team Gewiss–Ballan when he won the Giro, having warmed up with an eye-catching victory at Liège–Bastogne–Liège. The Gewiss–Ballan team, it should be noted, comes with a health warning. Their doctor at the time was EPO guru Michele Ferrari and subsequent investigations by Danmarks Radio, *L'Equipe* and *La Republique* unearthed data recording eye-popping haematocrit level variations within most team members, including Berzin, for the period 1994–5. A reading in excess of 50 per cent was not proof positive of doping but it was considered indicative. Of course, this is an era few cycling historians have any great trust in but, with a definitive test for EPO not developed until 2000, few cheating riders were 'outed' and competition results remain.

Pantani lights up the 1994 Giro

After Indurain had reduced the Giro to a low-key promenade for two years, Berzin's arrival from virtually nowhere was, however, generally welcomed and he was, of course, riding for an Italian team. From Vyborg, blond and very Nordic and relatively outgoing, he was very different from Indurain and that contrast was also welcomed. But the personality who lit up the 1994 Giro was undoubtedly Pantani who, while never really threatening to get on terms with Berzin, claimed two sublime mountain stages in a manner which suggested to the *tifosi* that a potential *campionissimo* might finally be moving among them again. With Chiappucci struggling a little and Pantani seemingly out of contention in tenth place at 6.28, the young Italian was given licence to attack in the mountains on stage 14 when in the wet conditions he demonstrated his descending as well as climbing skills to win ahead of the pink jersey group. That was just the warm-up act for the following day when the snowy north face of the Stelvio awaited, not to mention the Mortirolo and Santa Cristina. This was the Tappone where the race would probably be won and lost. As usual there was a flurry of debate and possible controversy as the weather closed in and there were rumours of a possible cancellation or rejigging of the stage, but eventually the peloton headed into the mountains. Initially everybody was cautious and neither Berzin nor Indurain were really equipped to attack on a climb like the Stelvio so it was on the Mortirolo that Pantani launched his offensive, in that athletic, fluid style that characterised his climbing. Berzin briefly attempted to match the Italian but then thought better of it. Pantani still wasn't an out-and-out threat to his *maglia rosa* and the probable result of trying to match him would be Berzin cracking. Much better to drop back and just ride tactically against Indurain.

So Pantani was up the road, there was a long way to go and flattish terrain before the final climb, the Santa Cristina. The clever thing to do would be to throttle back a little and wait for somebody to join him and then ride tempo together to the Cristina where he would again attack and close out the stage. With adrenalin running high and the crowd urging him on, such considered tactics were almost counter-intuitive, and throughout most of his career Pantani committed totally from the start of a climb or break, which is one of the reasons why he was so popular. But on this occasion he was right to box clever. This was a stage win that needed finessing. Indurain, sensing that this might be his opportunity to recoup lost ground on Berzin, made his way up to the soft-pedalling Pantani along with Nelson Rodríguez, and together they settled in to consolidate the break. They worked well but when the Santa Cristina hoved into view there was only one outcome as Pantani started dancing on his pedals and disappeared up the mountain, finishing the day nearly 3 minutes ahead of his supposed team leader, Chiappucci, with whom he had endured a strained relationship from the moment he joined the team. Indurain was at 3.30 while Berzin had rallied to finish just 30 seconds behind Indurain which was his main objective. It was a spectacular performance from Pantani and cemented his place in Italian hearts. Pantani in full flow, sprinting effortlessly up a mountain, was an iconic sight, as beautiful, carefree and confident on a bike as he was gawky, preoccupied and just plain odd when he dismounted. Like other great climbers he adopted a different persona on his chosen battleground. The showman came out and the Italian crowds loved him for it. As he prepared for action – and Pantani rarely disappointed and failed to attack on the key climb of a stage – there were a few theatrical flourishes that signalled the start of his latest performance. He would remove his bandana and throw it to a fan on the roadside. Sometimes the sunglasses as well. A nose stud would be prised out and thrown to the masses. He would demolish the last of his favourite jam rolls – he eschewed the power bars and cereal cakes that were coming into vogue – a final gulp from his bidon and he was off. From now on it was him and the mountain. Everybody knew what was coming: he could hardly have signposted it any better. Pantani's coup that day earned him second place overall in 1994 and a glorious Giro career seemed assured, but for one reason or another it was another three years before he raced in the Giro again and a further 12 months after that before he finally fulfilled his potential in his home race.

As it happened 1995 was the year of Tony Rominger, an exceptionally talented all-rounder, who had broken the world Hour record twice in a matter of days in Bordeaux in 1994 – when the now disgraced Dr Michele Ferrari was in his corner advising his every move – while he also claimed his third consecutive Vuelta a España that year. For three or four years Rominger vied with Indurain as the sport's pre-eminent Grand Tour rider and 1995, after a six-year absence, was the year he planned a serious assault on the Giro where he had only previously ridden as a *gregario*. Rominger took control of the race on day two, an 18km TT from Foligno to Assisi, and in truth he never looked back as he became the third Swiss rider to win the Giro behind Koblet and Clerici. Rominger claimed that he wasn't particularly seeking the jersey so early in the race and wasn't overly bothered about defending. With long time trials on stages ten and 17 in which to impose his authority there was probably a good deal of truth in that but, equally, it was the first time he had worn the jersey, and been at the epicentre of the race, and his Mapei-GB team were riding strongly. Deliberately manoeuvring to gift the jersey to another team can go against the grain and so Rominger kept tapping away and the challenge never really came. Tactically their main opponents, Gewiss–Ballan, with Berzin and Latvian Piotr Ugrumov in their ranks, also got it wrong. That twin-pronged attack had the potential to at least inconvenience Rominger but the two Eastern Bloc riders didn't get on and each had individual ambitions. Second and third respectively looks quite impressive in the record books but from a position of some strength they never threatened the eventual winner. At one point, on stage 14, Ugrumov even rode with Rominger against Berzin when the Russian began to struggle in the mountains.

It was another Russian, Pavel Tonkov, dubbed 'the Tsar', possibly on account of his rather stylish and regal riding style, who took the honours in 1996 having finished a creditable sixth in 1995. Tonkov was another *rouleur* who could climb well and only once finished outside the top ten in the ten Giri he contested. To celebrate both the centenary of *Gazzetta dello Sport* and the founding of the modern-day Olympics, the Giro decided it would start in Athens and there were three sprint stages in Greece before it transferred back to Italy for stage four. That transfer included a rather comical element with the Italian police planning a raid on all the teams as they alighted on the Italian mainland only to be thwarted by *Gazzetta* who not only got wind of the raids but obtained detailed plans and decided to publish them all the day before they were due to be carried out. With the element of surprise blown the Italian police conceded defeat and cancelled their investigations for the time being. That apart, the first fortnight was largely uneventful but Tonkov made an appearance in pink after stage 13 when he went very well on a lumpy stage and, although he lost the *maglia rosa* in the race's only time trial the following day, he recovered the jersey in splendid fashion on stage 21 which took in the Mortirolo, a ride which clinched the race. It was by no means a classic and, with Enrico Zaina in second place and Abraham Olano third, the 1996 podium was a little short on stardust but Tonkov was a considerable rider. All the normal caveats to riders of this era apply but the Russian was always there or thereabouts.

Tonkov was certainly at the start line the following year when a particularly mountainous course had frightened off many top riders, especially those with designs on the Tour de France. Combining the two was now considered nigh on impossible although Marco Pantani was to disprove that in 1998. Pantani, after missing the two previous Giri, made a welcome return in 1997 to boost a lacklustre field that, in addition to those who had opted for the Tour, also found itself without Chiappucci who had recorded a haematocrit level of 50.8 per cent towards the end of the Tour of Romandie and copped a two-week ban that ruled him out of the Giro.

Pantani had been in the wars since his second place in the 1994 Giro. In 1995 he had been showing good early season form but early in May was involved in a training accident, crashing into a team car and suffering bad bruising. Much worse was to follow that autumn with a very nasty crash in the Milano–Torino race when he hit a car head-on and broke various bones in his left leg. That random injury nearly cost Pantani his career and he missed the entire following season as he tried to recover and then regain fitness. For a long while it was touch and go. Meanwhile, the Giro organisers and RAI kept his name to the forefront by getting him to sing the theme song which accompanied the opening credits of their daily coverage, a bouncy Eurotrash number which is far from being the worst foray into song we have heard from a prominent sports star. The Milano–Torino crash was to come back to haunt him in 1999 when the Turin public prosecutor, finally looking into the incident, recorded that blood tests taken at the hospital where Pantani was operated on just hours after the crash indicated a haematocrit level of 60.1 per cent, so abnormally high as to be virtually inexplicable by natural causes.

After a promising start Pantani's 1997 Giro ended in tears on a nothing day when the bunch had let an escape go 14 minutes up the road on the way to Amalfi and were promenading to the finish. As they descended the Valico di Chiunzi a cat darted across the road and Pantani went tumbling. The fate of the cat is not recorded but Pantani was badly bruised and shaken and lost 12 minutes on the leaders. Overnight he abandoned but he was clearly in decent form that season and kicked on to finish third overall at the Tour.

With Pantani gone Italian hopes rested mainly with specialist climber Ivan Gotti from the Gewiss–Ballan team who had ridden strongly in the mountains in 1996. Gotti took the lead on stage 14 and retained that advantage by limiting his losses to just 40 seconds in the 40km TT from Baselga di Pinè to Cavalese where Tonkov had reckoned on wiping out the 51-seconds deficit, and some. The reigning champion really did have a fight on his hands. There were dramas elsewhere as well. After being thwarted in 1996 the *carabinieri* successfully managed to conceal their intentions from *Gazzetta* 12 months later and launched a well-directed raid on the hotel where MG-Technogym riders were staying. There they 'discovered' 20 boxes of anabolic steroids, growth hormones and EPO. Their DS, Giancarlo Ferretti, tried to defend the indefensible but within hours the team had been thrown off the Giro. A tough final day in the mountains awaited but Gotti remained strong to close out the race and become the first Italian to win the Giro since Franco Chioccioli in 1991.

And so to 1998 and one of the most absorbing modern-day Grand Tours, the start of Pantani's golden year when for three months or so he was untouchable on a bike. Gotti's win in 1997 had been a little bonus to keep the *tifosi* going, but what they really craved was a Pantani victory and his return to form in the 1997 Tour had offered much hope for the 1998 Giro. At first glance, however, the course hardly appeared tailor-made for him with two 40km time trials seeming to favour the consistent Tonkov who was strong against the clock and in the mountains. Another likely contender was the Swiss rider Alex Zülle of the soon-to-become-infamous Festina team, who had won the Vuelta a España in September 1997. Still, there were some meaty mountain days for Pantani to get stuck into and hope sprang eternal.

For the first two weeks of the race it was Zülle who looked in commanding form while Michele Bartoli, essentially a one-day specialist, attacked furiously whenever possible and lit up the race. Those two headed up the GC but after the climb to San Marino on stage 11 Pantani was handily placed in fourth at 51 seconds, just 1 second behind Tonkov. Pantani, like Bartoli, had also ridden aggressively and, although looking short of a gallop in the early stages, seemed to be coming into form. Pantani continued to chip away at that lead and after winning stage 14 on the ascent of the Piancavallo had closed to within 14 seconds before it all seemed to go wrong in the first TT.

Zülle predictably romped home, averaging a jaw-dropping 53.77kmh, catching Pantani, his two-minute man, in the process and eventually routing his closest rival by nearly 3 and a half minutes. At first glance it looked all over but that was more or less the deficit Pantani had expected and, if not exactly in good spirits, he was a long way from throwing in the towel. He was still in third place overall behind Zülle and Tonkov with the race now entering the high mountains. Once there he lost no time in going to work on stage 17, the Tappone, where the Duran, Staulanza, Marmolada and Sella provided a fearsome second half of the stage. Tonkov attacked on the Marmolada, Pantani joined him along with another Italian climber, Giuseppe Guerini, and, confronted by that three-pronged attack, Zülle cracked. The leading trio forged on until Tonkov lost contact and the Italian combo sped up the Sella Pass. Pantani was riding himself into pink while Guerini was rewarded with the stage win.

Tonkov recovered well the following day to take stage 18, Selva di Val Gardena to Alpe di Pampeago, but Pantani was in close attendance in second place which set the scene for stage 19 – Cavalese to Plan di Montecampione – when Pantani started the day 27 seconds ahead of Tonkov. Stage 19 was truly spectacular with the final long, hot climb into Montecampione serving up a remarkable 45-minute head-to-head between Pantani and Tonkov up the 19km climb to the finish. With a final time trial yet to come, in which Tonkov was widely expected to claw back time, Pantani had to not only win but try and eke out his lead as much as possible. By common consent he needed to win by 1 minute, probably more. He knew it, a grim-faced and suffering Tonkov knew it, as did the roadside fans and watching millions on TV. Time and time again Pantani got up on his pedals and started to accelerate, yet every time the muscular Tonkov, usually known for his smooth style, shuddered with the physical effort as he closed the gap.

With approximately 2.8km remaining the Russian was still on Pantani's wheel, a remarkable effort on his part, but then with a final throw of the dice Pantani accelerated one last time, not forcefully because he himself was on the limit. He just got up out of the saddle, as he had already done scores of times that day, and upped the tempo again. Head down, Pantani at no stage looked back. As he had done all afternoon he judged Tonkov's response from observing the Russian's shadow on the road. For 50m or so Tonkov held firm; still he didn't yield, the shadow could still be seen at the same angle. And then, finally, the elastic snapped. One minute Tonkov was there, the next he had gone. Tonkov had simply soaked up too much punishment on the way up and could take it no longer. In the final two kilometres Pantani, roared on by his fans, buried himself to finish 57 seconds ahead of Tonkov who was close to collapsing when he crossed the line. It had been a career-defining ride by Pantani, but was it enough? He now led Tonkov by 1 minute 28 seconds, which was just about the exact time the pundits and, indeed, his team thought he might concede to Tonkov if the Russian rode to his known time-trialling form over 34km. On paper there was now every possibility of the 1998 Giro being the closest in history.

What happened at that final, decisive, time trial is that Pantani, to widespread incredulity, defeated Tonkov by 5 seconds to finish third on the stage behind Serhiy Honchar and that Giro-winning performance can be viewed from various angles. Perhaps Tonkov, having given his all in the preceding days in the mountains, had emptied the tanks and given a below-par performance in his time trial. A possibility without question. Or perhaps Pantani – a better TT rider than was normal for 'pure' climbers – was inspired by the jersey, the crowd and the prospect of winning his home Tour. Another possibility that cannot be dismissed. Or was it down to doping? On the morning of the time trial his room-mate and *gregario* for the last three weeks, Riccardo Forconi, was withdrawn from the race after a blood test revealed his haematocrit level had risen above 50 per cent. Why would a foot soldier be displaying such a suspiciously high level on a day when his performance in the time trial was of no relevance other than he needed to make the cut? That, of course, sparked renewed rumours of doping within the team generally or even the possible swapping of the samples by the two riders – which would have involved some form of complicity among officialdom. The Italian public, however, were not in the mood to doubt their new hero over this incident. There was no appetite to taint what appeared to be a glorious victory and the triumphant emergence of a rider who could potentially compare with the great Italian riders of yesteryear. Twelve months later, however, the events of that morning before the final time trial in 1998 resonated loudly when Pantani, seemingly cruising to the most commanding of wins, was kicked off the race for the same offence. In the meantime, however, he revelled in his popularity and celebrity, a situation which was only enhanced in July when he also won the Tour de France. For a while at least he was the most popular and recognisable sportsman in a sports-mad country.

13

PANTANI EXPULSION HERALDS DARK DAYS (1999–2007)

The 1999 Giro should have been a formality for Marco Pantani; he could have won it comfortably riding well within himself and saved his main efforts for the Tour and a rare double-double. Instead he seemed intent on embellishing his reputation with a series of stellar performances that were adored by the *tifosi* but rather alarmed officialdom generally and the UCI dope controllers in particular. They finally swooped on the morning of stage 21, which started in Madonna di Campiglio, and tested Pantani. His haematocrit level was recorded at 53 per cent, which led to his summary and controversial expulsion from the race, a decision that ultimately sounded the death knell for Pantani's career and sent him into a mental decline that, arguably, contributed to his death from an apparent cocaine overdose five years later. The circumstances of these blood tests and expulsion from the race have become a cause célèbre and possibly the most discussed and debated controversy in Giro history. And that debate seems as 'live' today as it ever was.

When Pantani woke up on the morning of that stage 21 there was no bigger sports star and celebrity in Italy. After the tough years of crashes and rehabilitation he was about to win his third Grand Tour on the bounce and financially the big time awaited. There was no hotter property but by lunchtime he was being bundled into the back of a car and driven off in disgrace. For a while the fans continued to believe and support him but the wider cycling world grew angry at being taken for fools. Up until stage 21 Pantani had been unstoppable as he reeled off four mountain stage wins of increasing brilliance – Gran Sasso d'Italia, Santuario di Oropa, Alpe di Pampeago and Madonna di Campiglio – which more than compensated for the time he lost to Laurent Jalabert and Serhiy Honchar in the two time trials. After crossing the line alone at Madonna di Campiglio he was over 5 and a half minutes up on second-place Paolo Savoldelli with just two stages left. Stage 21 was admittedly the Tappone but climbs such as the Gavia, Passo del Mortirolo and Valico di Santa Cristina would surely only underline his superiority and see his lead grow to even bigger, more legendary proportions.

The atmosphere was, however, a little tense after that stage win at Madonna di Campiglio and Pantani was the target, now open to both scepticism and criticism. The scepticism was beginning to mount because his day-on-day brilliance and effortless powers of recovery were testing the limits of credibility. The direct criticism, meanwhile, came from those who, although accepting his dominance, felt he and his team were stifling the race and that Pantani didn't have to contest every stage victory to comfortably take the title. In the 20 stages up to this point not one breakaway had prevailed, which was killing the Giro as a spectacle. Pantani was becoming like Eddy Merckx in his absolute need to win everything. Certainly at the press conference that evening after stage 20 he felt the need to defend himself a little: 'I hadn't planned to attack today but Simoni had a go and then Jalabert and I ended up on Jaja's wheel. I am not a rider who should be on Jalabert's wheel in the mountains so I left. And when I was on my own I felt even better, I was in a state of grace. We didn't light the fuse. It would have suited me to let the breakaway go. The others brought it back. When Simoni and Jalabert attacked it seemed right to take up the challenge.'

Pantani headed for his team hotel – the Hotel Touring in Madonna di Campiglio – while across the road the UCI medical team checked into the Hotel Majestic. Just about everybody saw them and as a result Mercatone Uno and the other teams staying at the Hotel Touring will have known what was coming their way the following morning. Later that evening Pantani, apparently unconcerned, was seen in the restaurant dining with *Gazzetta* sports editor Claudio Cannano. Or, rather, Cannano was dining, Pantani was contenting himself with a meagre rice dish. That evening he had already, it later emerged, tested his haematocrit levels with a simple centrifuge testing device which recorded a permissible level of 48.6 per cent. It was nonetheless a pretty high figure for the third week of a Grand Tour, when the level should have been plummeting, and some might well wonder why a 'clean' rider would ever own a centrifuge with which to conduct his own daily tests in the first place. Pantani's own figure, it should be noted, was also higher than the one previous official spot test he had undergone during the Giro, on the morning of stage 12 well over a week earlier when he recorded 47.4 per cent.

The following morning Pantani was called to give a sample at the comparatively late time of 7.25 with the rider required to appear under UCI protocol ten minutes later. In the event he wasn't tested until 7.46 a.m. Pantani was tested with three UCI doctors present and the samples immediately taken to a room at the Majestic, along with the others, to be evaluated. Unlike tests for a specific doping agent – the presence of a banned substance in the blood – haematocrit testing takes a matter of minutes. By 9 a.m. the press had somehow been tipped off regarding a Pantani positive and were converging on the Hotel Touring although for a few minutes the man himself was unaware. That soon changed and when informed an enraged Pantani punched his bedroom window in fury and cut his hand. The police were called and he and his team immediately lodged a complaint of fraud which required police action. Meanwhile, at 10.12 a.m. the result of Pantani's test – 53 per cent – was officially released and he was withdrawn from the race. As an exercise in clutching defeat from the jaws of victory it could scarcely be bettered.

Just after 1 p.m. Pantani, apparently close to a state of collapse and, guarded by uniformed police officers, stopped briefly on the steps of his hotel to address the media:

I have already been controlled twice [presumably he was also referring to the pre-race test as well]. I already had the pink jersey. I had a haematocrit level of 46 per cent [it was in fact 47.4 per cent]. And today I wake up with a surprise. I believe there is definitely something strange here. And I have to say that starting again this time ... I've started again after serious accidents but morally this time we have reached rock bottom.

With that Pantani was bundled into a car and driven away from the Giro at high speed. Still fuming, they stopped at the Santa Maria della Scaletta Hospital in Imola and requested a blood test. The hospital obliged and issued a certificate confirming that their tests showed Pantani's level at between 47 and 48 per cent. At roughly the same time Pantani's samples collected at Madonna di Campiglio were being retested in a laboratory in Como, along with the other samples collected from other riders. A result of 53 per cent for Pantani was confirmed. Those samples were then seized by the police to be examined independently by Professor Vittorio Rizzoli, Director of Hematology at the University of Parma. Again 53 per cent was the level recorded. At a later date, when this was challenged, DNA from Pantani was used to confirm that the samples being examined were unquestionably his.

The Pantani expulsion was a huge story and soon all sorts of other information came to light such as his sky-high haematocrit levels when involved in the Milano–Torino crash in 1994. Further massively strong circumstantial evidence of long-term EPO use came when *La Stampa* obtained confidential details of hundreds of blood tests for a dozen or so top Italian riders in the mid-nineties, including Pantani. These demonstrated highly suspicious readings. In 1994, when he finished second in the Giro, he had recorded a level of 40.7 per cent on 16 March but on 23 May – midway through the Giro – it had risen to 54.5 per cent. The awful reality began to dawn on Italian fans and others that Pantani had been systematically cheating – doping – from early in his career. Still he raged although perhaps that anger was at being caught rather than the implications per se. While he was under a dark cloud others – much lesser riders who were very possibly doping themselves – rode on. Such thoughts were enough to spark an alarming mental decline in Pantani and he was later diagnosed as being bipolar, with all this being further aggravated by his copious use of recreational drugs, notably cocaine. In the ensuing years there were very occasional moments of lucidity and hints at a comeback but generally it was very much a downhill trend.

It is nonetheless a controversy that refuses to go away and further fuel was thrown on the fire in March 2016 when Italian police in Forlì, having interviewed members of the Mafia, confirmed in a 30-page report that they believed a branch of the Camorra Mafia in Naples had been actively involved in plotting Pantani's disqualification in 1999 in order to avoid paying out on massive illegal wagers on Pantani's victory. According to those police reports, the Mafia was suspected of bribing unnamed members of the medical staff that carried out the tests on behalf of the UCI in Madonna di Campiglio. It was suspected, so the report alleges, that they used a technique of deplasmation to raise Pantani's haematocrit above the 50 per cent limit. The doctors concerned have always denied any wrongdoing and the Italian police confirmed that, because of the statute of limitations, they will not be pursuing the case further. This latest train of inquiry came to an end in July 2016 when the case was formally closed and archived by High Court judge Monica Galass who concluded that the evidence obtained was not capable of identifying perpetrators of any alleged offences – conspiracy, sports-fixing, threats and extortion.

What we do know for certain now, after the French Senate investigation of old blood samples in 2013, is that Pantani was using EPO at the 1998 Tour de France, and we also have the compelling evidence of his sky-high haematocrit level at various other stages of his career.

Meanwhile, at the 1999 Giro, on stage 21 Ivan Gotti worked himself into a powerful three-man break with Roberto Heras and Gilberto Simoni to comfortably take the GC from Paolo Savoldelli, with Simoni in third place.

The 2000 Giro began inauspiciously when Evgeni Berzin, the 1994 winner, was withdrawn from the race on the eve of the start because his haematocrit level was above 50 per cent. Berzin was by now a busted flush anyway; he had finished 52nd the previous year, and he immediately parted company with his team Mobilvetta Design-Formaggi Trentini. An inglorious end to what had once been a significant career. Pantani, meanwhile, at least made it to the start line after a difficult winter which included more cocaine binges, interspersed with more cogent periods when he trained hard in the winter sun on Tenerife and hinted briefly at past glories. But he was in no condition to lead the Mercatone Uno team and was instead going to ride as a *gregario di lusso* for Stefano Garzelli, a versatile rider who was useful on all terrain and a good enough climber to win the 1998 Tour of Switzerland. He was no Pantani – although there was a striking similarity in looks – but as it turned out he was good enough to win the race.

Cristian Moreni, later to write his own footnote in the sport's doping history when he tested positive in the 2007 Tour de France for testosterone, featured prominently in the early stages of this Giro before the race settled down and Francesco Casagrande took ownership of the pink jersey. Casagrande, a consistent one-day and Grand Tour performer, led the UCI world rankings that year and was considered the favourite by many but he came with baggage, having been banned for nine months in 1998 for testing positive for testosterone at the Tour of

Romandie. Garzelli clung on to the jersey until stage 20 but came under increasing pressure and the cracks had started to appear on stage 19 between Saluzzo and Briançon in France when the peloton spent much of the day climbing at high altitude on the Colle dell'Angelo and the Col d'Izoard. Pantani, banishing his demons and demonstrating his class for one of the last occasions on a bike, played a fine hand on behalf of Garzelli by attacking hard on some sectors of the stage to unsettle Casagrande while dropping back on others to assist his 'leader' Garzelli, who maintained an even tempo during a gruelling day in an attempt to conserve energy for a formidable-looking 34km mountain time trial the following day.

The Mercatone tactics worked well with Pantani taking second in the stage and a fresh-looking Garzelli riding home alongside a visibly fatigued Casagrande 25 seconds later. The pay-off came the following day when Garzelli put more than 2 minutes into Casagrande in the time trial over the Col de Montgenèvre to move into a comfortable lead with just one stage left. The race was his but, as he posed for pictures with Pantani – who had finished 28th overall – the media dubbed him 'il *Piratina*', 'the Little Pirate'. The perceived hierarchy was still Pantani followed by the others. Neither the public nor the media had fully grasped the depths of Pantani's decline. Nor, indeed, had Garzelli who immediately took steps to find himself a new team believing there would be no chance to ride for GC at Mercatone and defend his title next year when Pantani was expected to be fully restored as team leader.

2001 and the San Remo drugs raids

By 2001 doping was clearly rife in the peloton and although a rudimentary test to identify EPO was introduced earlier in the year, the authorities still appeared to be fighting a losing battle as riders began regular micro dosing – rather than occasional big injections – to cheat the system. The cycling authorities, often much maligned but becoming proactive at this stage in the drugs war compared with some sports, were, however, on their case and were backed up in Italy at least by the government making doping a criminal offence. The 2001 Giro became a battleground remembered now for the mass raids in San Remo in the same way that the 1998 Tour de France is remembered for the 'Festina Affair' and the raids that followed. The evidence of widespread doping was overwhelming and, although it was still fiendishly difficult to bring matters to court and enforce a ban, there was at least a willingness to try. The race as such in 2001 featured a battle between the great new hope of Italian cycling – the apparently 'dope-free' Dario Frigo – and the increasingly wily old fox Gilberto Simoni. Frigo, a talented all-rounder and particularly strong in the time trials, had warmed up for the Giro with wins at Paris–Nice and Romandie and was seen as big contender, along with Simoni and Garzelli. As for Pantani, the *tifosi* and media alike waited with bated breath. The first thing was to get him to the start line in one piece and that at least was successfully accomplished. For the best part of two weeks Frigo generally held sway but he lost a little ground to Simoni on the first big mountain stage and then failed to capitalise fully on the long 55km TT centred on Lake Garda so that by the time they reached San Remo and stage 17 the writing was on the wall. Frigo might only have been 15 seconds behind in second place but with two demanding days in the mountains to come there was, barring accidents, no way he could realistically challenge Simoni. Indeed, he would do well to hang on to his podium place.

It was in San Remo that the 2001 Giro fell apart. The stage itself was uneventful in racing terms although it did spawn two positives for EPO in Pascal Hervé and Riccardo Forconi, the latter of course being Pantani's *gregario* and room-mate in 1998 when he had famously been pulled from the time trial for adverse haematocrit levels. It was later that evening in San Remo, though, that the Italian police went to work with a vengeance, with 200 officers descending on the team hotels and car parks in coordinated raids, sparking off a mass panic among the riders and team helpers as illegal substances were flushed down lavatories and thrown randomly out of windows.

Obtaining prosecutions was a difficult and long process. Banned substances were found in Frigo's room and he was immediately kicked out of the race but it was four years before he received a suspended six-month prison sentence and $14,500 fine. By that time he was also facing charges in France after a boot full of performance-enhancing products was found in his wife's car at the Tour de France. Giuseppe Di Grande and Alberto Elli also received six-month suspended sentences and $14,500 fines after the San Remo raids while Domenico Romano and Ermanno Brignoli each received shorter suspended sentences. Trainer Primo Pregnolato copped an eight-month suspended sentence and a $7,260 fine. US Postal rider Gianpaolo Mondini was subsequently sacked after growth hormones were found in his room. Former Giro champion Ivan Gotti received a suspended sentence and an undisclosed fine when doping products were found in the campervan driven by his father while initially Pantani, who decided to withdraw from the race after San Remo pleading a fever, was banned for six months after an insulin syringe was discovered in his room. This ban was later lifted on appeal. It was the tip of the iceberg and, frankly, a frightening snapshot of the doping subculture that existed in professional cycling and the Giro at the time.

Emergency meetings were held between defensive riders, team directors and organisers apparently shocked by the scale of the problem. At one stage it seemed the rest of the race would be cancelled but eventually a compromise was agreed whereby only the next stage was lost. 'The Giro has lost an arm and I have lost part of my heart,' declared race organiser Carmine Castellano but generally the sport went into denial. UCI President Hein Verbruggen, instead of supporting the Italian police, complained of their draconian attitudes while, with an election to win, Italian presidential candidate Silvio Berlusconi promised that when he was in power no such raids would be tolerated. Eventually the race limped shame-faced back into Milan and, with Frigo eliminated from the scene, Simoni promenaded home unopposed well over 7 minutes ahead of second-place Abraham Olano with Unai Osa completing the podium. It had been the roughest of rides and nobody was quite sure what would happen next. Cycling and the Giro were in a very dark place.

In fact, the Giro simply muddled on. It was too big a national institution to fold and historically the truth is that it has always enjoyed, and prospered from, a little infamy. Nor was it suffering in isolation; there was a growing realisation of just how prevalent the problem was generally in cycling and soon a long list of doping scandals at the Tour de France was, to a certain extent, to divert the attention away from the Giro's problems in that respect.

It was still going on, though, no question of that, and although the 2002 Giro in fact offered up a compelling race on face value the heavy doping undertones continued. Nicola Chesini left the race abruptly after stage five when police found performance-enhancing drugs in his hotel room, while Roberto Sgambelluri and Faat Zakirov became the first professional cyclists to test positive for NESP, a refined and stronger version of EPO. Bigger-name riders also found themselves in trouble. Stefano Garzelli, the Giro winner just two years earlier, tested positive for the banned diuretic and masking agent probenecid and was kicked off the race. He protested his innocence long and hard, claiming a spiked drink, but was sent home and later received a nine-month ban. Meanwhile, before the start of stage ten it came to light that the previous year's winner, Simoni, had tested positive for cocaine in an out-of-competition test shortly before the start of the race. Simoni claimed it might have been related to a visit to the dentists and tried to brazen things out; indeed, he won the hilltop finish at Campitello Matese on stage 11 but the arrival of police officers at the team hotel that evening wanting to know more about the circumstances of his cocaine positive persuaded Simoni that he should withdraw from the race. The list of recent Giro winners, Pantani, Gotti, Garzelli and Simoni, was beginning to look a little tarnished to say the least.

Depressingly, doping was becoming the story, the constant narrative. It was a modern and extremely ruthless way of cheating but those tempted to look back at the 'good old days' should reflect that doping, in effect, was the logical conclusion of the 'whatever it takes' attitude that has always existed in cycling and especially the Giro and Tour de France. Skulduggery on the road has always existed in the Giro, the blatant taking of tows, organised teams of supporters pushing riders up mountains, while officialdom has sometimes moved in mysterious and inexplicable ways to favour some riders and not others, cancel some stages and not others. The Giro has always been a brutal, ruthless environment and doping was the unsurprising, some would say inevitable, result of those attitudes. No wonder some modern-day riders struggled to marry the reverence shown to, say, Coppi and Anquetil, who both admitted to doping during their careers albeit in a less sophisticated form, to this sudden clampdown on their own doping activities. Senior *directeurs sportifs*, once given to regaling their troops with stories of the old days, were now having to sack riders for similar misdemeanours. It was the new reality and cycling was struggling dreadfully to adapt, a process that in many ways is still continuing although there have been encouraging signs in recent years.

In the 2002 race itself Garzelli had looked the most likely rider from the off but after his unscheduled departure the *maglia rosa* reverted to the East German-born rider Jens Heppner, not a big name then or now although he has achieved a certain infamy in recent years as one of the names released by the French Senate in 2013 as being positive for EPO at the 1998 Tour de France. Heppner enjoyed his 11 days in pink but was immediately found out when the Giro hit the Dolomites, where a young Australian, former world mountain-bike champion Cadel Evans, rode strongly to briefly claim the race leadership. The following day was another mountainfest with five categorised climbs and Evans suffered a dramatic collapse, which opened the door for Paolo Savoldelli, a very fine climber and notably the best descender of his generation, so much so that he earned the self-explanatory nickname '*il Falco*'. Savoldelli had served notice of his Grand Tour potential with a second place overall in 1999 but since then had been troubled with a back injury and was rarely seen at his best. Hard on the heels of Savoldelli was Tyler Hamilton who was set to become one of the most notorious dopers of his generation with no fewer than three competition positives and bans. On this occasion Hamilton overcame a number of crashes to show remarkable endurance and finish a strong second place overall behind Savoldelli with Pietro Caucchioli in third place.

Pantani's last stand

Outwardly the 2003 Giro was quieter on the doping front with the only scandal being the retrospective disqualification of Lithuanian Raimondas Rumšas who had finished sixth overall, when a test midway through the race eventually came back positive for EPO. For this race Marco Pantani was again the centre of the pre-race hype with the irony of him somehow being seen as the poster boy and saviour of a badly damaged event somehow escaping those most closely involved. The Giro was undoubtedly in trouble. For the second year in succession Spanish TV had declined to cover it and, with no domestic TV back home to advertise their sponsors' interests, the Spanish teams had no compunction about boycotting the race. Pantani, ahead of the race, at least looked in reasonable physical condition which probably encouraged unrealistic expectations. In the absence of Savoldelli and Evans, who had both opted to concentrate on the Tour, the favourite was clearly Gilberto Simoni who had eventually been cleared of his cocaine charge. Apparently the cocaine had somehow been contained in boiled sweets a friend had brought back from Peru.

Initially the new big-name sprinter on the block, Alessandro Petacchi, enjoyed the best part of a week in the pink and indeed the quick men monopolised the headlines for a while with Mario Cipollini nipping in for the two stage wins he needed to surpass Alfredo Binda's all-time record. He broke the record on stage nine from Arezzo to Montecatini amidst much celebration. Cippo raced one more Giro in 2004, the only time he didn't win a stage, and after announcing his retirement in April 2005 was allowed to ride a ceremonial Prologue at the 2005 Giro when he wore a fluorescent skinsuit which listed his 42 stage wins.

After the sprinters had briefly commanded centre stage, the GC race took over in 2003 with Garzelli relieving Petacchi of the pink jersey before Simoni took a firm grip on the leadership and race on stage 12 when the Giro featured the Zoncolan climb, with its 20 per cent sections, for the first time. The steeper it became the more confident and dominant Simoni appeared, but for much of a spectacular day the crowd were treated to one last glimpse of the genuine genius of Pantani as he attacked and counter-attacked in trademark fashion. Only right at the end did his lack of true racing form and condition kick in as he faded a little but fifth place still represented a very decent effort on such a crucial stage. Never again was Pantani to be seen at the sharp end of a bike race. It was a poignant moment. Simoni continued on his way and really rubbed salt into Garzelli's wounds by beating him in the stage 15 time trial which really should have suited the latter. Simoni was on his way and he signed off with his third and final stage win of that year's Giro with an imperious flourish in the mountains on stage 18, the Tappone, which was an old-fashioned snowy epic with the Esichie and Fauniera in almost wintry condition. Simoni made the stage so hard and fast that 35 riders missed the cut, which on this occasion officialdom chose to implement.

After the race much of the debate still centred on Pantani. He had finished 14th and enjoyed that one very fine day in the mountains.

Perhaps it *wasn't* all over for him? Perhaps the magic *could* be rekindled and he could secure a guest ride for a team in the Tour de France? Still people were not seeing the reality of the situation. While talk of a Tour de France ride continued in June, Pantani was forced to book himself into a rehabilitation clinic in an attempt to cure his now chronic cocaine addiction. It was over for him; he was spiralling out of control. There was never and could never be another ride at the Tour. Later that year he spent a good while in Cuba where his 'friend' Diego Maradona had gone to be cured of drug-related health problems, but with no structure to his life, no training or racing, Pantani was dangerously adrift. For a while he was off the radar but somehow, although shocking, it was no surprise when on 14 February 2004 came reports that he had been found dead in a hotel room in Rimini, the victim of an apparent cocaine overdose. He was 34.

Italian cycling was still reeling three months later when the 2004 Giro got underway on 8 May. Happy chance provided two storylines to divert and entertain the cycling public. The first was the classic new young star on the block rising to the occasion to usurp his team leader and win the race – this time Damiano Cunego, from Verona, who was inevitably quickly dubbed '*il Piccolo Principe*', 'the Little Prince'. Cunego started the race very much as Saeco's Plan B to Gilberto Simoni but that is not how he viewed the situation and he was to be proved right. Secondly, a muscular, snarling sprinter punching great holes in the peloton in the sprint finishes is always good value and for a few years around this time Alessandro Petacchi was the sprint king, and at the 2004 Giro he won no fewer than nine stages, bringing to mind some of the stage-winning orgies of earlier years and quickly making up for the absence of the newly retired Mario Cipollini.

Cunego was an exciting prospect, a climber who could time-trial adequately and didn't mind the rough and tumble of the one-day Classics and Monuments. A junior world champion at just turned 18 in 1999 he was well established with Saeco who he joined in 2002. Going into the 2004 Giro, aged 23, he had won the traditional warm-up, the Giro del Trentino, and was undeniably in good form but there was nothing to really suggest he would pose a threat to Simoni. Indeed, the name Cunego scarcely warranted a mention in the previews but despite that the race very quickly developed into a two-way tussle between the erstwhile colleagues. Simoni enjoyed four days in pink but Cunego was still riding brilliantly and, save for a brief intervention from Yaroslav Popovych, took over the *maglia rosa* again up to stage 18 which included the Gavia and a summit finish at the ski station Bormio 2000. Stage 18 always felt like it would be the crucial stage and it was where Simoni would certainly have been expected to put his upstart young colleague in his place. This was prime Simoni territory and Cunego, well into the third week of a Grand Tour for the first time in his career, would surely begin to falter.

The stage was ignited by an attack on the snowy Gavia by Garzelli, who was riding strongly, but the elite bunch, led by Saeco, eventually caught him at the foot of the Bormio 2000 climb at which point Simoni launched his attack, the move that everybody expected would decide the race. Simoni, though, wasn't climbing with the fluency of old; in fact he was labouring by his standards and couldn't shake off an elite group of Serhiy Honchar, Emanuele Sella, Dario Cioni, Julio Alberto Pérez Cuapio and Cunego who, lest we forget, had been back in pink for two days and started the day fully 2 minutes 38 seconds ahead of Simoni but only 1.14 ahead of Honchar.

A rare sprint finish on a mountain stage loomed and Cunego was always the best equipped to win that. The two Saeco riders were at odds and/or simply not communicating. Simoni's assault on the pink jersey had come to nothing but he was in denial; he still believed he was the main man and his team's best bet. That moment had long gone but still he seemed to be looking for a long lead-out and stage win which additionally would earn him a 20-second time bonus. With one more mountain stage to come that would at least vaguely keep Simoni in the game. In his mind, anyway. Meanwhile, the cards had fallen perfectly for Cunego. Simoni's big push had been a tame affair; he just didn't look to have the legs, and as the leader of the Giro Cunego now had absolute licence to press on and close out the race. Technically you could argue that he started to lead out Simoni but he deceived nobody. Very quickly Cunego produced a savage acceleration and the reigning champion just couldn't get in his wheel as the young tyro pulled away to beat Cioni and Honchar by 5 seconds with Simoni a further 4 seconds back. Cunego was quickly surrounded at the finish line by journalists who reported that as Simoni passed the huddle he pointed at Cunego and shouted, 'You are a bastard ... you are really stupid.'

There was clearly no love lost and the following day Simoni joined forces with Garzelli to attack his 'team-mate' and race leader on the Mortirolo, with Slovenian Tadej Valjavec adding firepower to the breakaway. Cunego was potentially exposed and vulnerable but, paced by the Saeco *gregario di lusso* Eddy Mazzoleni, he pegged the breakaway at about 1 minute and in fact when Garzelli led the breakaway over the line Cunego was only 52 seconds back. He had defended his lead well and, with just the sprint stage into Milan remaining, was now unassailable. Italy had its new cycling hero although it is interesting to reflect on the generous reception 'the Little Prince' received after staging a coup within his team compared to that afforded to Stephen Roche.

For a long time the perceived wisdom concerning Cunego was that he burned himself out in 2004, when he raced and won all around the world, and his comparatively disappointing subsequent results represent a classic case of too much too young. His was seen as a potentially great career that never quite took off. That seems a harsh assessment. Many professionals would give their eye teeth for the three Monuments victories in the Giro di Lombardia, an Amstel Gold victory and the silver medal in the 2008 World Championships he recorded after his victory in the Giro. But what puts Cunego's achievements in a different light is the findings of an Italian court after a hearing in 2013 and early

2014 into alleged doping activities of the Lampre–Merida team which superseded the old Saeco squad. Not only was there not a shred of evidence against Cunego, there were in fact written notes in team records that Cunego repeatedly refused to have anything to do with the Spanish doctor, José Ibarguren Taus, who was allegedly at the hub of the doping activities. Not many riders from this era have had their results, performances and racing integrity validated in this way and his struggles against some riders we now know to have been doped up to the eyeballs should perhaps be considered more sympathetically in this light.

Doping or no doping, the 2005 Giro d'Italia was a furiously ridden race and compelling spectacle with the resilient and independently minded Paolo Savoldelli again proving that you don't always need a powerful team to emerge victorious. Savoldelli had demonstrated his ability to look after himself previously. In the controversial 1999 Giro he had eventually finished second despite riding for a Saeco team built largely to accommodate the needs of their sprinter and perennial stage-winner Mario Cipollini, while in 2002 he won the Giro even though his Index–Alexia team also tried to promote the needs of sprinter Ivan Quaranta. Come 2005 and Savoldelli was back at the Giro with the Discovery Channel team but the American-based squad was very much targeting Lance Armstrong's attempt at a seventh straight Tour de France and keeping their big guns back for July in France. When it came to the big mountain days Savoldelli was going be playing a lone hand.

The 2005 Giro was also nothing if not cosmopolitan with the 20 teams of the newly created Pro-Tour all entered which resulted in 140 non-Italian riders going to the start. Simoni and Cunego were still riding for the same team although it had now been rebranded Lampre–Caffita. Both also appeared to be in outstanding form so the potential for internal argument and strife was high again and provided an interesting dynamic. The young Ivan Basso was another rider to be reckoned with, along with another highly rated young Italian, Danilo Di Luca.

Initially there was something for everybody in a varied course and the leadership swapped hands regularly with five riders disputing the pink jersey in the first ten days, with one-day specialist Paolo Bettini winning or regaining the jersey on no fewer than three occasions. The big GC shakeout, however, came on the mountainous stage 11 from Marostica to Zoldo Alto when stage winner Savoldelli looked superb, closely followed by Basso who was projected into pink. Cunego suffered a collapse in form and finished over 7 minutes adrift alongside Garzelli who was still feeling the effects of a heavy crash on stage seven. With Cunego no longer a contender, at least Simoni now had complete authority within his team again and the stage was now set for a fascinating second half of the race. Savoldelli took over the leadership on stage 13, which was possibly a mixed blessing given the absence of a team really capable of defending the jersey, but he really had little choice. Riding in an elite group behind the break on a testing day that included five major climbs, it was clear that Basso was struggling with a stomach ailment and kept dropping off the back even though the other riders weren't pressing overly hard. Basso eventually finished 1 minute behind and Savoldelli found himself in pink. The following day on the Stelvio the ailing Basso fell out of GC contention altogether when he lost 40 minutes but, although the threat from that quarter had now disappeared, Savoldelli now had to contend with a Simoni who was getting stronger and more bullish by the day, a lively Di Luca and a relatively unknown Venezuelan, José Rujano, who tipped the scales at just over nine stone and was, predictably, an outstanding climber.

Savoldelli rode with much panache and cunning to resist all comers and was helped in that by Basso. Basso was now riding for stage wins, which enabled Savoldelli to concentrate on defending his lead within the lead group and, with his peerless descending to call upon, he could generally make up any time lost when distanced on a climb. He arrived at the penultimate stage with a 2 minutes 9 seconds lead over Simoni and exactly 3 minutes over Rujano but was far from safe. The new race director Angelo Zomegnan, in only his second race in charge and keen to make an impression, had come up with something very different as a finale with a final stage that included the first-ever appearance of the Colle delle Finestre climb, a 19km brute rising to 2,178m with an average gradient of well over 9 per cent. Additionally, the last eight kilometres, the steepest part of the climb with sections well over 15 per cent, was an unpaved white track, what the Italians called *strade bianche*. Zomegnan had listed the climb as *categoria speciale*. Bookending the stage were two separate ascents into Sestriere and coming so close to the finish of the race there was the potential for all sorts of drama.

Savoldelli had to have his wits about him and he stayed calm riding his own tempo when Simoni, Di Luca and Rujano, a trio with enormous firepower, predictably attacked hard up the Finestre. The temptation was to go with his closest rivals but that's exactly what they wanted. In a group of four they would have systematically worked him over and Savoldelli could well have cracked altogether on such a climb. Instead, head down, he kept tapping out his own rhythm. Over the top of the Finestre and the lead trio were well out of sight but Savoldelli produced one of the great descents in Giro history to peg that lead back to just over 2 minutes and then, on the final climb into Sestriere, the pacesetters started to pay for their day-long efforts. Simoni and Di Luca both began to slow as they cramped which allowed Rujano to slip away for the stage win. Simoni rallied a little, Di Luca hit the wall again and at the summit Savoldelli, seeming to grimace and smile at the same time, eventually crossed the line just 1 minute 29 seconds behind Simoni. A second Giro title was his.

If 2005 was a great race and spectacle with few caveats – there were actually no positive tests connected with the race although nobody doubted that doping was still occurring – the following year witnessed an astonishing climbing masterclass from Basso who had shown 12 months earlier what a force he was in the mountains. This time Basso, riding for the CSC squad, took a firm grip on stage eight, one of three mountain stages he won, as he routed the field and took the GC by over 9 minutes. He was imperious and, of course, given the climate of the time, there were those who were deeply suspicious. After the Giro Basso was strongly fancied to complete the Giro/Tour double but was one of those riders who withdrew on the eve of the Tour de France when their possible involvement in a blood-doping ring revolving around Dr Fuentes was revealed as details of the Spanish police Operación Puerto emerged. Basso denied all knowledge until May 2007, when he admitted to having been a client of Fuentes since 2004. Basso insisted that, despite being aware of Fuentes' blood-doping operation, he had not himself been involved and that he rode and won the 2006 Giro riding clean. His victory remains in the record books but later that year he was handed a two-year ban from the sport.

What with the reigning champion Basso prevented from racing, the doping debate very much dominated the 2007 race. Sprinter Alessandro Petacchi retrospectively had all five of his stage wins scrubbed from the record books and was banned for a year after testing positive for sabultamol. Italian climber Leonardo Piepoli also tested positive for salbutamol – in fact he produced a higher reading than Petacchi, but was cleared, although within two years he left the sport having acknowledged his use of PEDs at the 2008 Tour de France. The race winner Danilo Di Luca also aroused suspicion when a random test on the evening of his race-clinching stage win on Monte Zoncolan recorded irregular hormone levels compared with his mandatory blood test some hours earlier at the race finish. The results were highly suggestive of a blood transfusion but on this occasion a CONI commission concluded there was insufficient evidence to ban Di Luca.

14

STILL CRAZY AFTER ALL THESE YEARS. THE MODERN-DAY GIRO (2008–15)

Over the years, with the notable exception of the remarkable Miguel Indurain, the Giro d'Italia had been comparatively barren ground for Spanish riders. For decades the Vuelta's early season slot in the calendar, when Spanish riders were expected to compete flat out for their Spanish teams in their showpiece domestic race, militated against repeating such an effort often less than a week later, when the Giro started. The best of the Spanish riders usually preferred to rest up and then prepare for the Tour de France. It also has to be said that although Spain has always been blessed with talented climbers not all of them prospered in the often wintry conditions that frequently existed in the Dolomites and Alps in May and early June. Additionally, the Spanish media often tended to be lukewarm about the Giro and the expense of covering the event in addition to their own national Tour and the Tour de France. There were years when Spanish TV flatly refused to pay the Giro organisers' asking price for 'live' coverage and without that incentive for their sponsors Spanish teams simply didn't compete.

By 2008, however, the landscape was changing. After the retirement in 2005 of Lance Armstrong whose final *mea culpa* admission to systematic doping was still some way down the track, there was a vacuum to be filled. The sport lacked an obvious star rider and figurehead but after his victory in the 2007 Tour de France there was every reason to suspect that a slim but resourceful Spaniard, Alberto Contador, a climber of extraordinary fluidity and endurance, might be that man. Being the naughty noughties he also came with a little baggage. Contador was one of a number of ONCE-Eroski riders who had been withdrawn from the 2006 Tour de France on the eve of the race after possible links with the Operación Puerto investigation in Spain. Contador has always denied any links with Fuentes and investigations by the UCI and the Spanish Federation found no case to answer.

Despite being cleared by the UCI over the alleged Puerto links, Contador still seemed unlikely to race in the 2008 Giro with the organisers initially wanting to show their displeasure at the tainted Astana squad, who Contador had signed for at the end of 2007, by denying them an entry. Similarly ASO had made it clear that Astana would not be allowed to race at the 2008 Tour de France. As the start of the Giro in Sicily approached, however, the Italians wavered. Astana let it be known that, denied of the opportunity to race at the Tour de France, they would be fully committed to competing with their strongest available squad at the Giro if invited and that would include the reigning Tour de France champion Alberto Contador. It was a mighty draw and the Giro, mindful of the huge hike in media interest Contador would spark, ruthlessly 'uninvited' the wild-card entry, the NCS Medical team, in order to allow Astana to take their place at the start line. All is fair in love and war ... and bike races. So late was the call-up that Contador was enjoying a brief holiday sunning himself on a Spanish beach when he received the call but he was in good shape nonetheless. Early wins at the País Vasco and Castilla y León had seen him start the season with a bang.

Contador checked out of his beachside hotel and caught the first plane to Sicily where the start was being staged in Palermo. Under-standably he eased his way into the race a little, a process aided by an unlikely break on stage six which established Giovanni Visconti and his Quickstep team in pink for over a week. Visconti was a rider who was never going to win the Giro but somebody who would defend the jersey proudly which allowed the GC contenders a little longer to manoeuvre quietly under the radar before launching their challenges. Contador demonstrated his building form, however, when he finished second in a testing mountainous time trial on stage ten which moved him to fourth overall but ahead of all his main GC rivals. Not that Contador wasn't tested; he undoubtedly was, with a number of riders, not least Emanuele Sella, producing all sorts of pyrotechnics in the mountains. Sella took no fewer than three stage wins climbing at a scarcely believable pace. Contador, however, contented himself with defending the jersey at all times, riding consistently well, and although he didn't claim a stage win in 2008 he duly became only the second Spaniard to win the Giro.

Later that summer Sella was subjected to an out-of-competition doping control and tested positive for CERA, one of the latest EPO products for which a test had not existed a couple of months earlier in the Giro. Eventually he admitted the offence to CONI and, banned for a year, named his team-mate Matteo Priamo, the winner of stage six at the Giro, as the supplier of the drug. Priamo was subsequently banned for four years and never raced again. Strangely their stage wins and Sella's sixth place overall have not been scrubbed from the official Giro records. Meanwhile, Riccardo Ricci, who had produced a number of spectacular but suspicious rides during the Giro en route to second place behind Contador, tested positive for CERA at the Tour de France a couple of months later, after winning two stages, and was kicked out of the race and sacked by his team, Saunier Duval–Prodir. Suspicion immediately turned on his performances in the Giro. The UCI, using the updated tests, eventually revisited 82 samples from selected riders in the 2008 Giro and found six of the samples to be what they called 'presumptive positives'. The governing body, however, has declined to name who those riders were. Ricci's runner-up spot in 2008 stands but, after another drugs offence in 2011, when he fell seriously ill after an illegal blood transfusion, he was banned for 12 years.

The stench of drugs and doping still attached itself to the Giro with old habits dying hard and the 2009 podium was more tainted than most, but the organisers tried to put their best foot forward for what they termed the race's centenary although that only referred to the 100 years of its existence, not the actual editions of the race. The re-emergence, out of retirement, of Lance Armstrong also added superficial gloss and notoriety to the event although nobody expected him to seriously contest the honours, firstly on account of his four-year retirement and also an early season crash and broken collarbone had put him weeks, if not months, back in his preparations. Armstrong eventually finished 12th overall although that result was ultimately scrubbed from the records, along with all his other performances, by the UCI after his later admission of wholescale doping. Armstrong maintains to this day that he didn't dope in the 2009 Giro.

A team time trial up and down the Lido on the Venetian lagoon was as spectacular and photogenic as it gets for the start in 2009 and offered that rarity in Giro history, a British *maglia rosa* with sprinter Mark Cavendish leading his impressive HTC–Highroad team to a notable victory. Although losing the jersey to Alessandro Petacchi the following day, Cavendish went on to claim three individual stage wins to underline his growing reputation as the fastest sprinter in the peloton. Danilo Di Luca took over the jersey from the sprinters and opportunists on stage five before ceding it to Denis Menchov after a week and it was his daily fight with Menchov that provided the central theme to what was an enthralling race, one of the most absorbing in recent history. Menchov eventually won by 41 seconds, surviving a late scare in wet conditions on the final-day time trial when he slid off at a corner. It could all have come to grief there and then but luckily he avoided hitting the barriers or any spectators and was able to remount and continue on his way.

Absorbing as the contest was, it seems that seeing wasn't necessarily believing when it came to Di Luca. On 22 July it was announced that he had given not one but two positive tests during the race, firstly at the

Cinque Terre time trial and then on the Mount Vesuvius stage during the final week. A long legal battle ensued but he received a two-year suspension for his trouble and his results were struck from the record books. Third-placed Franco Pellizotti also retrospectively found himself in hot water when, nearly a year later and on the eve of the 2010 Giro, *Gazzetta* reported suspicious readings on his biological passport dating back to the previous season. He was eventually found guilty of doping in an appeal heard by CAS and received a two-year ban, backdated to 17 May 2009, which meant his results at the 2009 Giro and the Tour de France were rescinded. In a similar retrospective blood-passport offence Tadej Valjavec, riding for Ag2r, had his ninth place set aside. It was a sorry tale.

In 2010, with Di Luca and Pellizotti prevented from riding and Menchov concentrating on the Tour de France, not one of the previous year's top three was back to contest the Giro which started with three stages in the Netherlands. One rider who was back, however, was Ivan Basso, the winner in 2006 who had now served his Operación Puerto-related ban and was looking for redemption in a race he had once seemed set to dominate. Another interesting returner was Bradley Wiggins, a star of various Olympic and World track cycling championships, who had set out the previous year to see if he could reinvent himself as a Grand Tour rider having previously ridden on the road mainly as a *gregario* and specialist Prologue and time-trial competitor. Indeed, in many ways the 2009 Giro had been his Damascene moment when, having lost a stone in weight during the winter, he found himself riding comfortably with the lead group every day for Team Garmin, having been a fully paid-up member of the *gruppetto* 12 months earlier. After a fortnight he and his Garmin team took the conscious decision to conserve energy for the Tour de France, which was suddenly becoming a viable option, while there was also a final-day time trial at the end of the Giro that he had his eyes on. As it happened, encountering the worst of the conditions on a wet and blustery afternoon, he finished in second place in the time-trial, 1 second behind Ignatas Konovalovas. The following month Wiggins contested the Tour de France and finished fourth in GC, later upgraded to third. In 2010 he returned to the Giro, this time as the team leader of the newly formed Team Sky and, although it started well with a fine win in the time trial and a much-coveted pink jersey, the race soon fell apart badly for Sky. On the crash-prone roads of Holland, Wiggins was unlucky to be delayed by a spill that cost him the *maglia rosa* and then, on stage three, a day of high winds and rain, he and half his Sky team crashed nastily on a fast corner and lost 4 minutes. His GC challenge was all but over before the race had even reached Italy.

It might not have been a classic in terms of quality, but the 2010 Giro was already proving quite eventful with frequent changes of leadership, and the next talking point was a brutally hard but wonderfully photogenic stage seven, which included lengthy stretches of *strade bianche*, when gravelly white roads predictably deteriorated into muddy tracks when the rains came. There were crashes from start to finish that day – Wiggins and Carlos Sastre were badly affected – and by the end it was mainly a battle for survival with Australian Cadel Evans, riding with BMC, prevailing ahead of Damiano Cunego and Alexander Vinokourov who went into pink. In many ways the day had been a throwback to the wildest days with just a hint of the Eroica era and although not amused at the finish many of the riders, after the luxury of a bath and massage later that night, admitted to enjoying the novelty of it all and the media was full of iconic images the following day. The race continued on its slightly bizarre way and on stage 11 came the very odd sight of the leaders – Vinokourov, Evans, Basso and his young but very promising Liquigas colleague Vincenzo Nibali – allowing a 54-man break to disappear into the distance after just 20km. It had been a full-on Giro with three rough days in the Netherlands, a transfer, the 'Eroica stage' and GC action everywhere you looked and there is no doubt that the leaders were tired. They badly wanted a straightforward, uncomplicated day so a game of bluff and counter-bluff ensued with nobody really wanting to take up the chase although the responsibility seemingly rested mainly with Vinokourov's Astana team and Liquigas–Doimo. The former, though, were beset by illness that day although trying very hard to disguise that fact lest those in the chasing group gang up and launch another attack.

Meanwhile, up front Sky, who had endured a disappointing Giro thus far in their debut season, and Sastre's Cervelo team, who were also chasing a positive result, piled on the pressure in unison with young Australian Richie Porte, who had started the day sixth in GC at 2.06, the main beneficiary. By the time the breakaway finished nearly 13 minutes ahead of the pink-jersey group Porte was the new leader. Vinokourov, the leader when Astana signed on that morning, was now 12th, nearly 10 minutes back with Evans, Nibali and Basso packed closely behind him. The Giro hadn't seen drama like this in a long while. The breakaway had put the hammer down to such an extent that 41 riders missed the cut-off time of 39 minutes, although on this occasion they were treated leniently. It was way too early in the race to lose so many riders.

Yet ultimately Basso still won the race. How was that? With some difficulty is the short answer but at least Liquigas Doimo – who bore much responsibility for the mess-up – had time and mountain stages to make amends. All was not quite lost. They had the best climber in Basso and the best descender in Nibali and they had to make every kilometre count. From stage 11 onwards they had to ride a perfect race. The fightback started on stage 14 when nobody could stay with stage-winner Nibali followed by Basso, the duo putting over 2 minutes into the rest of the field while Basso piled in again the next day on the Zoncolan, this time taking nearly 6 minutes out of Porte. By that evening Basso has climbed back up to third place in GC, behind Porte and David Arroyo, who had taken the pink jersey from Porte. It had taken two mighty efforts, he was back in the game, but still Basso had to stay patient. The course flattened out considerably over the next four days; he would possibly have to wait until the penultimate day which took in the Gavia en route to a hilltop finish at Ponte di Legno to finish the job. It was going to be close and for one horrible moment it looked like snowy conditions on the Gavia might see that part of the stage cancelled and the sting drawn from Basso's attack, but the organisers eventually decided the stage could proceed as originally planned. Basso did everything that was needed behind stage winner Johann Tschopp to finish third on the day and overhaul Arroyo. Going into the final-day time trial, which was to finish in the Roman amphitheatre in Verona, Basso led by 1 minute 15 seconds, which he improved upon by 26 seconds. It had been some comeback and in many ways Basso's career highlight.

Tragedy strikes the Giro again

The 2011 Giro will be remembered for the saddest of reasons as the Belgian rider Wouter Weylandt suffered a fatal accident on stage three descending the Passo del Bocco near the town of Mezzanego. Weylandt was a flinty Belgian sprinter who had been a professional for seven seasons, mainly with Quick-Step–Davitamon and, although his form could be patchy, he had won a stage at the Vuelta a España in 2008 and also a stage of the 2010 Giro. He and Quick-Step had parted ways at the end of that 2010 season but the ambitious new team Leopard Trek had snapped him up as a lead-out rider for their number-one sprinter Daniele Bennati.

As a climb the Passo del Bocco – a steady 15km ascent to 956m at an average of 5.6 per cent – barely warrants a mention in the Giro pantheon although it was the venue for an important hill climb TT in 1994 that was won by Evgeni Berzin en route to his overall victory. The road however is very narrow, the tarmac condition is variable and there is a canopy of trees over many passages of the road making visibility difficult as riders move in and out of sunlight. There are also long sections of stone walling right next to the road and coming so early in the race with the peloton compact, animated and nervous, it was definitely a descent that commanded respect. Weylandt's crash was still horribly random, though. According to a number of the riders closest to him in the peloton, Weylandt, like all the riders travelling at considerable pace, probably in excess of 60kmh, had just momentarily glanced backward to check his position when he clipped a low stone wall on the left of the road. That catapulted him right across the narrow road where he landed heavily and, it would seem, died on impact. Race doctor Giovanni Tredici was almost directly behind the crash in a race vehicle and attended within seconds but later confirmed the rider was dead although they tried to resuscitate him, in vain.

Cycling is a tough sport and there have been plenty of examples of bad behaviour from riders and teams over the decades not least at the Giro d'Italia but there was an instinctive dignity and gravitas about the way the peloton marked the death of one of their own the following day. The longish 216km run from Quarto dei Mille to Livorno was neutralised by the organisers before the start of the day and, after a minute's silence and at the prompting of the *maglia rosa* David Millar, each of the teams rode approximately ten kilometres at the front in team classification order before Weylandt's team Leopard Trek took over for the final stint, arriving ahead of the peloton at the finish along with Weylandt's best friend and training partner Tyler Farrar from the Garmin team. Both Leopard Trek and Farrar withdrew from the race soon after they crossed the line. All the riders wore black armbands, many of the churches in the small villages and towns the peloton passed through tolled in mourning and at the end of the race Weylandt's race number of 108 was retired from the Giro in perpetuity. No results or timings from the day counted towards any of the race's classifications and after the stage, instead of any podium presentations, the four jersey classification leaders – Millar, Alessandro Petacchi, Gianluca Brambilla and Jan Bakelants – appeared on stage with the Leopard Trek team to lead another moment of silence.

The 2011 Giro, although a severe test, was virtually a benefit for Alberto Contador who dominated proceedings from early on, taking the leader's jersey on stage nine to win by over 6 minutes from Michele Scarponi and Vincenzo Nibali. Contador was a class apart and seemingly won while barely breaking sweat but he was riding under a cloud. At the 2010 Tour de France, which he won, he had tested positive for a minute amount of the banned substance clenbuterol on the second rest day in Pau – he blamed contaminated meat bought by the team's chef over the border in Spain – and had been vigorously protesting his innocence through the courts. The Spanish Cycling Federation cleared Contador, which enabled him to ride in the Giro, but both WADA and the UCI appealed that decision and the wheels were set in motion for a final hearing at the Court of Arbitration in Sport (CAS). That was a long and involved process but finally, on 6 February 2012 CAS adjudicated that Contador had given a positive test at the 2010 Tour de France and that his win in that race should be annulled, along with his commanding 2011 Giro d'Italia win. Runner-up Michele Scarponi was declared the new 2011 Giro d'Italia champion.

The 2011 Giro was ill-starred in so many ways and it wasn't just Contador who suffered retrospectively in its wake. Angelo Zomegnan, who had been the Giro race director for seven years, endured considerable criticism before and during the race. Right from the launch of the course there were mutterings about it being too difficult for the modern era, a course that might tempt riders into using PEDs. There were 40 categorised climbs, 409km of categorised climbing and seven summit finishes. Add in two stages – five and 20 – that featured long stretches of *strade bianche* and a number of transfers that were long even by Giro standards and the peloton wasn't happy. This manifested itself on stage 14 in which Zomegnan had intended to feature the truly spectacular Monte Crostis climb in the Friulian Alps – 14km at an average of

10 per cent with sections at 18 per cent on the upper ramparts – for the first time in the Giro. The climb is narrow and exposed and not suitable for a convoy of support cars and Zomegnan had already decreed that only team motorbikes could be used as back-up, but in the light of Weylandt's tragic death neither the riders nor the teams were in any mood to compromise on safety issues. They made representations to the UCI commissaries who on the evening before the planned stage ruled that the much-anticipated Crostis climb would have to be taken out.

The knock-on effect of that was massive with many fans, including local unpaid volunteers who had been working since the snows cleared early in April to make the road surface as good as possible, up in arms. When they learned of the decision they gathered in a small village at the bottom of the Tualis climb which Zomegnan had added to the stage at the last minute as an alternative to the Crostis. The mood was ugly and, amid chaotic scenes, the race was again diverted. Altogether it was an unsatisfactory day at the Giro and the race director was in the firing line again on the final day in Milan when the concluding time trial was suddenly shortened by nearly six kilometres because the local authorities found themselves under pressure with a bigger than expected turnout for local elections. Voters protested that planned road closures and general Giro-inspired chaos in the city centre would make it difficult for them to access polling stations, and again last-minute alterations to the route had to be made. That was the final straw for parent company RCS and a month later, although praising Zomegnan for his handling of events immediately after Weylandt's death, they sacked their race director although he was kept on as a consultant.

A Giro first for Hesjedal and Canada

The 2012 Giro was a much less contentious affair and offered up a pleasing storyline with Canada's Ryder Hesjedal, riding for Garmin, becoming only the second North American to win the race, squeezing home by 16 seconds from Joaquim Rodríguez on the final-day time trial after a ding-dong battle in the final week. That last-gasp, final-day win was only the second time in Giro history that this had been achieved – the first was Moser in the controversial 1984 edition – and it was a compelling race despite the absence of Contador who was still serving his ban.

Hesjedal, from Victoria on Vancouver Island in British Columbia, had initially made an impact on the cycling world as a mountain biker winning a silver medal at the 2003 World Championship and he was possibly heading for a gold medal at the 2004 Olympics in Athens when he punctured. He could climb all right but as a big, tall guy – 6ft 2in and prone to put on weight when not racing and training regularly – he had made his way in the professional road-racing peloton as an ultra-reliable *rouleur* and a superior sort of domestique who could also perform well in the longer time trials. Awareness of his full potential came on the 2010 Tour de France Queen stage, when Contador and Andy Schleck duked it out on the Tourmalet, and he finished a very creditable third on the day and impressive fifth overall. Not for the first time his team manager Jonathan Vaughters and experienced DS and Giro veteran Charly Wegelius, noticed that the Canadian had a tendency to finish long stage races strongly. In an ideal world Ryder Hesjedal would be competing in Grand Tours of four or five weeks' duration but, in the absence of such ultra-marathons, the Garmin think-tank of Vaughters and Wegelius very much liked the look of the 2012 Giro which finished with three mountain stages in the last five days and a decent length 28.2km TT on the final day. The *corsa rosa* also had a team time trial on stage four and Garmin around this time were outstanding in that discipline, claiming a notable win in the TTT at Les Essarts in the 2011 Tour de France. No Contador, Wiggins concentrating on the Tour de France, a backloaded final week and a heaven-sent team time trial? The stars seemed to be aligning if you looked in the right direction but could Hesjedal be convinced?

At the Garmin training camp in Boulder, Colorado, in November 2011 Vaughters and Wegelius set about persuading Hesjedal that he might be best served in 2012 switching from the Tour, which he had ridden in preference to the Giro for the last three seasons. He eventually came around to the idea and Garmin set about building a team that could protect him during the windy and sometimes chaotic opening three stages in Denmark, deliver a TTT triumph and then fight hard in the mountains. It was a tall order for a team that traditionally concentrated on stage wins and indeed they still turned up at the 2012 Giro also looking to contest the sprints with Tyler Farrar, but when the American crashed out early on the die was well and truly cast.

Hesjedal looked in good form from the start although probably only the cognoscenti noticed when he finished 17th in the opening day Prologue, some 30 seconds behind stage winner Taylor Phinney. The moot point, however, was that he was 14 seconds ahead of the next recognised GC contender, Joaquim Rodríguez, and those seconds were to prove very valuable indeed three weeks and 3,502km down the road. His team claimed a stunning win in the TTT in Verona on the race's first day back from Denmark and by stage seven he was in pink, a position he disputed for the rest of the race. In fact, Hesjedal assumed the jersey on three separate occasions – stages seven, 14 and 21. He was nothing if not consistent.

The key to actually winning the race was always finishing strong and that's how it worked out. Instead of losing time to Rodríguez on the very steep Alpe di Pampeago, as was expected by most, Hesjedal actually pulled 13 seconds back on the pink jersey. Then, on the penultimate day, which included the Stelvio, exemplary team riding and pacing from Christian Vande Velde and Peter Stetina saw him restrict his losses to Rodríguez to just 14 seconds on a day when the Spaniard might have expected to gain minutes. Going into the final trial, Rodríguez may have been in pink but with just a 31-second lead it was Hesjedal's race to lose. The Canadian was by some distance the better time-trial rider and even if a twisting technical city course wasn't ideally suited to his big engine, he was experienced enough to measure his effort well to deliver one of the most celebrated wins in Canadian sporting history. Vaughters summed it up like this: 'Basically Ryder won the Giro because he out-dieseled everybody. He wasn't spectacular at any time but he never faltered while everybody else gradually fatigued.'

Missing from the 2012 Giro was Vincenzo Nibali who, after a third place in 2010 and a runners-up spot in 2011, opted to try his luck at the Tour de France, where he finished third. He returned home to finally win the Giro in emphatic fashion in 2013, riding what most observers considered to be a nigh-on perfect race in horrid, testing conditions. Most of Europe experienced an unusually cold and wet late spring that year and those conditions certainly affected the Giro, with poor weather the norm and stage 19 – Ponte di Legno to Martell – being lost altogether to the snow. The following day's climb to Tre Cime di Lavaredo, which Nibali won, was also a wintry affair. Although a native of sun-kissed Sicily, indeed his nickname is 'the Shark of Messina', Nibali proved very at home in such conditions with his sublime descending and bike-handling skills serving him well coming off the big climbs. The early withdrawals of reigning champion Hesjedal and reigning Tour de France champion Wiggins through injury and illness respectively certainly paved his way but Nibali looked 'best in class' from early on. The Italian stamped his authority on the race from the moment he took the jersey after the stage eight time trial – which Alex Dowsett won from Wiggins in the all-British showdown – and was an increasingly dominant figure as he took overall victory from Rigoberto Urán with Thomas De Gendt in third. Elsewhere the race was also notable for five stage wins from British sprinter Mark Cavendish which saw him take the Points jersey and complete the clean sweep of Points win in the three Grand Tours, a feat only previously achieved by four other riders – Uzbekistan's Djamolidine Abdoujaparov, Italy's Alessandro Petacchi, Laurent Jalabert from France and Belgium's Eddy Merckx.

History was made in 2014 when diminutive climber Nairo Quintana became the first Colombian to win the Giro d'Italia and only the second rider from that cycling-mad country to win a Grand Tour after Luis Herrera who won the Vuelta a España in 1987. Just for good measure fellow countryman Rigoberto Urán finished runner-up and a third Colombian, Julián Arredondo, won the blue climber's jersey and the prestigious stage to Rifugio Panarotta. As a demonstration of the potential of modern Colombian cycling it could scarcely be bettered and there was also a feeling of the Giro breaking new ground with a spectacular overseas start in Belfast with two stages in Northern Ireland before a third stage finishing in Dublin in the Republic of Ireland. Early May weather in those parts can be as fraught as the Alps and Dolomites and, almost predictably, it rained for the best part of three days with the murk and poor visibility particularly unwelcome on stage two which took in long sections of the famous Antrim coast road, one of the most spectacular roads in the world on a good day. But overall the weather didn't seem to dampen the enthusiasm of the huge crowds and the riders stoically put up with driving rain and wind, the warm welcome offering much compensation. One thing that did dampen Irish spirits, however, was a crash, and broken collarbone, in the early stages of the opening-day time trial in Belfast for Dan Martin, the Irish rider with the best chance of bagging a few stage wins in the race and perhaps even featuring in the GC contest.

Once new sprinter Marcel Kittel had stolen the early headlines with his impressive turn of pace to win stages two and three, the main GC contenders took over and from early on Quintana, well protected from the rough and tumble by his Movistar team, looked ominously strong although there were spells in pink for both the ageless Cadel Evans and Urán. Quintana took a firm grip with a memorable win on stage 16 which took in a very snowy Stelvio. It wasn't without controversy, though, as such wintry days seldom are. As conditions worsened the race director announced some three kilometres before the race reached the top of the Stelvio Pass that, because of potentially dangerous conditions in the first part of the descent, riders were to follow race motorbikes down through the first six bends. So late was the call, however, and so problematic getting that message from team cars down the mountain to riders up the road, that not all of the peloton received it. Some radios were working, others weren't. Some riders were wearing earpieces, others had discarded then as impractical in the foul weather. Another batch of riders claimed to have heard that the whole of the descent was to be neutralised and there is no doubt that confusion reigned, as the official Giro Twitter feed acknowledged with a tweet at 2.57 p.m.:

'Wrong communication: no neutralization for the descent from the Passo dello Stelvio. Sorry for the wrong information. #giro'

Quintana was already going well when he crested the Stelvio with Ryder Hesjedal and Pierre Rolland and he certainly didn't hang around on the descent before the 22.35km climb up the Val Nartello which tops out at 2,059m, but he later denied attacking while others slowed in compliance with officialdom. Official timings show he gained 1.41 on the peloton by the end of the descent which he extended to 4 minutes 11 seconds by the top of the Val Martello climb. 'I realised we were ahead at the top of the Stelvio but we didn't attack on the descent,' he insisted afterwards. 'My team-mates didn't hear anything, I didn't hear, just an order from our team car to cover up well. I don't understand why there is an argument. I gained my time, above all, on the last climb, not on the descent. I just raced like everybody else.'

Quintana wasn't present the following year for the 2015 Giro and nor were Vincenzo Nibali or Chris Froome for that matter as they preferred to concentrate on the Tour de France. All of which left the field clear for Alberto Contador who firmly believed he could pull off the first Giro/Tour double since Pantani in 1998. As he put it himself before the race, 'I want to do something people will remember for ever.' Contador duly won the Giro – and his three-finger salute on the podium clearly demonstrated that he still believed it was his third race win, not second – but the battle took more out of him than he anticipated and he had to settle for a distant fifth place at the Tour. What made this Giro so difficult for Contador, other than the stubborn resistance of the Astana duo of Fabio Aru and Mikel Landa, was a nasty crash on stage six which resulted in a dislocated shoulder. Contador had taken the pink jersey the day before on the summit finish of the Abetone and everything seemed to be going to plan, but the following day – a fairly routine run from Montecatini Terme to Castiglione della Pescaia – he found himself in the wrong place at the wrong time as he coasted home in the bunch some 200m from the finish. On one side of the finishing straight a spectator leaned over the safety barriers to take a photograph and caused Daniele Colli from Nippo–Vini Fantani to crash, that in turn causing a ripple across the peloton that saw Contador come to ground painfully on the other side of the road. The dislocation of Contador's left shoulder was instantaneous and in the racing footage you can see Contador instinctively reaching for his shoulder to seemingly push it back in place. He remounted and finished but at the podium ceremony the shoulder popped out again and he was unable to put on the pink jersey as protocol normally insists, holding it aloft instead. Nor was he able to uncork the ceremonial bottle of champagne. It looked certain that Contador's Giro was over, and scans that night confirmed that there had been a dislocation but, equally, there appeared to be very little ligament damage or trauma. There was just a chance he might be able to take the start line the following day for the longest stage of the race, a 264km from Grosseto to Fiuggi. The Tinkoff-Saxo medics strapped him up expertly and in normal life he could have walked around in little pain or discomfort, but Contador was the leader of the Giro d'Italia and nearly 7 hours in the saddle over rolling terrain awaited.

Contador's defence of the pink jersey over the coming week, greatly aided by outstanding team support from the likes of Ivan Basso, Michael Rogers and Roman Kreuziger, was exemplary and although he lost it to the eager Aru on stage 13 the Spaniard hit back in stunning fashion the following day in a time trial of nearly 60km between Treviso and Valdobbiadene when he put over 3 minutes into Aru and Landa. Beginning to recover now, it gave Contador the buffer he needed in the mountains which, given his climbing style with the shoulder constantly in swaying motion, was going to be tricky. On the first of the final mountain stages which took in the Passo di Mortirolo, Contador gained a further 2 minutes on Aru and for a moment Landa looked the biggest threat. But thereafter Aru started to do himself justice and claimed two mountain wins. Contador, out of necessity, rode conservatively defending his hard-earned lead and finally reached Milan for one of the best Grand Tour wins of his very considerable career. 'I knew it would be a very demanding Giro, but I didn't think it would be so complicated,' admitted Contador. 'There was the crash and then the Astana team riding so strongly, it was exhausting just about every day from the long time trial onwards. It was a very hard-won race.' Contador was also unrepentant about his three-finger gesture on top of the winner's podium. 'People watching on TV, the riders, the fans … everyone knows it's my third victory.'

15

GIRO D'ITALIA - BRINGING UP THE CENTURY

As if on cue the Giro d'Italia teed up the 100th edition in 2017 with a spectacular and compelling race in 2016 that in many ways underlined its special and enduring appeal. Varied weather, a rugged route, stunning scenery – especially during three sun-blessed days in the snow-topped Dolomites – aggressive racing from start to finish, the emergence of new stars and personalities to fire the imagination and a dramatic late comeback in the snowy Alps by the home favourite and reigning champion Vincenzo Nibali. Nor, at the time of going to press anyway, were proceedings stained by any positive tests for doping.

The Giro made a tumultuous start, in perfect early summer weather, in the Netherlands where huge crowds again greeted the race. The Dutch rarely fail to put on a show and, of course, the likelihood of home favourite Tom Dumoulin winning the 9.6km Prologue in Apeldoorn and taking possession of the *maglia rosa* bolstered local interest. Dumoulin duly delivered and then held on to the pink jersey the following day when Marcel Kittel powered to victory in a sprint finish in Nijmegen. The big German was not to be denied the next day, however, when the organisers, looking to maximise the Giro's accessibility to fans, simply reversed the course of the previous stage and finished in Arnhem where Kittel took the stage and the overall lead. As the Giro and camp followers dashed for planes to southern Italy and the reappearance of the Giro on Italian soil at the start of stage three in Catanzaro, Kittel could reflect on four stage victories in his Giro career – one in Belfast, one in Dublin and two in Holland – without once winning in Italy.

It set the tone for a wonderfully eclectic Giro as the race worked its ways steadily up the peninsula. Dumoulin – who had shown his GC potential at the Vuelta a España in 2015 – regained the overall lead for four days but had no great designs on GC on this occasion. He was then succeeded in the leader's jersey by Italy's Gianluca Brambilla before young Bob Jungels became the first rider from Luxembourg to wear the *maglia rosa* since the days of Charly Gaul. There was also one day in pink for Andrey Amador which was celebrated in his native Costa Rica with the presidential palace being floodlit in pink for the evening.

The hardcore GC contenders took over on stage 14 – a sumptuous high mountain stage in the Dolomites between Alpago and Corvara. It was won in impressive style by young Esteban Chaves from an Orica GreenEDGE team that had switched from its normal modus operandi of hunting individual stage wins to getting fully behind the Colombian climber in the GC contest. The other big winner that day was another Dutchman – Steven Kruijswijk from the Lotto team – who underlined his growing reputation by cruising into pink where for five stages he looked to the manor-born and seemingly heading for a first Grand Tour victory. The tall and well-built Kruijswijk, with his coathanger American footballer shoulders, cut an impressive figure on his bike and was both climbing smoothly and avoiding any mishaps in the peloton. For a while his task was possibly made less complicated by a lacklustre Nibali who outwardly looked fit enough but was misfiring a little. Nibali clearly laboured on the gruelling stage 14 when he became detached from the pink jersey group but he is no quitter and dug very deep, using his great descending skills to limit his losses to 37 seconds and stay in contention. He might not have won the 2016 Giro that day but he could easily have tumbled out of contention. The following day when, as was revealed by his team after the Giro finished, he was suffering from a stomach upset,

Nibali was on the ropes again in a demanding 10.8km mountain time trial from Castelrotto to Alpe di Siusi when he both felt unwell and dropped a chain before requiring a bike change. Again it could all have gone horribly wrong but he went deep again to finish 25th on the day which was 2 minutes 10 seconds behind the stage winner Alexander Foliforov and resulted in Nibali dropping to third in GC, nearly 3 minutes behind a fresh-looking Kruijswijk. Nibali lost more time on the final climb on stage 16 and by the start of stage 19 on the final Friday was 4 minutes 43 seconds down on the Dutchman. He hadn't quite cracked as such but was clearly finding it incredibly difficult to get fully on terms with the young guns Chaves and Kruijswijk.

The Nibali debate was taking over the Giro. Some insisted an early season change in the length of his pedal cranks – they were apparently slightly lengthened – had altered his pedalling style and reduced his dynamism on the climbs while his worried Astana team sent him for medical tests and there was talk of him withdrawing to save further stress and perhaps to start preparing for the Tour de France. Nibali stopped talking to the media – rare for him – and the *tifosi* weren't sure whether to support or denounce their man. Remembering his past glories, they chose the former and were ultimately well rewarded for their loyalty. The tests revealed no illness or underlying problem and following that news the weight seemed to lift off his shoulders as he rode on. This was after all a rider who had finished 14 of the previous 15 Grand Tours he had ridden, a series that included seven podiums and three wins. Two torturous days beckoned in the Alps, but Nibali has always preferred the long, slightly easier gradients of the Alps to the Dolomites and indeed Pyrenees on the Tour. There were a couple of difficult and potentially dangerous descents beckoning on which to demonstrate his prowess in that department as well. Nibali's two main rivals were still both young men yet to achieve a top three in any Grand Tour. Indeed, between them they only had two top-ten finishes. Perhaps it wasn't quite their time after all. A lot could still happen.

And it did. Stage 19 from Pinerolo to Risoul was a one of the toughest seen in years and the 'race' was already well and truly on as Nibali – looking more confident and hopeful – started to apply the pressure on the leader's group three kilometres from the top of the Colle dell'Agnello, the Cima Coppi for the 2016 Giro at 2,774m. Chaves went with him, as did Kruijswijk, but Dutch journalists were already commenting that the latter wasn't looking as smooth and effortless as usual as they climbed up into the snowline and freezing mist. It was now or never if Nibali was to recoup anything from the race. A stage win at the very least would be nice. That was the priority; a climb back up into the reckoning for overall victory would be a massive bonus. Heading down the descent and still in the area of massed snowbanks and reduced visibility, Nibali took flight in trademark fashion and Chaves followed in his wheels, but Kruijswijk held back a little, opting to take his own line – disastrously so as he overcooked a fast left-hand bend and lost control on a rutted section of the road right next to the packed snowbanks. His bike cartwheeled off into the snow and Kruijswijk himself somersaulted before landing painfully on his back and ribs, half in the snow, half in the road. He bounced back up but there were cuts and abrasions on his arms and legs and X-rays were later to reveal a broken rib. Remounting, he headed off shakily down the road and soon needed a bike change and, although he fought bravely down the rest of the descent and in the valley that followed, the crash really hit home on the climb up to Risoul where he lost time badly. His pink jersey was disappearing. Both Nibali and Chaves also had team members up the road – Michele Scarponi and Rubén Plaza respectively – who dropped back to help their leaders. It was a desperate situation for the young Dutchman who paid a heavy price for his one moment of carelessness in an otherwise flawless race. Afterwards he conceded that the mistake and blame were entirely his and dismissed any suggestion that Nibali and Chaves should have waited for the jersey.

Kruijswijk wasn't the only one to feel the pressure as Nibali went for the jugular. Up that final climb into Risoul the previously unflappable Chaves suddenly lost 53 seconds to Nibali as well – and again we only discovered after the race that he was feeling unwell for much of the last three or four days of the Giro. The Colombian may have finished the day in pink but he was now only 44 seconds ahead of a rejuvenated Nibali who nonetheless slumped onto his bike and wept uncontrollably at the finish. It had been emotional. The battered Kruijswijk was now third overall at 1.05 but was clearly going to struggle the following day, another short but intimidating Alpine stage from Guillestre to Sant'Anna di Vinadio, the latter famed for its mineral water. Nibali was on a roll but remained patient before delivering the *coup de grâce* with the calm efficiency of a Sicilian hitman, leaving his big effort so late that his main contenders had no chance to respond. Descending brilliantly from the final big climb of the day – the Colle della Lombarda – Nibali then fought his way up a fierce, short ramp into Sant'Anna di Vinadio to claim his second Giro title in a race he might have quit just 54 hours earlier. Chaves, whose parents had flown in from Colombia in the hope of seeing their son's greatest moment, finished runner-up while Alejandro Valverde rode strongly on this final mountain stage to deny Kruijswijk even the consolation of a podium spot. The picture in *Gazzetta* the following morning was of Nibali consoling Chaves's parents while the main headline was *Dal buio al trionfo*: from darkness to victory.

It was unquestionably a dramatic victory and a timely reminder of sport's unpredictability and a strong counter-argument to fend off those who feel sport too often follows a predetermined script. Some bracketed it with other last-gasp Giro victories such as Coppi (1953), Gaul (1959) and Tonkov (1996), while others of a more suspicious disposition wondered exactly how his 'Lazarus-like' victory had been achieved during those final two days in the Alps. The Astana team had been under scrutiny for previous violations and there were high-profile team members with a considerable doping backstory, namely team manager Alexander Vinokourov and Nibali's *gregario di lusso* Michele Scarponi who enjoyed a very effective race indeed. Once the dust settled, however, it was possible to consider the objective reality of Nibali's win which offers another scenario. None of the other modern-day Grand Tour *galácticos* were present at the 2016 Giro – Alberto Contador, Chris Froome, Nairo Quintana – so Nibali wasn't riding away against the sport's absolute elite. And during those final two days, Kruijswijk's otherwise impressive challenge manifestly faltered in one instant, that nasty self-induced crash on stage 19. Chaves, meanwhile, started to labour a little through illness and fatigue. Both were Grand Tour novices compared to Nibali. Being in serious contention for a winner's jersey – and the pressures that brings – was new territory for them. Nibali demonstrated great spirit and resilience and no little skill, but the truth is the 2016 Giro was more a case of him going less slowly than the others at its denouement rather than riding away from the field with some superhuman, barely credible effort. The winning margins were narrow: 57 seconds over Chaves, 1.05 over third-placed Valverde.

'Believing until the very end was the secret of this victory,' said Nibali. 'It was a very hard Giro d'Italia, in so many ways. I started with the weight of being the favourite on my shoulders and that affected my race. Perhaps I'd convinced myself that I was going to dominate the race as I did in 2013. I always expect a lot from myself and that led me to make mistakes. I wasn't as focused as I should have been. It was only when I thought I'd almost lost the race that I managed to offload all the pressure that was weighing me down. I told myself that there was not a big difference between winning and losing but that I wasn't going to give up.'

The 2016 Giro was, however, a timely celebration of the race itself and above all it reminded us that the beauty of Italy remains unsurpassed as a backdrop for any sporting occasion and continues to be fundamental to the race, determining both the terrain and sometimes the mood.

The 2016 race was blessed with more than its fair share of early summer weather but May can always be a capricious month and there was enough drizzle, rain and high mountain hail and murk for those who enjoy the extremes. The roadside snowbanks were piled high and threatening to topple onto the road during the deciding Alpine stages and a reminder of what a chancy business it is scheduling such important race-deciding stages so late in proceedings in a part of the world where the snows depart late and winter can return overnight. And yet those distinctive and perennial images are what marks out the Giro from any other major bike race in the world.

The Giro remains the love child of *Gazzetta dello Sport* and the paper's owners RCS, and they continue to feed off each other, even if there have been many moments of tension and estrangement during their long relationship. Cycling, in the form of the Giro, remains the only sport in Italy that can occasionally usurp football even in May when the big football competitions are coming to their conclusion. The Giro's live TV coverage has noticeably improved, with most of the big mountain stages now being covered from kilometre zero which has opened the eyes of new fans. In 2016, glorious crisp, cloudless weather greeted the stunning stage 14 which featured the Pordoi, Sella, Gardena, Campolongo, Giau and the Valparola. Commentators raved about its beauty – rightly so – and social media went into meltdown proclaiming it, scenically, as probably the most spectacular stage in Grand Tour history. That might well be the case – it's certainly difficult to recall any stage that surpasses it – but those mighty climbs and passes have appeared in the Giro for many decades and been the scene of many a drama. They haven't just suddenly appeared, their beauty isn't new, it's more that improved technology – and the growing demand for real-time coverage – has pushed them to the forefront. The armchair fan can enjoy the terrain in its full glory and not just rely on the word of an excitable correspondent perhaps given to hyperbole and outbreaks of purple prose.

One notable way in which the Giro has changed over the years is the shedding of its 'Italy only' reputation. For many decades it was undeniably an inward-looking race, and perhaps with good reason. The racers, in many ways, were gathered to glorify and promote the still-fledgling nation of Italy while revisiting – geographically – its difficult but extraordinary past and doffing a cap to the many regions, once rivals and even enemies, but now united under the one flag. But times change. Italy is now confident of its own identity. Yes, there are still a high proportion of Italian winners – largely down to top Italian riders continuing to place a Giro victory over and above a Tour win and making it their priority for the season – but the race has become remarkably diverse. In 2016 just six team leaders among the 22 teams competing were Italian, and stages were won by riders from Germany, Slovakia, Belgium, the Netherlands, Spain, Colombia, Russia, Costa Rica and Estonia as well as Italy. The top team was from Kazakhstan and the best young rider from Luxembourg. The Giro has become a glorious melting pot.

Another interesting modern development, in stark contrast with the past, is the quick-fire mountain stages towards the end of the final week. In 2016 those two final, decisive mountain stages were 162km and 134km respectively, short sprints compared with some of the mountainfests of yesteryear. The action was full on and concentrated which in turn produced compelling TV. It's a formula we can expect to be repeated.

The Giro has come a long way in its first 99 editions: 373,755km to be precise, almost the distance from the Earth to the Moon. The regular overseas departs have become a fact of life – among other things they help pay the bills and balance the books – but they can also be spectacular, almost evangelical affairs spreading the word, which was certainly the case in Apeldoorn in 2016. Just as the 100th edition of the Tour in 2013 didn't stray outside of France, the 100th Giro will not be going out of Italy – but the race will continue to spread its wings thereafter. There has been talk of staging the Grande Partenza in North America, the Middle East and Japan, considered fanciful by some, but this is a race that is developing year on year and nothing should be discounted.

The centenary route, unveiled in Milan in October 2016 with 20 former race winners in attendance, met with widespread approval. Starting with three days in Sardinia, there appeared to be something for everybody as the *corsa rosa* moved to Sicily, with a mountain finish on Mount Etna, before transferring to the Italian mainland and working its way northwards as expediently as possible with the minimum of transfers. Two individual time trials – one mid-race between Foligno and Montefalco and one in Milan on the final day – offered up a degree of a balance to set against the many iconic climbs. The mighty Stelvio featured not once but twice on Stage 16, while Stage 18, the Tappone, highlighted the Dolomites taking in the Passo Pordoi, Passo Valparola, Passo Gardena, Passo di Pinei Panider Sattel and the Pontives.

'We've created a wholly Italian race, one that visits as much of Italy as possible, to celebrate the race and also the history of Italy,' said Mauro Vegni, head of cycling at RCS. 'There are stages that recall Bartali, Coppi, Girardengo, Gimondi and Pantani – the biggest protagonists in the history of our race. We visit as much of Italy as possible, 17 of the 21 regions, in fact. The route climbs into the Alps, the Apennines, mountains in the south like Mount Etna and of course the Dolomites. We are still right to describe the Giro as the world's toughest race in the world's most beautiful place. This route validates that claim.

'The 2017 Giro d'Italia is also the start of the next 100 years of the race. We have modernised the Giro d'Italia in lots of ways in recent years and made it more famous around the world, that's why so many countries and major cities want to host the Grande Partenza. The Giro d'Italia helps promote Italy and all the great things that Italy is known for globally. It is a bike race but it is more than a bike race at the same time.'

APPENDIX

Giro d'Italia GC Podiums & Jersey Winners

Year	GC 1st place	GC 2nd place	GC 3rd place	Mountains jersey	Points jersey
1909 (2,448km)	Luigi Ganna (ITA) 25 points 89hr 48min 14sec	Carlo Galetti (ITA) 27 points	Giovanni Rossignoli (ITA) 40 points	–	–
1910 (2,980km)	Carlo Galetti (ITA) 28 points 114hr 24min	Eberardo Pavesi (ITA) 46 points	Luigi Ganna (ITA) 51 points	–	–
1911 (3,530km)	Carlo Galetti (ITA) 50 points 132hr 24min	Giovanni Rossignoli (ITA) 58 points	Giovanni Gerbi (ITA) 84 points	–	–
1912 (2,444km)	Team Atala (Ganna, Galetti, Micheletto, Pavesi) (ITA) 33 points 101hr 32min 57sec	Team Peugeot (Durando, Gremo, Agostoni, Allasia) (ITA) 23 points	Team Gerbi (Gerbi, Rossignoli, Albini, Bordin) (ITA)	–	–
1913 (2,932km)	Carlo Oriani (ITA) 37 points 135hr 15min 56sec	Eberardo Pavesi (ITA) 43 points	Giuseppe Azzini (ITA) 48 points	–	–
1914 (3,162km)	Alfonso Calzolari (ITA) 135hr 17min 56sec	Pierino Albini (ITA) @ 1hr 57min 26sec	Luigi Lucotti (ITA) @ 2hr 4min 23sec	–	–
1915–1918: First World War					
1919 (2,964km)	Costante Girardengo (ITA) 112hr 51min 29sec	Gaetano Belloni (ITA) @ 51min 56sec	Marcel Buysse (BEL) @ 1hr 5min 31sec	–	–
1920 (2,632km)	Gaetano Belloni (ITA) 102hr 44min 33sec	Angelo Gremo (ITA) @ 32min 24sec	Jean Alavoine (FRA) @ 1hr 1min 14sec	–	–

1921 (3,107km)	Giovanni Brunero (ITA) 120hr 24min 39sec	Gaetano Belloni (ITA) @ 41sec	Bartolomeo Aymo (ITA) @ 19min 47sec	—	—
1922 (3,095km)	Giovanni Brunero (ITA) 119hr 43min	Bartolomeo Aymo (ITA) @ 12min 29sec	Giuseppe Enrici (ITA) @ 1hr 35min 33sec	—	—
1923 (3,202km)	Costante Girardengo (ITA) 122hr 58min 17sec	Giovanni Brunero (ITA) @ 37sec	Bartolomeo Aymo (ITA) @ 10min 25sec	—	—
1924 (3,613km)	Giuseppe Enrici (ITA) 143hr 43min 37sec	Federico Gay (ITA) @ 58min 21sec	Angiolo Gabrielli (ITA) @ 1hr 56min 53sec	—	—
1925 (3,520km)	Alfredo Binda (ITA) 137hr 31min 13sec	Costante Girardengo (ITA) @ 4min 58sec	Giovanni Brunero (ITA) @ 7min 22sec	—	—
1926 (3,429km)	Giovanni Brunero (ITA) 137hr 55min 59sec	Alfredo Binda (ITA) @ 15min 28sec	Arturo Bresciani (ITA) @ 54min 41sec	—	—
1927 (3,758km)	Alfredo Binda (ITA) 144hr 15min 35sec	Giovanni Brunero (ITA) @ 27min 24sec	Antonio Negrini (ITA) @ 36min 6sec	—	—
1928 (3,044km)	Alfredo Binda (ITA) 114hr 15min 19sec	Giuseppe Pancera (ITA) @ 18min 13sec	Bartolomeo Aymo (ITA) @ 27min 25sec	—	—
1929 (2,920km)	Alfredo Binda (ITA) 107hr 18min 24sec	Domenico Piemontesi (ITA) @ 3min 44sec	Leonida Frascarelli (ITA) @ 5min 4sec	—	—
1930 (3,907km)	Luigi Marchisio (ITA) 115hr 11min 15sec	Luigi Giacobbe (ITA) @ 52sec	Allegro Grandi (ITA) @ 1min 49sec	—	—

(Continued)

Giro d'Italia GC Podiums & Jersey Winners (Continued)

Year	GC 1st place	GC 2nd place	GC 3rd place	Mountains jersey	Points jersey
1931 (3,012km)	Francesco Camusso (ITA) 102hr 40min 46sec	Luigi Giacobbe (ITA) @ 2min 47sec	Luigi Marchisio (ITA) @ 6min 15sec	–	–
1932 (3,235km)	Antonio Pesenti (ITA) 105hr 53min 50sec	Joseph Demuysère (BEL) @ 11min 9sec	Remo Bertoni (ITA) @ 12min 27sec	–	–
1933 (3,343km)	Alfredo Binda (ITA) 111hr 1min 52sec	Joseph Dumuysère (BEL) @ 12min 34sec	Domenico Piemontesi (ITA) @ 16min 31sec	Alfredo Binda (ITA)	–
1934 (3,548km)	Learco Guerra (ITA) 121hr 17min 17sec	Francesco Camusso (ITA) @ 51sec	Giovanni Cazzulani (ITA) @ 4min 59sec	Remo Bertoni (ITA)	–
1935 (3,577km)	Vasco Bergamaschi (ITA) 113hr 22min 46sec	Giuseppe Martano (ITA) @ 3min 7sec	Giuseppe Olmo (ITA) @ 6min 12sec	Gino Bartali (ITA)	–
1936 (3,766km)	Gino Bartali (ITA) 120hr 12min 30sec	Giuseppe Olmo (ITA) @ 2min 36sec	Severino Canavesi (ITA) @ 7min 49sec	Gino Bartali (ITA)	–
1937 (3,849km)	Gino Bartali (ITA) 112hr 25min 40sec	Giovanni Valetti (ITA) @ 8min 18sec	Enrico Mollo (ITA) @ 17min 38sec	Gino Bartali (ITA)	–
1938 (3,645km)	Giovanni Valetti (ITA) 112hr 49min 28sec	Ezio Cecchi (ITA) @ 8min 52sec	Severino Canavesi (ITA) @ 9min 6sec	Giovanni Valetti (ITA)	–
1939 (3,011km)	Giovanni Valetti (ITA) 88hr 2min 0sec	Gino Bartali (ITA) @ 2min 59sec	Mario Vicini (ITA) @ 5min 7sec	Gino Bartali (ITA)	–

APPENDIX

Year (km) / Winner	2nd	3rd		
1940 (3574km) Fausto Coppi (ITA) 107hr 31min 10sec	Enrico Mollo (ITA) @ 2min 40sec	Giordano Cottur (ITA) @ 11min 45sec	Gino Bartali (ITA)	—
1941–1945: Second World War				
1946 (3,188km) Gino Bartali (ITA) 95hr 32min 20sec	Fausto Coppi (ITA) @ 47sec	Vito Ortelli (ITA) @ 15min 28sec	Gino Bartali (ITA)	—
1947 (3,843km) Fausto Coppi (ITA) 115hr 55min 7sec	Gino Bartali (ITA) @ 1min 43sec	Giulio Bresci (ITA) @ 5min 54sec	Gino Bartali (ITA)	—
1948 (4,164km) Fiorenzo Magni (ITA) 124hr 51min 52sec	Ezio Cecchi (ITA) @ 11sec	Giordano Cottur (ITA) @ 2min 37sec	Fausto Coppi (ITA)	—
1949 (4,088km) Fausto Coppi (ITA) 125hr 25min 50sec	Gino Bartali (ITA) @ 23min 47sec	Giordano Cottur (ITA) @ 38min 27sec	Fausto Coppi (ITA)	—
1950 (3,981km) Hugo Koblet (SUI); 117hr 28min 3sec	Gino Bartali (ITA) @ 5min 12sec	Alfredo Martini (ITA) @ 8min 41sec	Hugo Koblet (SUI)	—
1951 (4,153km) Fiorenzo Magni (ITA) 121hr 11min 37sec	Rik Van Steenbergen (BEL) @ 1min 46sec	Ferdi Kübler (SUI) @ 2min 36sec	Louison Bobet (FRA)	—
1952 (3,964km) Fausto Coppi (ITA) 114 hr 36min 43sec	Fiorenzo Magni (ITA) @ 9min 18sec	Ferdi Kübler (SUI) @ 9min 24sec	Raphaël Géminiani (FRA)	—
1953 (4,035km) Fausto Coppi (ITA) 118hr 37min 26sec	Hugo Koblet (SUI) @ 1min 29sec	Pasquale Fornara (ITA) @ 6min 55sec	Pasquale Fornara (ITA)	—

(Continued)

Giro d'Italia GC Podiums & Jersey Winners (Continued)

Year	GC 1st place	GC 2nd place	GC 3rd place	Mountains jersey	Points jersey
1954 (4,337km)	Carlo Clerici (SUI) 129hr 13min 7sec	Hugo Koblet (SUI) @ 24min 16se	Nino Assirelli (ITA) @ 26min 28sec	Fausto Coppi (ITA)	–
1955 (3,873km)	Fiorenzo Magni (ITA) 108hr 56min 13sec	Fausto Coppi (ITA) @ 13sec	Gastone Nencini (ITA) @ 4min 8sec	Gastone Nencini (ITA)	–
1956 (3,523km)	Charly Gaul (LUX) 101hr 39min 49sec	Fiorenzo Magni (ITA) @ 3min 27sec	Agostino Coletto (ITA) @ 6min 53sec	Tied: Federico Bahamontes (ESP) Charly Gaul (LUX) M. Del Rio (ITA)	–
1957 (3,926km)	Gastone Nencini (ITA) 104hr 45min 6sec	Louison Bobet (FRA) @ 19sec	Ercole Baldini (ITA) @ 5min 59sec	Raphaël Géminiani (FRA)	–
1958 (3,341km)	Ercole Baldini (ITA) 92hr 9min 30sec	Jean Bankart (BEL) @ 4min 17sec	Charly Gaul (LUX) @ 6min 7sec	Jean Brankart (BEL)	–
1959 (3,657km)	Charly Gaul (LUX) 101hr 50min 26sec	Jacques Anquetil (FRA) @ 6min 12sec	Diego Ronchini (ITA) @ 6min 16sec	Charly Gaul (LUX)	–
1960 (3,481km)	Jacques Anquetil (FRA) 94hr 3min 54s	Gastone Nencini (ITA) @ 28sec	Charly Gaul (LUX) @ 3min 51sec	Rik Van Looy (BEL)	–
1961 (4,004km)	Arnoldo Pambianco (ITA)	Jacques Anquetil (FRA) @ 3min 45sec	Antonio Suárez (ESP) @ 4min 17sec	Vito Taccone (ITA)	–

1962 (4,180km)	Franco Balmamion (ITA) 123hr 7min 3sec	Imerio Massignan (ITA) @ 3min 57sec	Nino Defilippis (ITA) @ 5min 2sec	Angelino Soler (ESP)	—
1963 (4,063km)	Franco Balmamion (ITA) 116hr 50min 16sec	Vittorio Adorni (ITA) @ 2min 24sec	Giorgio Zancanaro (ITA) @ 3min 15sec	Vito Taccone (ITA)	—
1964 (4,119km)	Jacques Anquetil (FRA) 115hr 10min 27sec	Italo Zilioli (ITA) @ 1min 22sec	Guido De Rosso (ITA) @ 1min 31sec	Franco Bitossi (ITA)	—
1965 (4,151km)	Vittorio Adorni (ITA) 121hr 8min 16sec	Italo Zilioli (ITA) @ 11min 26sec	Felice Gimondi (ITA) @ 12min 49sec	Franco Bitossi (ITA)	—
1966 (3,976km)	Gianni Motta (ITA) 111hr 10min 48sec	Italo Zilioli (ITA) @ 3min 57sec	Jacques Anquetil (FRA) @ 4min 40sec	Franco Bitossi (ITA)	Gianni Motta (ITA)
1967 (3,572km)	Felice Gimondi (ITA) 101hr 5min 34sec	Franco Balmamion (ITA) @ 3min 36sec	Jacques Anquetil (FRA) @ 3min 45sec	Aurelio González Puente (ESP)	Dino Zandegù (ITA)
1968 (3,917km)	Eddy Merckx (BEL) 108hr 42min 27sec	Vittorio Adorni (ITA) @ 5min 1sec	Felice Gimondi (ITA) @ 9min 5sec	Eddy Merckx (BEL)	Eddy Merckx (BEL)
1969 (3,731km)	Felice Gimondi (ITA) 106hr 47min 3sec	Claudio Michelotto (ITA) @ 3min 35sec	Italo Zilioli (ITA) @ 4min 48sec	Claudio Michelotto (ITA)	Franco Bitossi (ITA)
1970 (3,292km)	Eddy Merckx (BEL) 90hr 8min 47sec	Felice Gimondi (ITA) @ 3min 14sec	Martin Van den Bossche (BEL) @ 4min 59sec	Martin Van den Bossche (BEL)	Franco Bitossi (ITA)

(Continued)

Giro d'Italia GC Podiums & Jersey Winners (Continued)

Year	GC 1st place	GC 2nd place	GC 3rd place	Mountains jersey	Points jersey
1971 (3,567km)	Gösta Pettersson (SWE) 97hr 24min 3sec	Herman Van Springel (BEL) @ 2min 4sec	Ugo Colombo (ITA) @ 2min 35sec	José Manuel Fuente (ESP)	Marino Basso (ITA)
1972 (3,725km)	Eddy Merckx (BEL) 103hr 4min 4sec	José Manuel Fuente (ESP) @ 5min 30sec	Francisco Galdós (ESP) @ 10min 39sec	José Manuel Fuente (ESP)	Roger De Vlaeminck (BEL)
1973 (3,796km)	Eddy Merckx (BEL) 106hr 54min 41sec	Felice Gimondi (ITA) @ 7min 42sec	Giovanni Battaglin (ITA) @ 10min 20sec	José Manuel Fuente (ESP)	Eddy Merckx (BEL)
1974 (4,001km)	Eddy Merckx (BEL) 113hr 8min 13sec	Giambattista Baronchelli (ITA) @ 12sec	Felice Gimondi (ITA) @ 33sec	José Manuel Fuente (ESP)	Roger De Vlaeminck (BEL)
1975 (3,963km)	Fausto Bertoglio (ITA) 111hr 31min 34sec	Francisco Galdós (ESP) @ 41sec	Felice Gimondi (ITA) @ 6min 18sec	Andrés Oliva (ESP)	Roger De Vlaeminck (BEL)
1976 (4,161km)	Felice Gimondi (ITA) 119hr 58min 15sec	Johan De Muynck (BEL) @ 19sec	Fausto Bertoglio (ITA) @ 49sec	Andrés Oliva (ESP)	Francesco Moser (ITA)
1977 (3,968km)	Michel Pollentier (BEL) 107hr 27min 16sec	Francesco Moser (ITA) @ 2min 32sec	Giambattista Baronchelli (ITA) @ 4min 2sec	Faustino Fernández Ovies (ESP)	Francesco Moser (ITA)

Year (distance)					
1978 (3,610km)	Johan De Muynck (BEL) 101hr 31min 22sec	Giambattista Baronchelli (ITA) @ 59sec	Francesco Moser (ITA) @ 2min 19sec	Ueli Sutter (SUI)	Francesco Moser (ITA)
1979 (3,301km)	Giuseppe Saronni (ITA) 89hr 29min 18sec	Francesco Moser (ITA) @ 2min 9sec	Bernt Johansson (SWE) @ 3min 13sec	Claudio Bortolotto (ITA)	Giuseppe Saronni (ITA)
1980 (4,025km)	Bernard Hinault (FRA) 112hr 8min 20sec	Wladimiro Panizza (ITA) @ 5min 43sec	Giovanni Battaglin (ITA) @ 6min 3sec	Claudio Bortolotto (ITA)	Giuseppe Saronni (ITA)
1981 (3,895km)	Giovanni Battaglin (ITA) 104hr 50min 36sec	Tommy Prim (SWE) @ 38sec	Giuseppe Saronni (ITA) @ 50sec	Claudio Bortolotto (ITA)	Giuseppe Saronni (ITA)
1982 (4,010km)	Bernard Hinault (FRA) 110 hr 7min 55sec	Tommy Prim (SWE) @ 2min 35sec	Silvano Contini (ITA) @ 2min 47sec	Lucien Van Impe (BEL)	Francesco Moser (ITA)
1983 (3,922km)	Giuseppe Saronni (ITA) 100hr 45min 30sec	Roberto Visentini (ITA) @ 1min 7sec	Alberto Fernández (ESP) @ 3min 40sec	Lucien Van Impe (BEL)	Giuseppe Saronni (ITA)
1984 (3,808km)	Francesco Moser (ITA) 98hr 32min 20sec	Laurent Fignon (FRA) @ 1min 3sec	Moreno Argentin (ITA) @ 4min 26sec	Laurent Fignon (FRA)	Urs Freuler (SUI)
1985 (3,998km)	Bernard Hinault (FRA) 102hr 46min 51sec	Francesco Moser (ITA) @ 1min 8sec	Greg LeMond (USA) @ 2min 55sec	Luis-Jose Navarro (ESP)	Johan Van de Velde (NED)
1986 (3,858km)	Roberto Visentini (ITA) 102hr 33min 56sec	Giuseppe Saronni (ITA) @ 1min 2sec	Francesco Moser (ITA) @ 2min 14sec	Pedro Muñoz (ESP)	Guido Bontempi (ITA)

(Continued)

Giro d'Italia GC Podiums & Jersey Winners (Continued)

Year	GC 1st place	GC 2nd place	GC 3rd place	Mountains jersey	Points jersey
1987 (3,915km)	Stephen Roche (IRE) 105hr 39min 40sec	Robert Millar (GBR) @ 3min 40sec	Erik Breukink (NED) @ 4min 17sec	Robert Millar (GBR)	Johan Van de Velde (NED)
1988 (3,579km)	Andrew Hampsten (USA) 97hr 18min 56sec	Erik Breukink (NED) @ 1min 43sec	Urs Zimmermann (SUI) @ 2min 45sec	Andy Hampsten (USA)	Johan Van de Velde (NED)
1989 (3,418km)	Laurent Fignon (FRA) 93hr 30min 16sec	Flavio Giupponi (ITA) @ 1min 15sec	Andrew Hampsten (USA) @ 2min 46sec	Luis Herrera (COL)	Giovanni Fidanza (ITA)
1990 (3,450km)	Gianni Bugno (ITA) 91hr 51min 8sec	Charly Mottet (FRA) @ 6min 33sec	Marco Giovannetti (ITA) @ 9min 1sec	Claudio Chiappucci (ITA)	Gianni Bugno (ITA)
1991 (3,715km)	Franco Chioccioli (ITA) 99hr 35min 43sec	Claudio Chiappucci (ITA) @ 3min 48sec	Massimiliano Lelli (ITA) @ 6min 56sec	Inaki Gaston (ESP)	Claudio Chiappucci (ITA)
1992 (3,843km)	Miguel Indurain (ESP) 103hr 36min 8sec	Claudio Chiappucci (ITA) @ 5min 12sec	Franco Chioccioli (ITA) @ 7min 16sec	Claudio Chiappucci (ITA)	Mario Cipollini (ITA)
1993 (3,702km)	Miguel Indurain (ESP) 98hr 9min 44sec	Piotr Ugrumov (LAT) @ 58sec	Claudio Chiappucci (ITA) @ 5min 27sec	Claudio Chiappucci (ITA)	Adriano Baffi (ITA)
1994 (3,721km)	Evgeni Berzin (RUS) 100hr 41min 21sec	Marco Pantani (ITA) @ 2min 51sec	Miguel Indurain (ESP) @ 3min 23sec	Pascal Richard (SUI)	Djamolidine Abdoujaparov (UZB)
1995 (3,736km)	Tony Rominger (SUI) 97hr 37min 50sec	Evgeni Berzin (RUS) @ 4min 13sec	Piotr Ugrumov (LAT) @ 4min 55sec	Mariano Piccoli (ITA)	Tony Rominger (SUI)

Year (distance)	Winner				
1996 (3,990km)	Pavel Tonkov (RUS) 105hr 20min 23sec	Enrico Zaina (ITA) @ 2min 43sec	Abraham Olano (ESP) @ 2min 57sec	Mariano Piccoli (ITA)	Fabrizio Guidi (ITA)
1997 (3,889km)	Ivan Gotti (ITA) 102hr 53min 58sec	Pavel Tonkov (RUS) @ 1min 27sec	Giuseppe Guerini (ITA) @ 7min 40sec	José Jaime González (ESP)	Mario Cipollini (ITA)
1998 (3,811km)	Marco Pantani (ITA) 98hr 48min 32sec	Pavel Tonkov (RUS) @ 1min 33sec	Giuseppe Guerini (ITA) @ 6min 51sec	Marco Pantani (ITA)	Mariano Piccoli (ITA)
1999 (3,757km)	Ivan Gotti (ITA) 99hr 55min 56sec	Paolo Savoldelli (ITA) @ 3min 35sec	Gilberto Simoni (ITA) @ 3min 36sec	José Jaime González (ESP)	Laurent Jalabert (FRA)
2000 (3,675km)	Stefano Garzelli (ITA) 98hr 30min 14sec	Francesco Casagrande (ITA) @ 1min 27sec	Gilberto Simoni (ITA) @ 1min 33sec	Francesco Casagrande (ITA)	Dimitri Konyshev (RUS)
2001 (3,577km)	Gilberto Simoni (ITA) 89hr 2min 58sec	Abraham Olano (ESP) @ 7min 31sec	Unai Osa (ESP) @ 8min 37sec	Fredy González (COL)	Massimo Strazzer (ITA)
2002 (3,349km)	Paolo Savoldelli (ITA) 89hr 22min 42sec	Tyler Hamilton (USA) @ 1min 41sec	Pietro Caucchioli (ITA) @ 2min 12sec	Julio Alberto Peréz Cuapio (MEX)	Mario Cipollini (ITA)
2003 (3,477km)	Gilberto Simoni (ITA) 88hr 40min 43sec	Stefano Garzelli (ITA) @ 7min 6sec	Yaroslav Popovych (UKR) @ 7min 11sec	Fredy González (COL)	Gilberto Simoni (ITA)
2004 (3,435km)	Damiano Cunego (ITA) 88hr 40min 43sec	Serhiy Honchar (UKR) @ 2min 2sec	Gilberto Simoni (ITA) @ 2min 5sec	Fabian Wegmann (GER)	Alessandro Petacchi (ITA)

(Continued)

Giro d'Italia GC Podiums & Jersey Winners (Continued)

Year	GC 1st place	GC 2nd place	GC 3rd place	Mountains jersey	Points jersey
2005 (3,465km)	Paolo Savoldelli (ITA) 91hr 25min 51sec	Gilberto Simoni (ITA) @ 28sec	José Rujano (VEN) @ 45sec	José Rujano (VEN)	Paolo Bettini (ITA)
2006 (3,502km)	Ivan Basso (ITA) 91hr 33min 36sec	José Enrique Gutiérrez (ESP) @ 9min 18sec	Gilberto Simoni (ITA) @ 11min 59sec	Juan Manuel Garáte (ESP)	Paolo Bettini (ITA)
2007 (3,489km)	Danilo Di Luca (ITA) 92hr 59min 39sec	Andy Schleck (LUX) @ 1min 55sec	Eddy Mazzoleni (ITA) @ 2min 55sec	Leonardo Piepoli (ITA)	Alessandro Petacchi (ITA)
2008 (3,404km)	Alberto Contador (ESP) 89hr 56min 49sec	Riccardo Riccò (ITA) @ 1min 57sec	Marzio Bruseghin (ITA) @ 2min 54sec	Emanuele Sella (ITA)	Daniele Bennati (ITA)
2009 (3,289km)	Denis Menchov (RUS) 86hr 3min 11sec	Danilo Di Luca (ITA) @ 41sec	Franco Pellizotti (ITA) @ 1min 59sec	Stefano Garzelli (ITA)	Danilo Di Luca (ITA)
2010 (3,484km)	Ivan Basso (ITA) 87hr 44min 1sec	David Arroyo (ESP) @ 1min 51sec	Vincenzo Nibali (ITA) @ 2min 37sec	Matthew Lloyd (AUS)	Cadel Evans (AUS)
2011 (3263km)	Michele Scarponi (ITA) 84hr 11min 24sec	Vincenzo Nibali (ITA) @ 46sec	John Gadret (FRA) @ 3min 54sec	Stefano Garzelli (ITA)	Michele Scarponi (ITA)

2012 (3,502km)	Ryder Hesjedal (CAN) 91hr 39min 2sec	Joaquim Rodríguez (ESP) @ 16sec	Thomas De Gendt (BEL) @ 1min 39sec	Matteo Rabottini (ITA)	Joaquim Rodríguez (ESP)
2013 (3,338km)	Vincenzo Nibali (ITA) 84hr 53min 28sec	Rigoberto Urán (COL) @ 4min 43sec	Cadel Evans (AUS) @ 5min 52sec	Stefano Pirazzi (ITA)	Mark Cavendish (GBR)
2014 (3,4455km)	Nairo Quintana (COL) 88hr 14min 32sec	Rigoberto Urán (COL) @ 2min 58sec	Fabio Aru (ITA) @ 4min 4sec	Julián Arredondo (COL)	Nacer Bouhanni (FRA)
2015 (3,474km)	Alberto Contador (ESP) 88hr 22min 25sec	Fabio Aru (ITA) @ 1min 53sec	Mikel Landa (ESP) @ 3min 5sec	Giovanni Visconti (ITA)	Giacomo Nizzolo (ITA)
2016 (3,463 km)	Vincenzo Nibali (ESP) 86hr 32min 49sec	Esteban Chaves (COL) @ 52sec	Alejandro Valverde (ESP) @ 1min 17sec	Mikel Nieve (ESP)	Giacomo Nizzolo (ITA)

Young rider classification (maglia bianca)

1976 Alfio Vandi (ITA)
1977 Mario Beccia (ITA)
1978 Roberto Visentini (ITA)
1979 Silvano Contini (ITA)
1980 Tommy Prim (SWE)
1981 Giuseppe Faraca (ITA)
1982 Marco Groppo (ITA)
1983 Franco Chioccioli (ITA)
1984 Charly Mottet (FRA)
1985 Alberto Volpi (ITA)
1986 Marco Giovannetti (ITA)
1987 Roberto Conti (ITA)
1988 Stefano Tomasini (ITA)
1989 Vladimir Poulinkov (USSR)
1990 Vladimir Poulinkov (USSR)
1991 Massimiliano Lelli (ITA)
1992 Pavel Tonkov (RUS)
1993 Pavel Tonkov (RUS)
1994 Evgeni Berzin (RUS)
1995–2006 (not awarded)
2007 Andy Schleck (LUX)
2008 Riccardo Ricci (ITA)
2009 Kevin Seeldraeyers (BEL)
2010 Riche Porte (AUS)
2011 Roman Kreuziger (CZE)
2012 Rigoberto Urán (COL)
2013 Carlos Betancur (COL)
2014 Nairo Quintana (COL)
2015 Fabio Aru (ITA)
2016 Bob Jungels (LUX)

Days in pink

1 Eddy Merckx (BEL) 77 (5 wins)

2 Alfredo Binda (ITA) 65 (5)

3 Francesco Moser (ITA) 50 (1)

4 Giuseppe Saronni (ITA) 48 (2)

5= Gino Bartali (ITA) 42 (3)

5= Jacques Anquetil (FRA) 42 (2)

7= Fausto Coppi (ITA) 31 (5)

7= Bernard Hinault (FRA) 31 (3)

9 Miguel Indurain (ESP) 29 (2)

10= Costante Girardengo (ITA) 26 (2)

10= Roberto Visentini (ITA) 26 (1)

Multiple winners

Five

Alfredo Binda (ITA) 1925 1927 1928 1929 1933

Fausto Coppi (ITA) 1940 1947 1949 1952 1953

Eddy Merckx (BEL) 1968 1970 1972 1973 1974

Three

Giovanni Brunero (ITA) 1921 1922 1926

Gino Bartali (ITA) 1936 1937 1946

Fiorenzo Magni (ITA) 1948 1951 1955

Felice Gimondi (ITA) 1967 1969 1976

Bernard Hinault (FRA) 1980 1982 1985

Two

Carlo Galetti (ITA) 1910 1911

Costante Girardengo (ITA) 1919 1923

Giovanni Valetti (ITA) 1938 1939

Charly Gaul (LUX) 1956 1959
Jacques Anquetil (FRA) 1960 1964
Franco Balmamion (ITA) 1962 1963
Giuseppe Saronni (ITA) 1979 1983
Miguel Indurain (ESP) 1992 1993
Ivan Gotti (ITA) 1997 1999
Gilberto Simoni (ITA) 2001 2003
Paolo Savoldelli (ITA) 2002 2005
Ivan Basso (ITA) 2006 2010
Alberto Contador (ESP) 2008 2015
Vincenzo Nibali (ITA) 2013 2016

Victories by nation

Italy 69
Belgium 7
France 6
Spain 4
Switzerland 3
Russia 3
Luxembourg 2
Sweden 1
Ireland 1
USA 1
Canada 1
Colombia 1

Maglia Nera (last-placed rider)

1946 Luigi Malabrocca (ITA) Milan-Gazzetta 69hr 41min 54sec
1947 Luigi Malabrocca (ITA) Welter 121hr 47min 27sec
1948 Aldo Bini (ITA) Benotto 128hr 59min 43sec
1949 Sante Carollo (ITA) Wilier Triestina 135hr 22min 57sec

1950 Mario Gestri (ITA) Bartali 122hr 28min 37sec
1951 Giovanni Pinarello (ITA) Bottecchia 124hr 37min 48sec

Cima Coppi climbs and winners

1965 Passo dello Stelvio 1,958m (6,424ft) Graziano Battistini (ITA)
1966 Passo Pordoi 2,239m (7,346ft) Franco Bitossi (ITA)
1967 Tre Cime di Lavaredo 2,320m (7,612ft) Felice Gimondi (ITA)
1968 Tre Cime di Lavaredo 2,320m (7,612ft) Eddy Merckx (BEL)
1969 Passo Sella 2,214m (7,264ft) Claudio Michelotto (ITA)
1970 Passo Pordoi 2,239m (7,346ft) Luciano Armani (ITA)
1971 Grossglockner 2,506m (8,222ft) Pierfranco Vianelli (ITA)
1972 Passo dello Stelvio 2,758m (9,049ft) José Manuel Fuente (ESP)
1973 Passo di Giau 2,236m (7,336ft) José Manuel Fuente (ESP)
1974 Tre Cime di Lavaredo 2,320m (7,612ft) José Manuel Fuente (ESP)
1975 Passo dello Stelvio 2,758m (9,049ft) Francisco Galdós (ESP)
1976 Vajolet Towers 2,758m (9,049ft) Andrés Gandarias (ESP)
1977 Valparola Pass 2,200m (7,218ft) Faustino Fernández Ovies (ESP)
1978 Passo Valles 2,033m (6,670ft) Gianbattista Baronchelli (ITA)
1979 Passo Pordoi 2,239m (7,346ft) Leonardo Natale (ITA)
1980 Passo dello Stelvio 2,758m (9,049ft) Jean-René Bernaudeau (FRA)
1981 Tre Cime di Lavaredo 2,320m (7,612ft) Beat Breu (SUI)
1982 Col d'Izoard 2,361m (7,746ft) Lucien Van Impe (BEL)
1983 Passo Pordoi 2,239m (7,346ft) Marino Lejarreta (ESP)
1984 Passo Pordoi 2,239m (7,346ft) Laurent Fignon (FRA)
1985 Passo del Sempione 2,005m (6,578ft) Reynel Montoya (COL)
1986 Passo Pordoi 2,239m (7,346ft) Pedro Muñoz (ESP)
1987 Passo Pordoi 2,239m (7,346ft) Jean-Claude Bagot (FRA)
1988 Passo dello Stelvio 2,758m (9,049ft) Cancelled due to severe weather
1989 Passo di Gavia 2,621m (8,599ft) Cancelled due to severe weather
1990 Passo Pordoi 2,239m (7,346ft) Maurizio Vandelli (ITA), Charly Mottet (FRA)
1991 Passo Pordoi 2,239m (7,346ft) Franco Vona (ITA), Franco Chioccioli (ITA)

1992 Passo Pordoi 2,239m (7,346ft) Claudio Chiappucci (ITA)

1993 Passo Pordoi 2,239m (7,346ft) Miguel Indurain (ESP)

1994 Passo dello Stelvio 2,758m (9,049ft) Franco Vona (ITA)

1995 Colle dell'Agnello 2,744m (9,003ft) Cancelled

1996 Passo di Gavia 2,621m (8,599ft) Hernán Buenahora (COL)

1997 Passo Pordoi 2,239m (7,346ft) José Jaime González (COL)

1998 Passo Sella 2,214m (7,264ft) Marco Pantani (ITA)

1999 Passo di Gavia 2,621m (8,599ft) José Jaime González (COL)

2000 Colle dell'Agnello 2,744m (9,003ft) José Jaime González (COL)

2001 Colle Fauniera 2,511m (8,238 ft) Cancelled because of protestors

2002 Passo Pordoi 2,239m (7,346ft) Julio Alberto Pérez Cuapio (MEX)

2003 Colle d'Esischie 2,366m (7,762ft) Fredy González (COL)

2004 Passo di Gavia 2,621m (8,599ft) Vladimir Miholjevic (CRO)

2005 Passo dello Stelvio 2,758m (9,049ft) José Rujano (VEN)

2006 Passo di Gavia 2,621m (8,599ft) Juan Manuel Gárate (ESP)

2007 Colle dell'Agnello 2,744m (9,003ft) Yoann Le Boulanger (FRA)

2008 Passo di Gavia 2,621m (8,599ft) Julio Alberto Pérez Cuapio (MEX)

2009 Sestriere 2,039m (6,690ft) Stefano Garzelli (ITA)

2010 Passo di Gavia 2621m (8,599ft) Johann Tschopp (SUI)

2011 Passo di Giau 2,236m (7,336ft) Stefano Garzelli (ITA)

2012 Passo dello Stelvio 2,758m (9,049ft) Thomas De Gendt (BEL)

2013 Tre Cime di Lavaredo 2,320m (7,612ft) Vincenzo Nibali (ITA)

2014 Passo dello Stelvio 2,758m (9,049ft) Dario Cataldo (ITA)

2015 Colle delle Finestre 2,178m (7,146ft) Mikel Landa (ESP)

2016 Colle dell'Agnello 2,744m (9,003ft) Michele Scarponi (ITA)

Overseas departs

1965 San Marino (San Marino)

1966 Monte Carlo (Monaco)

1973 Verviers (Belgium)

1974 Vatican City

1996 Athens (Greece)

1998 Nice (France)

APPENDIX

2002 Groningen (Netherland)

2006 Seraing (Belgium)

2010 Amsterdam (Netherlands)

2012 Herning (Denmark)

2014 Belfast (Northern Ireland)

2016 Apeldoorn (Netherlands)

BIBLIOGRAPHY

Bartali, Gino, with Mario Pancera, *La Mia Storia, Gazzetta dello Sport*, Milan, 1962

Bobet, Jean, *Tomorrow We Ride*, Mousehold Press, 2008

Buzzati, Dino, *The Giro d'Italia: Coppi versus Bartali at the 1949 Tour of Italy*, Velopress, 1999

Deering, John, *Team on the Run*, Mainstream, London, 2000

Denson, Vin, *The Full Cycle*, Mousehold Press, 2008

Drake, Geoff, with Jim Ochowicz, *Team 7-11*, Velopress, 2012

Fignon, Laurent, *When We Were Young and Carefree*, Yellow Jersey Press, London, 2010

Foot, John, *Pedalare! Pedalare!*, Bloomsbury, London, 2011

Fotheringham, William, *A Century of Cycling*, Octopus Publishing, London, 2003

—, *Fallen Angel: The Passion of Fausto Coppi*, Yellow Jersey Press, London, 2010

—, *Bernard Hinault and the Rise and Fall of French Cycling*, Yellow Jersey Press, London, 2015

Friebe, Daniel, *Eddy Merckx: The Cannibal*, Ebury Press, London, 2012

—, and Peter Goding, *Mountain High and Mountain Higher*, Quercus, London, 2011 and 2013

Healy, Graham, *That Shattered Peloton*, Breakaway Books, 2014

McConnon, Ali, and André McConnon, *Road to Valour*, Weidenfeld & Nicolson, London, 2012

BIBLIOGRAPHY

McGann, Bill and Carol, *The Story of the Giro d'Italia*, vols 1 and 2, McGann Publishing, 2012

Millar, David, *The Racer*, Yellow Jersey Press, London, 2015

Moore, Richard, *In Search of Robert Millar*, HarperSport, London, 2007

Moore, Tim, *Gironimo!: Riding the Very Terrible 1914 Tour of Italy*, Yellow Jersey Press, London, 2014

Penazzo, Sergio, and Daniel Schamps, *Tour 79 (Kennedy Brothers)*

—, and Pierre Martin, *Tour 80* (Kennedy Brothers)

—, *Tour 81* (Kennedy Brothers)

Penazzo, Sergio, Pierre Martin, Daniel Schamps and Cor Vos, *Tour 82* (Kennedy Brothers)

—, *Tour 83* (Kennedy Brothers)

—, Dante Baration and Cor Vos, *Tour 85* (Kennedy Brothers)

—, *Tour 86* (Kennedy Brothers)

—, *Tour 87* (Kennedy Brothers)

—, *Tour 88* (Kennedy Brothers)

—, *Tour 89* (Kennedy Brothers)

—, *Tour 90* (Kennedy Brothers)

Rendall, Matt, *The Death of Marco Pantani*, Weidenfeld & Nicolson, London, 2006

Roche, Stephen, with Pete Cossins, *Born to Ride*, Yellow Jersey Press, London, 2013

Strouken, Tonny, and Jan Maes, *Merckx 69*, Bloomsbury, London, 2014

Sykes, Herbie, *Coppi: Inside the Legend of the Campionissimo*, Rouleur Books, 2012

—, *Maglia Rosa: Triumph and Tragedy at the Giro d'Italia*, Rouleur, 2013

Vanwalleghem, Rik, *Eddy Merckx: The Greatest Cyclist of the 20th Century*, Velopress, 1996

Witherell, James L., *Bicycle History*, McGann Publishing, 2010

ACKNOWLEDGEMENTS

The Giro d'Italia – and those warrior riders and driven individuals who wage war with the roads and topography of the Italian peninsular – has a rich associated literature but a number of publications stand out and warrant special mention and thanks.

The 'Bible' – and now the starting point for all writers on the race – is Bill and Carol McGann's monumental *The Story of the Giro d'Italia* which offers up the final statistical word in terms of classification winners, results and timings on any given day over the last 99 editions of the race. That is no small matter when trying to piece together what actually happened in the early decades when much of the race took place away from the public gaze and record-keeping was sometimes sketchy. A comparatively recent discovery – to me anyway – was Dino Buzzati's *The Giro d'Italia: Coppi versus Bartali at the 1949 Tour of Italy*, one of the most lyrical sporting books imaginable. So much more than an account of that well-documented sporting rivalry, it provides an extraordinary technicolor snapshot of what the Giro was actually like over 70 years ago. Herbie Sykes's splendid and all-encompassing *Maglia Rosa* was also inspirational in the way it portrays the race.

The welcome invitation to write *Corsa Rosa* came from Charlotte Atyeo at Bloomsbury for which heartfelt thanks. Charlotte also edited the book with a sure hand, sharing my enthusiasm for the Giro and ensuring I didn't linger too long in any one era, no matter how tempting. On the occasion of the Giro's 100th edition the broad sweep was paramount. A big thanks also to Holly Jarrald and Richard Collins for their very considerable assistance.

Finally, a big thanks to my wife Mary, not least for accepting the loss of our spare bedroom for over a year as it became inundated with maps of Italy, old Giro route books and programmes and various dusty tomes and magazines.

INDEX

INDEX

INDEX

INDEX

INDEX

INDEX